German Yearbook on Business History 1988

German Yearbook on Business History 1988

Edited by
the German Society for Business, History, Cologne

In Cooperation with
the Institute for Bank-Historical Research, Frankfurt/Main

Editors:
Hans Pohl (Editor in Charge) and Bernd Rudolph

Editorial Staff:
Beate Brüninghaus, Monika Pohle and Manfred Pohl

Springer-Verlag Berlin Heidelberg New York
London Paris Tokyo Hong Kong

ISBN-13: 978-3-642-75514-9 e-ISBN-13: 978-3-642-75512-5
DOI: 10.1007/978-3-642-75512-5

Softcover reprint of the hardcover 1st edition 1990

Typesetting: Satz u. Grafikstudio Tanomvet, Beindersheim

2142/7130-543210

Table of Contents

List of Contributers and Translators

Contributors

Beate Brüninghaus M.A.
Geschäftsführerin
Gesellschaft für Unternehmensgeschichte e.V.
Bonner Str. 211
D-5000 Köln 51

Professor Dr. Lothar Burchardt
FB Philosophie und Geschichte
Universität Konstanz
Postfach 5560
D-7750 Konstanz

Professor Dr. Volker Hentschel
FB Rechts- und Wirtschaftswissenschaften
Johannes-Gutenberg-Universität
Postfach 3980
D-6500 Mainz

Professor Dr. Johannes Houwink ten Cate
p/a Herengracht 474
NL-1017 CA Amsterdam

Dr. Jürgen Mura
Sparkassenhistorisches Dokumentationszentrum
Deutscher Sparkassen- und Giroverband e.V.
Simrockstr. 4
D-5300 Bonn 1

Monika Pohle M.A.
Geschäftsführerin
Institut für bankhistorische Forschung e.V.
Goetheplatz 9
D-6000 Frankfurt am Main

Dr. Harm G. Schröter
Zentralinstitut für sozialwissenschaftliche Forschung (ZI 6)
Arbeitsbereich Witschafts- und Sozialgeschichte
Freie Universität Berlin
Hittorfstr. 2–4
D-1000 Berlin 33Dr.

Horst A. Wessel
Mannesmann AG – Mannesmann Archiv
Mannesmannufer 2–4
D-4000 Düsseldorf 1

Translators

Eva Marshall
Mannesmann AG
Postfach 5501
4000 Düsseldorf 1
(report by Horst A. Wessel)

Eileen Martin
19 Evelyn Gardens
GB – Richmond Surrey TWg 2 PL
(articles by Volker Hentschel, Johannes Houwink ten Cate, Monika Pohle, Harm G. Schröter, reports by Monika Pohle)

Ingrid Scheeben
Akazienstr. 9
D-5357 Swisttal
(report by Jürgen Mura)

Anne Wegner
Königin-Sophie-Str. 19
5340 Bad Honnef 1
(articles by Lothar Burchardt, Beate Brüninghaus)

Between War Profits and War Costs Krupp in the First World War

Lothar Burchardt

I. Preliminary Remarks*

Whoever takes a closer look at the German war and armament economy during the First World War cannot fail to come across Fried. Krupp AG in Essen. The size and complexity of the company, its controlling position within the Ruhr industries and its outstanding importance as a weapons manufacturer all lifted Krupp above the mass of the German industrial companies and gave the firm an important position. It was in particular in the later years of Wilhelm II. that Krupp was almost a national institution. The Kaiser's participation in the fates of the company and family leant strength to this position.

However the company did not only meet with goodwill. It was in particular its participation in the German and international armament business which made it increasingly suspect for left liberal and especially for the social democratic critic. An opportunity for renewed attacks and exposures arose in 1912/13 when in the course of the so-called "Kornwalzer Affair" a Krupp employee was found guilty of bribing army and naval officers.[1] This proved not only to the German but also to the foreign sceptics that they were right to believe that the company would stop at nothing in pursuit of its interests. In 1905 George Bernard Shaw had already, in his play "Major Barbara", not been sparing with his insinuations. In 1913 even the serious American journal "The Iron Age" wrote, following the facts revealed during the Kornwalzer affair, that Krupp was obviously recently prepared to go to any lengths to agitate a war.[2] Even before the First World War had really started, H.G. Wells had already decided who was the real culprit. "In the centre of this disaster which has finally become a world catastrophe is Kruppism, the dirty violent trade with the tools of death."[3] It was shortly afterwards that the often repeated but never conclusively proved allegation arose that the then company boss Gustav Krupp v. Bohlen und Halbach had been informed by the Kaiser months in advance of the imminent war,

* Renate Köhne-Lindenlaub and Jürgen Lindenlaub (Essen) have played an important role in the creation of this essay. I would like to take this opportunity of thanking them.

1 Cf. in detail W. Manchester, Krupp. German edition Munich 1968, pp. 269ff. A. Zimmermann, Der Prozeß Brandt und Genossen. Berlin 1914 provides a comprehensive contemporary picture. The relevant archive material is to be found in the Historisches Archiv at Fried. Krupp GmbH Essen (from now on shortened to HA Krupp), WA IV. 1414ff.

2 Gustav Krupp v. Bohlen to Minister for Culture (retd.) v. Studt, 22.5.1913 (W.A. Boelcke (Ed.), Krupp und die Hohenzollern in Dokumenten. 2nd edition, Frankfurt/M. 1970, p. 218).

3 Cit. in Manchester, p. 275.

even of the time it would start, and had accordingly adjusted his factories. The allies concluded that Krupp was hardly less of a war criminal that the Kaiser himself.[4]

In particular the company was accused at home and abroad of profiting (too much) from the war. Even though Krupp v. Bohlen had publicly stated at the beginning of the war that he was against earning a direct war profit[5], this statement impressed the contemporary critics as little as it has many historians since. The American Krupp-historian William Manchester calls this basically "ridiculous nonsense" and talks vaguely of "gross earnings" of approximately 432 million marks which the company made between August 1914 and autumn 1918.[6] Other estimates of profit vary from between the profit of 182 million marks shown on the books and the "at least 800 million marks" estimated as the Krupp war profits by the (then) Marxist journalist Bernhard Menne in 1937.[7]

Neither of the authors mentioned above looked carefully at the question as to what war profits really are, how they could be calculated in the Krupp case, and of what use they were in the end to the company and its shareholders.

The author of this article cannot hope to completely cover these and other connected questions. Some of the material appears to have been lost, other pieces have only partially survived the decades since the First World War. The remaining archive material only slowly opens itself to the user (in particular when he is not a trained accountant) and does not provide clear answers to all questions.

A further difficulty arises in the area of basic decision making in that the minutes of the meetings of the board of directors, the so-called directorate, have not survived for the years of the war. The minutes of the supervisory board meetings are availabe, however upon looking at them more closely they prove to be a very brief recording of the decisions and do not provide much insight into motives or background information. And in particular: even contemporary experts ceded occasionally to the complexity of the Krupp company. In the war years this included, in addition to the factories in Essen, which as "Gußstahlfabrik" (cast steel factory) composed the actual core of the company, amongst others the following:

- the Friedrich-Alfred-Hütte in Rheinhausen,
- the Stahlwerk Annen,
- the Grusonwerk in Magdeburg and
- the Germania-Werft in Kiel.

Altogether the Gußstahlfabrik, its satellite administrative offices and branches (which will now be called "subsidiaries" according to the Krupp terminology) employed almost 80,000 people in the summer of 1914. No other German company could boast similiar figures. These subsidiaries and the Gußstahlfabrik provided one another with goods at unknown internal offset prices, exchanged company secrets,

---

[4] Manchester, p. 275 and 302. Cf. also G.v. Klass, Die drei Ringe. Tübingen 1953, p. 352 and 356; W. Benz, "Der Fall Mühlon". in: Vjh. f. Zeitgeschichte 18, 1970, p. 348. Krupp was possibly named in an Allies list of war criminals from 1919. Cf. on this the Miszelle by J.W. Brügel in: Vjh. f. Zeitgeschichte 6, 1958, pp. 263–270.

[5] W. Berdrow, Alfred Krupp und sein Geschlecht. Berlin 71.–100. tsd. 1943, pp. 222f. Cf. also below, note 100.

[6] Manchester, p. 302 and 307.

[7] W. Engelmann, Krupp. Legende und Wirklichkeit, Paperback edition Munich 1970, p. 268.

information and occasionally top employees, provided balance sheets en bloc and appeared to the outsider to be an almost impenetrable thicket of all sorts of entanglements.

An analysis of the complex organism "Fried. Krupp AG" has in the mean time hardly become any easier. Therefore, this report does not attempt to investigate the entirety of the Krupp imperium. It will mainly confine itself to looking at some points about the Gußstahlfabrik. This is in as much permissible in that it was by far the largest company complex and employed almost twice as many people as all the subsidiaries together. Additionally it probably secured about 80–90% of the company profits during the period under investigation. Above all it was not only the historical basic unit of the company but was also considered, to a much greater extent than the subsidiaries, to be the personification of everything, good and bad, associated with the name Krupp. Occasionally – for example in connection with the accounts, dividends or financial reserves – statements must be made for the entire company. Only in these cases will the "entire company" or "Krupp AG" or similar names be mentioned, otherwise it will be the Gußstahlfabrik.

The following report starts with a short investigation into the position of the cast steel factory in the summer of 1914 and then attempts to follow in summary the development of the production and turnover during the war years. Following this the production costs are analysed and an attempt is made to arrive at an estimate of the profits through the comparison of turnover and costs. After this the use of the attained profits is investigated. Finally in conclusion the position of the cast steel factory or rather – as much as is necessary – the entire company towards the end of 1918 is looked at.

II. Production and Sales

During the last year before the war the Gußstahlfabrik had sales totalling 216.4 million marks.[8] Of this at least 35% came from the production of "peace materials" which included wheels, axles, rails, supports, sheet metal etc. A further 11% of the turnover arose from the sale of armoured plate or from its use on the war ships building at the Germania Werft. The remaining 54% belong to the area "war materials". This included, in addition to artillery ammunition, gun-carriages and vehicles, in particular cannons and howitzers of all calibers up to the 42cm mortars (developed at the firm's own cost and then top secret), the "Dicke Berthas" which became famous soon after the start of the war. It was this area of "war materials" which was decisive to the Krupp image: "the international name of the company Krupp" as the chief designer of the time Rausenberger occasionally stressed "is closely connected with the company's pionieering activities in the area of the production of war materials".[9]

In the summer of 1914 the monthly production capacity of the Gußstahlfabrik was 280 light or medium and 4 heavy guns. In addition there were at least 150,000

[8] This and the following figures refer to the business year 1913/14. The business year went from July 1 until June 30 of the following year. More exact data is provided in Table 2.

[9] Rausenberger to Krupp v. Bohlen, 3.10.1915 (HA Krupp, FAH IV. C 73b pp. 204–212).

shells and 230 000 detonators. The company had 270 000 square metres of shop floor and almost 6000 machines at their disposal for the manufacture of their military and civil products.[10] The monthly production of 200 field and 144 torpedo boat guns, for which the cast steel factory was granted permission in the mobilisation plans, is roughly comparable to the figures of the pre-war production.[11] Since the war was only expected to be short, the military administration did not initially express any further wishes. Once this hope was dashed following the Marne battle, the army started to press for higher production figures. From 1915 onwards additional machines were produced for this purpose.[12] The Grunsonwerk also became more involved in the manufacture of guns than it had been in the pre-war years.

At the end of August 1915 the army administration demanded of the company Krupp that "they once again ... should adapt their level of performance in manufacturing to suit the drastically increased demand."[13] Thereupon the cast steel factory again increased their capacity but did not reach the limit of their capabilities. As long as the army and marine administration only gave short term contracts, such a deep involvement would have been risky since there was still no certainty that Krupp would receive more orders and the necessary workforce.[14]

The breakthrough came with a discussion between Krupp von Bohlen and the third OHL shortly after they took office. On 9/8/1916 Hindenburg and Ludendorff asked the head of the company for his full support. In exchange for this they gave the company what amounted to a purchase guarantee.[15] This meeting, at which Carl Duisberg, the general director of Bayer, was also present, is occasionally referred to in the literature as a sort of "direct issuance of orders to the High Command by the monopolies".[16] I do not consider that the sources quoted in this connection support this interpretation. Rathermore they lead one to believe that the cause of this change is to be found in the greatly increased use of ammunition resulting from the heavy material battles in the summer of 1916. In particular I am not aware of any material from Fried. Krupp AG which indicates this sort of initiative on their part. However, once the demands of the OHL had been stated[17] and Ludendorff had promised to supply the additional workforce necessary for their realisation, they were immedia-

---

[10] According to lists in HA Krupp, WA VII. f 1116, p. 77 and 82.

[11] Boelcke, p. 223.

[12] According to an assessment by Krupp v. Bohlen (HA Krupp, WA VII. f 1075, pp. 1–3). The framework of this first expansive construction included the Kanonenwerkstatt III., the Granatendreherei VI and the Bremszylinderwerkstatt I.

[13] Cit. In: HA Krupp, WA VII. f 1116, p. 38.

[14] Notes on a discussion between representatives of the Fried. Krupp AG and the Chef der Feldzeugmeisterei within the Prussian war ministry on 23.10.1915 (HA Krupp, WA IV. 1394, pp. 90–95).

[15] Paper by Krupp v. Bohlen, "Richtlinien für das KM-Geschäft", p. 6 (HA Krupp, WA VII. f 1075). This work gives the date as 6.9 but I consider Ludendorff's dating of 8.9 to be more plausible. Cf. E. Ludendorff, Meine Kriegserinnerungen. Berlin 1920, p. 216.

[16] As in H. Weber, Ludendorff und die Monopole. Berlin (–0) 1966, p. 48 and (in a slighlty more moderate form) F. Klein (Ed.), Deutschland im 1. Weltkrieg. Vol. 2, Berlin (–0) 1968. p. 462.

[17] The OHL demanded amongst other things an increase in the production of artillery shells from 2.5 to 9 million per month, the production of cannon barrels from 1300 to 3000 etc, (HA Krupp, WA VII. f 1077). A list of the demands on the Fried. Krupp AG can be found in WA VII. f 1116, p. 67.

tely acted upon. Looking back Krupp v. Bohlen noted with satisfaction that the company had been able to react with unusual speed due to the specific structure of the distribution of shares in Krupps case.[18] Then there was a wave of expansion, such as never experienced by the company before. Inspite of an occasional fairly serious lack of construction labour and material, numerous new production plants for war material were built.[19] By the end of the war the workshop area within the Gußstahlfabrik dedicated to this production had risen to at least two and a half times the area used before the war. Faced with the increasingly threatening scale of lack of labour, the machine park was more rapidly developed (and here mainly the particularly efficient machines with electric drive); by the end of the war it was triple the peacetime level.[20] The production capacity for light and medium sized guns rose by at least five times, the detonator production by almost four times and the production of shells by as much as nine times that of before the war.[21]

Generally they worked to full capacity. Although there were difficulties in obtaining the necessary production factors – in particular the labour force – these could be overcome. With almost one third of the market in shells and one tenth of the ammunition production[22] Krupp was by far the largest and most vital German munitions supplier and as such enjoyed a certain priority in the allocation of scarce resources. Table 1 shows the rise in the production.

Table 1. The munitions production of Fried. Krupp AG 1913/14 – 1918[23]

	1.8.1914–31.7.1915	1.8.1915–31.7.1916	1.8.1916–31.7.1917	1.8.1917–31.7.1918	1.8.118–end of war
New guns (number)	1264	2481	2276	3408	1195
Repaired guns (number)	1535	2044	2536	1690	1067
New gun barrels (number)	476	1582	2108	3111	553
Repaired gun barrels (number)	49	357	687	931	440
Empty shells (million)	3,25	9,14	18,90	22,42	9,22
War ship units	29	25	26	23	1

[18] Krupp's commentary is to be found in the work mentioned in note 15, p. 7.

[19] Details are to be found in the work HA Krupp, WA VII. f 1116, pp. 42–51. This expansion programme will be discussed later. Diagrams of the monthly production capacity are in HA Krupp WA VII. f 1320.

[20] Cf. the lists in the work mentioned in note 19, p. 77. Boelcke provides further information, p. 225.

[21] Cf. the work mentioned in note 19, p. 82.

[22] Ibid., p. 95.

[23] Put together according to papers in HA Krupp, WA VII. f 1116, p. 96 (ammunition), WA VII. f 1320, p. 23 (artillery) and WA VII. f 1320, p. 41 (ships). The figures include repaired booty.

Everything produced was also sold.[24] Since the beginning of the war Fried. Krupp AG in general and the Gußstahlfabrik in particular had never experienced any appreciable sales problems. Of course the market diminished in that only a minimum could be exported. The reduction of the market to Germany also meant that the army and navy administrations could in effect monopolize the demand for war materiel and armour plate and could make far-reaching regulations relating to the type, number, and composition of the products.

These institutions additionally controlled the company in that they could to a certain degree regulate both the supply of workers and of the food which those workers required. The more industry considered itself to be dependant, in a period of increasingly scarce workers, on the release of qualified skilled workers from military service, the stronger grew the power of the military offices which decided upon such requests for release. In short: the start of the war even forced upon vast firms like Fried. Krupp AG various restraints which tended to increase rather than decrease with the progression of the war. They noticeably reduced the discretionary capacities and courses of action of the management and even occasionally almost reduced them to recipients of orders from military departments.

This is however in as much only one side of the coin in that the start of the war also brought huge advantages. Although the firm was up against a state demand monoply there was on the other hand if not quite a seller monoply at least an oligopoly. The number of competitive German ammunition producers was limited and could not in the short term be indefinately extended. The initiation of the Hindenburg programme was the latest point at which the military supply offices could afford to do without the largest firm of this group.

There was in effect a two-sided dependance from which Krupp, in addition to the disadvantages already discussed, also drew benefit. Whilst the company in times of peace had to win over customers and to compete with the competition, there was now to all effect a market guarantee:

As long as one oriented oneself to the state product and quality demands one could be certain that there was a buyer for the production. And even more: a seller could be more and more certain that the provisions officers were primarily concerned with the quality and number of the products and less with their price. Once it had been shown that an effective price control was almost impossible under these circumstances, a certain amount of resignation arose on this front. As long as the increase in prices was not disproportionate, the military was increasingly prepared to let the producers decide. Even if the Reichstag did try to exert some sort of parliamentary munitions control it was not successful against the united front of the manufacturers and the provisions office.[25]

The constellation which has just been outlined provided optimal conditions for a strong growth in the sales of the cast steel factory, as is shown clearly in Table 2. There was a constant annual rate of growth in the turnover during the war of 46–48%, which rose to 60% only in the business year 1917/18. This development most probably continued in the last months of the war but as turnover was assessed yearly,

---

[24] Cf. Table 1 above.

[25] Cf. on this W. Wette's interesting paper, "Reichstag und 'Kriegsgewinnlerei' (1916–1918) ..." in: Militärgesch. Mitteilungen 2/1984, pp. 31–56.

Table 2. The Cast Steel Factory turnover in contemporary prices according to areas of production[26]

	1913/14	1914/15	1915/16	1916/17	1917/18	1918/19
War Materials (million m.)	115.9	247.8	383.1	581.6	935.9	841.1
War Materials (in % of the applicable total sales	54	79	82	84	85	83
War Materials (in % of 1913/14)	100	214	331	502	808	726
War Materials (in % of the previous year)		214	155	152	161	90
Armour plate (million m.)	23.9	19.4	27.5	37.2	61.1	46.4
Armour plate in % of the applicable total sales	11	6	6	5	5	4
Armour plate (in % of 1913/14)	100	81	115	156	256	194
Armour plate (in % of the previous year)		81	142	135	164	76
Peace material (million m.)	76.6	48.4	56.1	73.1	109.1	127.6
Peace material in % of the applicable total sales	35	15	12	11	10	13
Peace material (in % of 1913/14)	100	63	73	95	142	167
Peace material (in % of the previous year)		63	116	130	149	117
Total sales (million m.)	216.4	315.6	466.7	691.9	1106.1	1015.1
Total sales (in % of 1913/14)	100	146	216	320	511	469
Total sales (in % of the previous year)		146	148	148	160	92

these figures are hidden by the loss of turnover in the first months after the war. Altogether turnover in 1917/18 rose nominally to more than five times that of the last years of peace.

The productivity also developed favourably. It is true to say that a comparison of yearly average outputs (expressed in marks per employee) is misleading; it rose nominally from about 4320 marks in the (not particularly good) year 1913/14 to

[26] Put together from the accounts in HA Krupp, WA IV. 2429–2433. The figures refer to the business year.

approximately 11 400 marks in the year 1917/18[27], that is by about 165%. However if one treats these figures for the inflation of about 40%[28] which had arisen in the mean time there is still a real increase of almost 60%.

As is well known, the turnover of a company is dictated on the one hand by the price per unit and on the other by the number of units sold. The development of unit prices during the period under investigation obviously showed – as did all other inner German prices – a clearly rising tendency. Closer scrutiny does not always provide a clear picture, a fact which even then occasionally led to sharp controversy among contemporaries as to how high the rise in the price of iron production and processing actually was.[29] Since, in the special case of the Gußstahlfabrik, the calculation of the preliminary work done by the company's factories would cause difficult problems and in addition to this the basic data is incomplete, no attempt will be made here to follow the development of prices closely.

Altogether the cast steel factory certainly went through a phase of extremely dynamic sales increas. This also showed up in a marked increase in the frequency of capital turnover, i.e. the quotient of sales to company capital.[30] No far-reaching conclusions should be drawn from these non-treated figures however, since the real rise in sales was considerably slower. On average, the mark lost 15% of its purchasing power annually during the war years, in 1916/17 even as much as 20%.[31] By the end of the war its value had sunk to about half that of the pre-war gold mark. If one corrects the nominal values accordingly, the sales look less imposing.[32] However they still were impressive enough and in 1917/18 had probably reached a real level of at least three times the sales of the last years of peace.

The relative importance of the three branches of war materials, peace materials and armour plate shifted markedly during the war years. The field of war materials (which were to all effect guns and their parts) accounted for 54% of the sales in the last years before the war. In face of the continuously increasing demand this proportion rose to 79% in the first years of the war and finally settled down at about 85%. This development was for obvious reasons to the detriment of peace materials, the quota of which sank slowly from 35% to 10%.

---

27 Calculated according to personnel data in HA Krupp, WA 41/6–5 and the sales figures in WA IV 2429–2433.

28 Calculated according to the rate of exchange of the mark against the Dutch guilder which can be considered to be a relatively stable comparison. The development of the rates of exchange become obvious from the Vierteljahreshefte f. d. Statistik des Deutschen Reiches, 1919 I., 1920 IV. etc.

29 Cf. for example the rise in the price of rod iron, billets and heavy plate between mid-1914 and mid-1917; the manager of the Verein Deutscher Eisen- und Stahlindustrieller stated that it was on average 39%, the war office claimed 100% and the industry critic Erzberger almost 150%. The figures relating to this are in: Stahl u. Eisen 1925, p. 4 (Industry); Bundesarchiv Koblenz, R 13 I 188, p. 124–126 (war office), report from the Bavarian Hauptmann Hartmann dated 14.1.1918 in Bayerisches Hauptstaatsarchiv (war archive) Munich, MKr 17270 (Erzberger).

30 For the calculations cf. R. Hofmann, Bilanzkennzahlen. 4th ed. Wiesbaden 1977, pp. 136–140 and 306f. The company capital consists of the share capital (at nominal value), reserves and non-distributed profits.

31 Cf. note 28.

32 The turnover treated for inflation was in 1914/15 about 290 million, for 1915/16 about 330, for 1916/17 almost 480, for 1917/18 about 670 and for 1918/19 less than 500 million marks.

Armour plate for battle ships and cruisers had never played the central part, either in Krupp's total sales or in the entire Ruhr industry, with which it was often credited by some of the opponents of the German fleet build-up.[33] In the cast steel factory it did not account for much more than one tenth of the total sales even during the main period of war ship construction. Since the construction of large fighting ships stagnated during the war, and even declined for a period, the proportion of sales accounted for by the production of armour plate sank finally to little more than 5%.

III. Production Costs, Earned Surplus and Welfare Costs

The real rise in sales was comparable to a slightly slower but all the same remarkable increase in the labour force. Table 3 gives a summary of this process.

Table 3. Size of the labour force of the Gußstahlfabrik and average wages of the male and female workers[34]

	1913/14	1914/15	1915/16	1916/17	1917/18	1918/19
Size of the labour force (blue and white collar workers)	39 090	56 680	69 710	87 385	104 072	105 741
Percentage woman	0.0	7.0	17.4	21.9	24.8	24.9
Male and female blue collar workers	33 321	50 405	64 184	80 908	97 256	97 463
Average wages of the female blue collar workers (marks/shift)	1.99	2.52	3.58	4.53	5.89	6.76
Average wages of the male and female blue collar workers (marks/shift)	5.73	6.01	6.68	7.50	9.97	12.12
Average female wages in % of average male wages	34.6	41.6	50.4	55.0	52.4	50.1

In the beginnings the additionally required work force was fairly easy to find around Essen. Once this source had been depleted the Gußstahlfabrik was forced to cover its requirements from more distant markets.[35] In addition to this, as has been

[33] This is proved in detail by G. Leckebusch, Die Beziehungen der deutschen Seeschiffswerften zur Eisenindustrie an der Ruhr in der Zeit von 1850–1930. Cologne 1963, p. 58–94 and 112–115. For Krupp in particular cf. pp. 84–89.

[34] According to papers in HA Krupp, WA 41/6–5 (size of workforce) and WA VII. f 1105 (wages). Fixed day for the size of workforce is always june 30, for the wages the 4th quarter. The wage payments do not include overtime.

[35] Information about the effectivity of these acquisitions, which can only be touched on here, is given in HA Krupp, WA IV. 1697 and WA VII. f 1105, pp. 15ff.

mentioned above, it increasingly tried to proctect key workers from national service and thereby keep them for the factory.[36] The various problems involved in the change of place of work – the recruitment and enticing away of employees, complications resulting from the enforcement of the Vaterländisches Hilfsdienstgesetz etc. – cannot be entered into here. Suffice it to note that the labour force requirements could not really be adequately met by any of the means mentioned.

Help was sought on the one hand by increasing plant efficiency – the extension of electrification and general mechanisation have already been mentioned – and on the other hand by searching for other work force reserves. Here the firm had two alternatives, namely the introduction of foreigners (either volunteers or conscripts), and the recruitment of women.

The Gußstahlfabrik took both paths with differing intensity. Prisoners-of-war were first offered to the factory at the end of April 1915[37] and apparently arrived during the summer. At first there were only about 200 prisoners. In the following years their numbers rose considerably, but they never amounted to more than about 1% of the entire workforce: Secrecy and security reasons did not favour using all too many prisoners in Germany's largest munitions factory.[38]

Beginning in November 1916, the Reich government started to conscript Belgian unemployed into the Reich.[39] This measure proved to be a dead loss, even leaving aside the international law aspects, and finally failed in the spring of 1917 due to the negative reaction of the international press. Whereas these "conscript Belgians" were never of any great importance to Krupp, the firm had more success with the recruitment of volunteer labour in Belgium and neutral foreign countries. Whilst at the beginning of 1916 only a few Dutch and barely 100 Belgians were working in Essen, there were at the end of the war about 7600 volunteer workers from almost 20 countries (mainly Belgians and Dutch), and these accounted for 7.5% of the labour force.[40]

The most effective step however proved to be the employment of women. At Krupp, as in most of heavy industry, there were hardly any female workers before the beginning of the war.[41] It was apparently the detonator factory which was the first

---

[36] In 1915 they numbered about 5000, in 1916 over 13 000, in 1917 almost 25 000. Additional data in HA Krupp, WA IV. 1697, p. 55–66 and WA IV. 1394.

[37] A notice from Heinemann about a meeting in the Prussian war ministry on 29.4.1915 (HA Krupp, WA IV, 1394, pp. 25–34).

[38] In 1917 and 1918 there were on average 840 prisoners of war working at the Gußstahlfabrik. More detailed data is in HA Krupp, WA 41/6–5 and WA VII. f 1105, p. 9. On payment of this workforce cf. ibid. p. 40.

[39] Cf. on this generally F. Zunkel, "Die ausländischen Arbeiter in der deutschen Kriegswirtschaftspolitik des 1. Weltkrieges". In G.A. Ritteer (ed.), Entstehung und Wandel der modernen Gesellschaft. Festschr. f. H. Rosenberg, Berlin 1970, p. 280–311. Additional material is to be found in HA Krupp, WA IV. 1242 and in the Bavarian war archives.

[40] Precise quarterly lists according to country of origin can be found in HA Krupp, WA VII. f 1105, p. 54 and Table 2. On the acquisition of this workforce cf. O. Heinemann, Kronenorden Vierter Klasse. Düsseldorf 1969, p. 154. The author – the father of the later Federal President – was then the head of the office for worker affairs at the Gußstahlfabrik.

[41] Paper "Änderungen im Personalbestand" (HA Krupp, WA IV. 1697, pp. 55–66.) Alfred Krupp's "Generalregulativ" of 1872 even contains the sentence that women and children do not work at the Gußstahlfabrik.

to break with this tradition; even in the first year of the war it doubled its low number of female employees[42] with good results. In the following years the proportion of female blue and white collar workers rose in the entire Gußstahlfabrik, most significantly in the shell and particularly in the detonator factories where the positive early experiences had proved themselves. Finally, more than two thirds of that labour force were women.[43] The proportion of women for the entire Gußstahlfabrik was at the end of 1917 about 26 000 or 25% of the total workforce. Workers and unions observed this development with mixed feelings[44] since they feared competition which would lower the wages. Their fears were not completely unjustified. As summarised in Table 3, the wages of the women in the Gußstahlfabrik (as in the entire heavy industry) were far below those of the men. Whether we compare the median or the average wages in Table 3[45], we always find that the women's wages lag far behind the wages of the men. Many contemporaries justified this fact by stating that women in heavy industry could only be employed in subordinate support tasks and could therefore, with respect to their wages, not be compared with their more highly qualified male colleagues. This may be true in some cases, – the long service "Kruppians" did have a sounder training and more long-term experience than the women who had just arrived. However if we compare the piece wages, where these arguments did not hold, we find a similar relationship.[46] It is therefore permissible to presume that female workers ceteris paribus were underpaid by about 30–50%. In a period of rapidly rising nominal wages this wage policy offered the company considerable advantages since it could keep the wage costs for about one quarter of its labour force to at the most two thirds of those which would have been required for male labourers.[47] This atypical wage cost relationship allows the development of the personnel cost intensity[48] to appear in a more favourable light than is justified by the facts. If it was possible to slow down the (unfavourable) rise of this figure in the business year 1915/16 and in the two following years and then even to reverse it[49], this was not only due to the increased efficiency which had been attained in the mean time but also to this structural change of the labour force.

---

[42] Letter from the detonator workshop to the board of directors from 8.12.1915 (HA Krupp, WA 41/6–160). On 30.9.1914 there were 510 women working in the detonator production (HA Krupp, WA IV. 1697, pp. 55–66).

[43] Precise lists are to be found in HA Krupp, WA VII. f 1116, p. 80 and WA 41/6–5. Cf. also Table 3.

[44] Cf. eg. "Vorwärts", Nr. 296 v. 26.10.1915, p. 1 or the "Werkverein" from 27.11.1915 (one copy in HA Krupp, WA 41/5–160).

[45] Quarterly figures about median wages are to be found in HA Krupp, WA 41/6–107.

[46] Cf. eg. the data from the detonator manufacture in the letter of the Deutscher Metallarbeiterverband, the Christlicher Metallarbeiterverband and the Gewerkverein der Metallarbeiter to the Krupp company dated 24.11.1915 (HA Krupp, WA 41/6–169). Even then the women received for the same work 50% of the mens' piece rate wage.

[47] If we presume that a quarter of the workforce received 60% of the mens' wages ceteris paribus, then we arrive at a saving of 10% of the wage costs.

[48] The intensity of the personnel costs is the quotient between personnel costs and turnover. On the calculation cf. Hofmann, p. 324.

[49] The following values arise for the cast steel factory: 1913/14: 68.9; 1914/15: 68.1; 1915/16: 75.5; 1916/17: 81.8; 1917/18: 75.8. The data used are to be found in HA Krupp, WA IV. 2429–2433.

However, in all, the wage cost development tended to be negative for the company. With the increasing scarcity of the production factor work more and more workers were for the first time in a position to choose the most attractive of several offers. The high fluctuation at Krupp[50] shows that they realised and used this opportunity. The companies were forced to react to this with increased wages. As a result of this the average shift wages in the Gußstahlfabrik rose between the business year 1913/14 and the end of the war by 135% for men and by about 240% for women.

This mirrors almost exactly the rise in wages in the metal industry as a whole, which however started at a lower basic wage than that paid in the Gußstahlfabrik:[51] The Krupp wages were, during the war years, always a few percent above the branch average, a fact that may explain the favourable position of the cast steel factory in the battle for the decreasingly available workers.[52] Even in comparison with the entire German wage structure the wages in Essen were probably fairly high. If one compares the average wages paid in several industrial branches during the war with those of the Gußstahlfabrik, one finds that only the branch average of the machine construction and electronical industry attain this wage level.

However Table 3 gives a too favourable picture in so much that it shows the nominal wages. A comparison of the Krupp wages with the cost of living shows that even these high wage increases were swallowed up to a large extent by the rise in the cost of living. For example, in the years 1915/16–1917/18 the shift wages for the men employed at the cast steel factory rose by 59% on the average.[53] If we compare this with the cost of living for the same period, for which the Kaiserliches Statistisches Amt gives us very plausible calculations, then we find there a rise of almost 44%. Other authors come to even more unfavourable results.[54]

Thus even at Krupp the real wages rose only slightly – if a all. The clarity with which the workforce of the Gußstahlfabrik were aware of this fact can be gathered from the large number of letters personally addressed to individual members of the management as well as to the board of directors and to Gustav Krupp v. Bohlen asking for a pay raise.[55] They reflect the quandary of a workforce which faced increasing physical stress while experieneing a depreciation in the food and provisions and in addition to this had to live with a general inflation almost from the first day of the war onwards.

---

50 Between the 1.10.1914 and the 31.10.1916, 6847 female workers and 38 660 male workers left the Gußstahlfabrik in order to look for better paid work. On the other hand, the Gußstahlfabrik acquired 80 944 new male workers and 21 742 female workers (HA Krupp, WA IV. 1697, pp. 55–66). Additional material is in WA IV. 1395, pp. 11–13 and 18.

51 Cf. in detail on this L. Burchardt, "Die Auswirkungen der Kriegswirtschaft auf die deutsche Zivilbevölkerung im 1. und 2. Weltkrieg". in: Militärgeschichtliche Mitteilungen 1/1974, pp. 65–97.

52 Cf. note 50.

53 Precise data can be found in: Kaiserliches Statistisches Amt (ed.), Beiträge zur Kenntnis der Lebenshaltung im 4. Kriegsjahr. Berlin 1919, p. 67.

54 Cf. eg. J. Kuczynski, Die Geschichte der Lage der Arbeiter unter dem Kapitalismus. Vol. 4, Berlin (–0) 1967, pp. 329–350f. Kuczynski estimates the rise to be above 84%, but I consider the calculations of the Kaiserliches Statistisches Amt to be more reliable.

55 They are to be found in HA Krupp, 41/6–160 and 161.

If the Gußstahlfabrik did not want to suffer in the battle for labour then its wages at least had to cover the cost of living, and if possible rise even more quickly. Since it resolutely adhered to this maxim – as is shown above – the wage costs rose rapidly (Table 4).

Table 4. Wage costs at the Gußstahlfabrik[56]

	2. Quarter 1914	4. Quarter 1915	4. Quarter 1916	4.Quarter 1917	4. Quarter 1918
Average wages costs per worker (marks per year)	1719	2004	2250	2991	3636
Average daily wage costs (tsd marks)	285	391	537	955	1153
Total wage costs per year (mio. m.)	57.1	117.4	161.1	286.5	345.8

Like the wages, the prices of raw materials and intermediate products rose continuously throughout the entire war and in particular during the last two war years. This price development was on the one hand dependent on the excessive pressure exerted on the available resources, and on the other hand upon the fact that the producers of the raw materials and their suppliers passed on to their clients the entire rise in production costs which they were also experiencing. Krupp was not affected by this development quite as much as many other companies. Since some requirements could be met internally, in that e.g. the Friedrich-Alfred-Hütte and the Annen Steel works supplied the cast steel factory or the Germania-Werft, the rise in costs could to a certain extent be contained. However these possibilities were limited since the rise in the suppliers' prices was generally a result of an increase in costs rather than an increase in the profit margins.

A few examples shall illustrate the development of the prices for raw materials and intermediate products.[57] Even the price for Thomas steel had risen by the end of the war to more than twice the peacetime level although the required ore could be mined in German territory. Bessemer steel, which came from Swedish ore, reached three times the level of the pre-war prices. Non-ferrous metals like copper, zinc and tin reached almost twice the pre-war price and were not easily obtainable even for

[56] These figures are for the male and female blue collar workers and do therefore not include the salaries of the white collar employees. They have been calculated according to HA Krupp, WA 41/6–107 and the papers mentioned in note 34. There was an annual average of 300 shifts. This figure was used for those calculations where there were no specific figures available for the number of shifts. Cf. additionally Table 3.

[57] For the following cf. the detailed price figures in Vierteljahreshefte f. die Statistik des Deutschen Reiches 1919 I, pp. 100f. On the provision of raw materials cf. additionally O. Goebel, Deutsche Rohstoffwirtschaft im Weltkrieg. Berlin 1930; A. Müller, Die Kriegsrohstoffbewirtschaftung 1914–1918 im Dienste des deutschen Monopolkapitals. Berlin (–0) 1955.

that price. Coal originally almost retained its pre-war price but, from 1916 onwards, became drastically more expensive and had by the end of the war more than doubled in price.

These rises were the result of increasing scarcity. This could be explained on the one hand by the increasing internal German requirements and on the other hand by the fact that the allied blockade had practically cut Germany off from the world markets. Originally some raw materials could be obtained in limited amounts from abroad[58] but this source soon dried up.

Thus the delivery of ore from countries which the allied blockade could not reach became ever more important. The Swedish ores became irreplaceable for Krupp since it was not possible to do without the Bessemer steel in some fields. In order to secure the supply of Swedish ore under all circumstances, Fried. Krupp AG in 1916/17 finally acquired shares in some Scandinavian ore mines.[59] From this transaction arose the so-called Sweden debt which was later to become a dangerous burden.[60]

Altogether the direct and periodical production costs which caused expenditures (and which did not include depreciation and welfare payments) developed for the Gußstahlfabrik as follows:

Table 5. The production costs of the Gußstahlfabrik[61]

	1913/14	1914/15	1915/16	1916/17	1917/18	1918/19
Production costs in million marks	149.2	214.9	352.9	566.1	834.4	829.1
Costs in % of the costs of 1913/14	100	144	236	379	562	556
Costs in % of the costs of the previous year		144	164	161	148	99
Costs in % of the sales	68.9	68.1	75.5	81.8	75.4	81.7

Table 5 shows two things in particular. Firstly, production costs rose considerably during the war years, which, bearing in mind the expansion of the company and production, may at first appear natural. However if one analyses the relationship between production costs and turnover a very clear deterioration is evident in comparison to the pre-war period. Secondly, whilst even in the rather slack business year 1913/14 costs were only 68–69% of the sales, the costs proportion during the

[58] Cf. on this in detail Manchester, p. 283.
[59] Minutes from the supervisory board meeting of 27.11.1916 and 16.4.1917 (HA Krupp 41/2–185).
[60] Cf. on this part VI.
[61] Compiled according to the accounts in HA Krupp, WA IV. 2429–2433. The figures given contain the freight costs which however were well below 1% and are therefore not treated seperately. For the turnover cf. above Table 2.

war rose to almost 82%. In other words; the production costs grew considerably quicker that the turnover. The balance from sales and production costs (direct, periodical costs which caused expenditures) is called the earned surplus. From this the social security payments, depreciation and a few smaller posts must be subtracted in order to arrive at the company profits. If we use the figures in Tables 2 and 5 we come to the following conclusions for the Gußstahlfabrik:

Table 6. The earned surplus of the Cast Steel Company broken down for the varios production Areas[62]

	1913/14	1914/15	1915/16	1916/17	1917/18	1918/19
War material (million marks)	36.9	80.1	91.5	98.7	215.7	151.1
War material (as % of the total earned surplus)	55	79	80	78	81	81
War material (as a % of 1913/14)	100	217	148	267	585	409
War material (as a % of the previous year)		217	114	108	219	70
War material (as a % of the total sales)	17	25	20	14	20	15
Armour plate (million marks)	13.8	10.1	10.8	10.0	25.8	15.0
Armour plate (as % of the total earned surplus)	20	10	9	8	10	8
Armour plate (as a % of 1913/14)	100	73	78	73	187	109
Armour plate (as a % of the previous year)		73	107	93	258	58
Armour plate (as a % of the total sales)	6	3	2	1	2	2
Peace materials (million marks)	16.5	10.6	12.1	17.2	26.1	20.0
Peace Materials (as % of the total earned surplus)	25	11	11	14	9	11
Peace materials (as a % of 1913/14)	100	64	73	104	158	121

[62] Compiled according to the accounts in HA Krupp, WA IV. 2429–2433.

Table 6. (continued)

	1913/14	1914/15	1915/16	1916/17	1917/18	1918/19
Peace materials (as a % of the previous year)		64	114	142	152	77
Peace materials (as a % of the total sales)	8	3	3	3	2	2
Total earned surplus (million marks)	67.2	100.8	114.4	125.9	267.6	186.1
Total earned surplus (as a % of 1913/14)	100	150	170	187	398	277
Total earned surplus (as a % of the previous year)		150	113	110	213	70
Total earned surplus (as a % of the total sales)	31	32	25	18	24	18
Total earned surplus after treatment for the loss in purchasing power (million marks)	67.2	92.7	81.2	86.9	157.9	93.1

As Table 6 shows the company profits rose continuously during the war. Particularly marked rises can be found in the business years 1914/15 in comparison to the relatively slow year previously and especially in 1917/18 when the Hindenburg programme made itself felt. The profits rose most quickly in the artillery and am munitions production where, in the business year 1917/18, they reached almost eight times the pre-war level. Compared to this the profits in the production areas armour plate and peace materials initially experienced two to three regressive years before they at least nominally reached the pre-war values. The actual driving force behind the development was therefore the area war material. Since the earned surplus in Table 6 represents nominal values it must be treated for the inflation caused by the war. The results of this correction can be seen in the last row of data in Table 6.

It is more instructive to express the earned surplus as a percentarge of the corresponding turnover. In addition this figures offers the advantage of being indifferent to inflation. If we calculate this quotient as in Table 6 we find that it does not rise to any great extent even in the area of war materials. Apart from the more favourable first year of the war it always settles down to about ± 3% of the 1913/14 values. On the average of all the war years it was only 1.8% higher than this value. For the two other production areas the relationship between earned surplus and sales worsened even during the the first year of the war and was on the annual average not more than one third of the pre-war values. Accordingly the ratio between earned surplus and total sales also worsened. Whilst in 1913/14 it was 31% and in the first year of the war even reached 32%, it sank considerably in the two succeeding years and even in the record year of 1917/18 did not reach the pre-war value by far. On average for the business years 1914/15–1918/19 the value remained at 23.4% – far below the pre-war level. These findings force us to conclude that the production of the Gußstahlfabrik became less and less profitable over the years.

This impression is strengthened when we include the costs for social and charitable activities in our calculations. These figures do not by any means appear for the first time in the Krupp balance during the war years: For several decades Essen had offered reasonably priced shopping possibilities, workers hostels and workers housing estates, jubilee gifts etc. The company management had always taken pride in its social activities.[63]

What was new however was the vastly changed dimensions of the resulting costs in comparison to peace times. Even the Kruppsche Konsumanstalt in Essen, which under normal circumstances was self-supporting, needed financial support from 1915 onwards so that the increase in the cost of food could be at last partially compensated for. The expansion of the company caused costs to rise particularly steeply in the area of board and lodging. Soon after the recruitment of the first skilled workers from outside Essen it became obvious that for price reasons the resettlement of these workers with their families could not be justified.[64] In addition to this it would have been difficult to find suitable accommodation. Since the company on the other hand was increasingly dependent on the arrival of these outside male workers (and since about 1917 also of female workers) there was no alternative but to bring this labour to Essen and to provide them with company lodgings and food.

As a result of this numerous new barracks and more canteens sprang up in addition to the singles homes which had long been in existence for young skilled workers and technicians and the so-called "Menagen" for unskilled workers. Altogether the number of beds provided by the Gußstahlfabrik rose during the war from 1204 to 22 653, and the capacity of the factory canteens increased from 3600 to 34 000 portions per meal.[65] The employees naturally had to pay for their board and lodging but these payments by no means covered costs. It was therefore necessary for the company to pay considerable subsidies, not to mention the building costs previously invested. On top of all this there was also the separation allowance for the families of these employees and several other smaller posts which we cannot report on here. Table 7 summarizes the social expenditures resulting from the war.

By the summer of 1919 these posts accounted for more than 143 million marks. They illustrate a problem which we will go into in more detail later: Since the vastly increased labour force of the war years could, for several reasons, only be slowly reduced after the end of the war, some of the wage and welfare costs caused by this increase lasted until long after the end of the war, with very little advantage to the company.

---

63 A presentation of the social activities according to the company's management is given in: Die Wohlfahrteinrichtungen der Gußstahlfabrik von Fried. Krupp zu Essen an der Ruhr. 3rd ed. Essen 1902.

64 On the following cf. the figures in HA Krupp, WA VII. f 1105, pp. 85ff.

65 Ibid., pp. 98–100.

Table 7. War related social payment of the Cast Steel Factory in thousand marks[66]

	1914/15	1915/16	1916/17	1917/18	1918/19	1919/20
Subsidy for the Kruppsche Konsumanstalt	–	830	2180	153	2112	1595
Displacement payments for employees moving to Essen with their families	0.3	103	158	104	41	14
Separation allowance for outside employees	13	1862	3729	5889	6344	24
Subsidies for the board and lodgimg for outside	157	2911	7723	29303	55132	8606
Other welfare expenditures	402	1059	978	2774	4 924	4887
Total	572	6765	14768	38222	68553	15116

Even more unproductive in an economic sense was another post. As the first Kruppians joined up with the start of mobilization, the question arose as to how their families should be cared for and by whom. Although since 1888, legislation provided for support from the Reich[67], this was barely enough to cover the needs of a family. Because of this, the local councils and often the previous employers were usually willing to augment the payments coming from the Reich. The Gußstahlfabrik did not hesitate for a moment to act accordingly. By 7/31/1914 it had already provided for the continuation of wages for the white collar employees who had joined up and announced a preliminary arrangement for company support for the families of these employees.[68]

As with the state payments this regulation often had to be adjusted to keep up with the rising cost of living; this can however not be followed in detail here.[69] Summarizing, it must at least be recorded that during the first two years of the war the cast steel factory provided on average about 30–35% of the total support that the family of a Krupp worker who had been called up received from the Reich, the town of Essen, and from other sources. With the increase in the state provisions in the second half of the war, the Krupp proportion slowly sank to about 20%.[70] A further 12–15% came from the so-called "Liebesgabensammlung", a sum of money which those factory employees, who had remained at the company, under the watchful eye of the Krupp administration gave, more or less voluntarily from their wages.

[66] Compiled according to the Tables in HA Krupp, WA 41/74–354. The figures are each for the period from August 1 to July 31 and therefore not for the business year but for the so-called war year.

[67] Cf. Burchardt (1974), pp. 83f.

[68] Publication of 31.7.1914 (HA Krupp, WA 41/44–352).

[69] Informative material on this is contained in HA Krupp, WA 41/74–352 and 74–353.

[70] These figures are valid for a family with 2 children. For smaller families the Krupp contribution made up a greater percentage, for the larger families a smaller percentage.

Additionally there were financial gifts from the company for those joining up, rent support for the soldiers' families, special payments for Christmas or confirmations etc.[71] (Table 8).

Altogether these payments added up to about 36.5 million marks, a fair proportion of which the Gußstahlfabrik had to provide under the difficult circumstances of the post-war period. The company was not obliged to carry out any of this. Besides, economic considerations counseled against these extra expenses since they strained the company budget without being of any measurable use. Even the idea that these payments were virtually meant to be Krupp's contribution to stabilisation of the German political system misses the point: Until 1917 there was no obvious need to question the inner stability of the Kaiserreich.

Table 8. Support from the Gußstahlfabrik to the families of company employees who had joined active service in thousand marks[72]

	1914/15	1915/16	1916/17	1917/18	1918/19	1919/20	1920/21
Wages for employees who had joined up	1456	3677	4247	3573	3175	241	17
Support for their families	1810	3231	3607	3103	3028	860	211
Other support payments	589	765	872	781	941	212	95
Total	3864	7673	8726	7457	7144	1313	323

The real motive was a social one. Krupp could look back on a long tradition of social engagement. It was not only aware of its special position as the largest employer far and wide but also knew that what ever it did or did not do had an exemplary effect on the entire Ruhr area and beyond. Gustav Krupp v. Bohlen had with his position also inherited from his in-laws a very strong readiness to shoulder this responsibility. It was from this position that he ordered the support payments with the same matter-of-factness with which the Gußstahlfabrik at the end of the war re-employeed thousands of ex-Kruppians, who had been released from active service, although there was originally no work for them.[73] Compared to this, all other motives receded in importance.

---

71 A detailed list of these allowances is contained in HA Krupp, WA IV. 1697.

72 Compiled according to papers in HA Krupp, WA 41/74–354 and 74–359. The years are always from 1.8 until 31.7.

73 Cf. on this below part VI.

IV. The Profits

The profit and loss calculations of the Fried. Krupp AG for the period under investigation contained the following positions.[74]

Debit	Credit
Tax	Earned surplus (after depreciation)
Blue and WhiteCollar Workers' Insurance	Interest
Welfare expenses	Diverse revenues
Pure profit	

Whilst these calculations were provided regularly for the entire company as part of the annual company report, they do not appear to be available for the Gußstahlfabrik. However since we have fairly accurate knowledge of the earned surplus before depreciation, the depreciation itself and the welfare expenses for the cast steel factory, it is possible to give at least a plausible estimate of the profits. The other values needed for this – tax, insurance, interest and diverse incomes – have been estimated as follows: since they are available for the entire company it was only necessary to suitably reduce the figures. For the insurance the figures of the published profit and loss calculations were reduced by the proportion of employees working for the entire company but not for the Gußstahlfabrik.[75] For the other figures it has been presumed that the Gußstahlfabrik apparently produced about 80–90% of the earned surplus during the war.[76] In order not to obtain too low a profit estimate, it was assumed that only 80% of the total given in the company report was attributable to the cast steel factory. Estimates produced according to these assumptions are given in Table 9.

The figures relating to the balance of the Totals I and II differ from the real pure profit in that they make no allowance for depreciation.[77] Since the area of depreciation is notoriously difficult and more often than not confuses rather than clarifies the profit levels, the balances provided in Table 9 in some ways probably offer a more realistic picture. Without depreciation, without re-investments and without (notable) extraordinary positions, the figures correspond roughly to the modern term of "cash flow" and therefore reflect the financial earnings capacity of the Gußstahlfabrik. They show that – with the exception of 1917/18 – the thus defined profits of the Gußstahlfabrik remained relatively constant at a nominal value of about 90 million per year.

According to these calculations we arrive at a total pure profit of 480 million marks for 1914/15 to 1917/18. Inclusion of the year 1918/19 would raise this figure by a further 94 million to 574 million Marks. If we express this pure profit as a

---

74 Compiled according to the company reports. I have refrained from listing the profits carried over from the preceding year which appear on both sides of the calculation since they cannot be calculated for the cast steel factory alone and they are, in this context, only of secondary importance.

75 This percentage remained fairly constant during the war at 37%. The figures for the profit and loss calculations were accordingly reduced by 37%.

76 This is supported by e.g. the breakdown of profits in HA Krupp, WA IV. 2430. Precise calculations do not appear to be available.

77 In the published profit and loss calculations of the entire company the depreciations have already been subtracted from the earned surplus.

percentage of total sales we find that on average for the business years 1914/15 to 1918/19 it reached about 17% of the sales.[78] Even the pure profit of the Gußstahlfabrik therefore remained very clearly below the value of 20%, which experts consider to be an average pure profit for the German munitions industry in the last pre-war years.[79] It was on the other hand about three times as much as was published as pure profit in the company accounts for the *total* company.

However, we must specify our findings. Firstly it is obvious that the pure profits as a proportion of the turnover did not rise – with the exception of the year 1917/18 – but fell. If this decline is more obvious here than in the comparison between earned surplus and turnover as given in Table 6 then this is because of the enormous rise of welfare costs (still contained in the earned surplus): In the business year 1914/15 this postion only swallowed up 3.9% of the profits made at the Gußstahlfabrik. During the following year it was almost 13% and in the year after that 18.7%. In 1917/18 the percentage of welfare expenses sank slightly to 17.1% and increased finally under the abnormal conditions of the business year 1918/19 to over 40%.

Table 9. The estimated pure profits of the Cast Steel Factory in million marks[80]

	1914/15	1915/16	1916/17	1917/18	1918/19
Earned surplus	100.8	114.4	125.9	267.6	186.1
Interest and div. incomes	4.5	6.0	11.8	11.8	5.0
Total I.	105	120	138	279	191
Tax	8.6	6.9	24.7	14.1	13.9
Employee insurance	3.7	4.4	5.2	6.9	7.8
Welfare expenses	3.9	14.5	23.5	45.7	75.7
Total II.	16	26	53	67	97
Balance from sums I & II before treatment for rise in cost of living (million marks)	89	94	85	212	94
Line 1 as a % of the sales	28.2	20.1	12.3	19.2	9.3
Balance from sums I & II after treatment for rise in cost of living (million marks)	81.9	66.7	56.7	125.1	47.0

Secondly it must be taken into consideration that the documented profit figures are nominal values. This does not change the (inflation neutral) proportion of the

[78] If one takes the average of the percentage turnover for each year then one arrives at 17.8%, if one calculates the quotient between turnover and profit totals then one arrives at 16%.

[79] Boelcke, p. 227.

[80] Company profits and welfare expenses as in Table 6–8, the other values according to the published company reports with the corrections as described in the text.

profits within the turnover, but it lets their absolute levels stand out too much. The profit values that have been treated for inflation are shown in the last line of Table 9. They show a clearly declining tendancy which was only interrupted in the business year 1917/18 – there however all the more clearly. If we total up these real profits we arrive for the years 1914/15 – 1917/18 at a figure of 332 million marks; if we include the following year, this increases to 379 million marks.

Thirdly the profits shown in Table 9 include, as has already been explained, the depreciation. Depreciation, as defined by a contemporary expert, was "a reduction in the value as calculated by the entrepreneur in order to allow for the actual reduction in value".[81] Thus it constituted a natural part of the company's financial policy; in fact, there was a legal obligation to allow for depreciation. The depreciation was and is "to be distributed over the entire period of use typical for the company".[82] Since the expected period of use cannot be precisely estimated in advance, much less fixed at a pre-determined level[83], a suitable depreciation value is often a moot point.

During the last years before the war Fried. Krupp AG depreciated the value of its machines annually by 8%, a figure reached in agreement with the appropriate assessment commission.[84] In its first war-time balance sheet, the company had used a depreciation level of 13.6% and in doing this had obviously annoyed the financial administration. Finally the matter was discussed in December 1915 between the Krupp financial head Haux and representatives of the Essen tax office at the district president's office.[85] Here the financial civil servants at first demanded that the depreciation value agreed on earlier was used. However Haux managed to convince them that the war demanded more from the machines and that, in addition to this, many machines would be useless after the war. The participants finally agreed on a level of 14% which accounted for this. But even in the 1915/16 accounts this level was clearly exceeded with 18.5%. As the balance sheets for 1916/17 were being prepared Krupp v. Bohlen noted the following "points to remember":

> "1. As much depreciation as possible..., so that F. (ried.) K. (rupp) does not have the dead weight of the new constructions when it competes nationally or internationally. 2. Low dividends in order to make the above point possible and in order to ensure against too high an asset assessment (sc. of the Krupp family) in case of a possible asset tax".[86]

The choice of a higher depreciation level was therefore meant to arm the company for the much feared "economic war after the war": If appropriate depreciations were not carried out and reserves built up, in good time the company would run into difficulties during the poor sales opportunities of the post-war period. The money needed for these precautionary measures was taken from the profits and therefore reduced the dividends. Foregoing a high dividend on the other hand did not effect the shareholders – still one of the richest families in Germany – too much and made

---

[81] W. Le Coutre, Grundzüge der Bilanzkunde, Vol. 1, Leipzig 1922, p. 59.
[82] Hofmann, p. 169.
[83] Le Coutre, pp. 62ff.
[84] Cf. the figures in the company reports and the minutes of the meeting of 29.12.1915 between the company representatives and the financial administration (HA Krupp, FAH IV. C71b, pp. 172–177).
[85] Cf. note 84.
[86] Hand-written notice of 8.8.1917 (HA Krupp, FAH IV. C 71b, p. 168).

a good impression on the public. On top of this it reduced the probability that the Krupp family would be too heavily burdened in a later tax on the asset gains from the war.

The firm acted accordingly in the business year 1916/17. New factory constructions were written off at 30%, short-term provisional buildings, such as the huts for the employees from far away, immediately.[87] This resolute depreciation practice could not of course remain unnoticed. In the end the governmental presidential office in Düsseldorf employeed an external expert to investigate the legality of the Krupp write-offs.

In his report this expert, Kommerzienrat Moritz Böker from Remscheid, came to the following conclusions: firstly he claimed that all the factory machines were under stronger stress due to the war and were therefore worn down quicker, and that in particular the machines built during the war were of poorer quality and therefore had a shorter life expectancy. Böker continued that all this applied to a number of factories important to the war effort. On the other hand Krupp was in a singularly unfavourable position with respect to the later use of the war-time constructions. It was impossible to picture an even approximately full use of them after the end of the war, "all the more so as a large part of the international markets will remain closed to the company for the foreseeable future". It also appared to be unfeasible to use them for other purposes "since we are considering here special equipment for the manufacture of cannons and gun-carriages". Summarising Böker concluded

> "that in the interests of the Fatherland the company Krupp has had unusually high obligations imposed on it which should at least to some degree be compensated by suitable depreciation levels"[88].

A glance at the assets account of the total company provides the following picture:

Table 10. The movements within the assets account of the Fried. Krupp AG[89]

	level at beginning of business year (book value mill. m)	Additions	Losses dismantling and sales etc. (million)	Depreciation			Level at end of business year (book value in mill. m)
				ordinary (mill. m.)	extra ordinary (mill. m.)	in % of balance col. 1–3	
1914/15	225	53	9	23	15	14.1	231
1915/16	231	86	34	28	27	19.4	228
1916/17	228	113	64	34	49	30,0	194
1917/18	194	225	103	50	19	21.8	247
1918/19	247	62	63	19	–	7.7	227
Totals		539	273	154	110		

[87] Directive from Haux to the book-keeping department of 7.11.1917 (HA Krupp, WA IV. 2433).

[88] Undated letter from Böker to the chairman of the appeals commission Düsseldorf from about 30.1.1918 (HA Krupp, FAH IV. C 71b, pp. 162–165). On Böker cf. the article in the Neue Deutsche Biographie.

[89] According to a list in HA Krupp, WA VII. f 1080. These figures do not always agree with those of the company report and are not fully compatible with them. The data for the cast steel factory, which are partially incomplete, can be found in WA IV. 2429–2433.

As shown in column 6 the the company obviously took the intervention of the tax office as a cause for reviewing its depreciation practices. However if we compare the published company reports with those of other large companies we detect a certain disparity (Table 11).

Table 11. The depreciation practices of large German companies (in % of book values)[90]

	1913/14	1914/15	1915/16	1916/17	1917/18	1918/19
Siemens & Halske	2.1	2.0	2.0	2.4	2.1	2.1
BASF	15.2	15.1	14.5	11.1	10.1	10.5
Fried. Krupp AG	8.1	13.6	18.5	25.5	20.5	26.0
MAN	12.4	6.7	17.2	14.8	14.4	5.9
Daimler-Benz	9.9	5.6	10.0	100.0	n.a.	59.3

Ignoring the special case of Daimler-Benz[91], we find that Krupp is almost always by a large margin at the top of the list. Whilst Siemens wrote off an annual average of about 2%, BASF of about 12.3%, MAN of about 13%, at Krupp it was nearly 21%.

The reason for these depreciation practices are given in the already mentioned Böker report. Krupp (and here in particular the Gußstahlfabrik) had to assume that a large proportion of the newly constructed machines would become redundant after the war. These machines were solely meant for the production of artillery and ammunition and constituted a considerable increase in the pre-war capacity for the production of war materials. Even the pre-war machines were, under normal conditions, seldom even approximately fully in use. If the grossly increased internal German demand of the war years fell oft at the end of the war and – as was to be expected – a large part of the foreign business too, the surplus capacity could on no account be used economically. Basically it was much more to be expected that they would remain inoperative as would the living barracks of the redundant workers. The barracks could therefore be fully depreciated immediately. It was only the not totally satisfactory earnings ratio and the expected opposition of the tax office that prevented the company management from writing-off the new machinery even quicker.[92]

Even knowledgable contemporary critics have basically acknowledged this necessity, at the same time also criticising that industry here occasionally exceeded the permissible levels.[93] This accusation also probably applies to a certain extent to Krupp. On the other hand it must be considered, in addition to the arguments already supplied, that the war years from the start were marked by an annual average

[90] Compiled according to the published company reports. The values are given as a percentage of the values of machines and buildings before depreciation.

[91] This case was reported by Wette in his interesting article mentioned in note 25.

[92] Cf. also the subsequently finished paper on the technique of balancing in HA Krupp, WA VII. f 1080, pp. 14f.

[93] In particular R. Fuchs, Die Kriegsgewinne der verschiedenen Wirtschaftszweige in den einzelnen Staaten... Zürich 1918, pp. 50f.

monetary depreciation of about 15% and that in the construction industry the prices rose slower but steadily.[94] One was faced with the fact that it was only possible to depreciate from the nominal cost of acquisition of previous times whilst the prices for investments were rising. The danger of a loss in substance connected with this offsets to a considerable amount the increased security attained through the unusually favourable order and sales situation of the war years. Once the war had stopped, the cast steel factory, more than any other German company, had to expect adaption difficulties which would be added to by the increasing construction costs. Cautious assessments of the inventory, the highest depreciation possible, and the build up of reserves were, under these conditions, tried methods of reducing the risk.

Furthermore our look at the depreciations only supplies an incomplete picture since objects removed from the assets sheets have not been taken into account. In times of peace this position was not of great importance. For example in 1913/14 it amounted to only 1.6 million marks, i.e., 14% of the ordinary and extraordinary depreciation of the Gußstahlfabrik. As shown in Table 12, the removals from the list of assets increased rapidly during the war and in 1917/18 even exceeded the amount of depreciation; proceeds from the sale of removed objects – if any – cannot be taken into account for the reasons mentioned above.

If we compare the totals from depreciation and deducted objects with that of the acquisitions[95] we find that in the years 1913/14 the quotient of both of these figures was about 67%. In other words: the Gußstahlfabrik at that time financed their investments to about two thirds with depreciation and deductions from their asset sheets. During the war this quotient increased and occasionally even exceeded the value of 1.00. On average the cast steel factory financed about 85% of their investments from depreciation and removals from the asset sheets. This meant a considerable increase in comparison to the pre-war years.

If we balance out the basic profits of the cast steel factory calculated above with its depreciations and removals then we arrive at the figures provided in Table 12.

Table 12. The pure profits of the Gußstahlfabrik in million marks[96]

	Basic Profit	Depreciation	Reductions	Pure profit		Pure profit in % of turnover
				nominal	real	
1914/15	89	21	1	67	61	19.3
1915/16	94	43	18	33	24	7.1
1916/17	85	51	38	– 4	–3	–
1917/18	212	40	60	112	66	10.1
1918/19	94	13	24	57	29	5.6
Summen	574	168	141	265	177	8.4

[94] In more detail in: H. Mauersberg, Deutsche Industrien im Zeitgeschehen eines Jahrhunderts... Stuttgart 1966, p. 323.

[95] The data is from Table 12 and 15. On the method of calculation cf. Hofmann, pp. 304f.

[96] Compiled according to Table 9 and the balance sheets in HA Krupp, WA IV. 2429–2433.

If we accept the Krupp depreciation rates and the removals from the asset sheets as given by the Gußstahlfabrik then according to Table 12 there is a pure profit for the business years 1914/14 to 1918/19 of about 265 million marks.[97] In addition to this there are also any possible earnings from the sales of dismantled machines. On average this pure profit would amount to about 8.4% of the turnover, a figure which is clearly above the figures provided in the company reports for the entire company, but far below the profit level of 20% of the sales which in the later pre-war years was occasionally mentioned as being normal.

There are however several indications that the removals shown in Table 12 have been calculated fairly high. For example one hardly needs to suppose that the business year 1916/17 finished with a loss. Even if we ignore the removals quoted by the Gußstahlfabrik and accordingly adjust upwards the pure profit given in Table 12 we would find the profit reaching 11.3% of the sales. This would be almost exactly half way between the values quoted in the company reports and the approximate values of 20% mentioned above.

In any case one can presume that the pure profits attained in the cast steel factory were – in absolute figures – enormous but that some of the global assertations floating about in the literature do need considerable correction. Looking at it in relation to the sales the Krupp profits do not by any means compare particularly favourably with those of other large German firms, the dividends of the company Fried. Krupp AG were even clearly below those of comparable companies.[98] Krupp could probably have increased the profits easily just by increasing the piece price. No later than the start of the Hindenburg programme the German ammunition production could not have functioned without Krupp, and the first timid attempts at state price control remained – as Wette has pointed out – in the end ineffective. In the special case of the Fried. Krupp AG there was the additional difficulty that the civil and military authorities did not consider themselves to be in a position of correctly estimating the prime costs due to the complexity of the company. It would only have been on the basis of these however that price examination and controls could have been carried out.[99]

If the company basically refused to take up this opportunity of unlimited enrichment then this had a lot to do with the personal attitude of the boss of the company. He by no means limited himself to speaking out in public against the attainment of war profits, but took conerete steps in the autumn of 1914 by giving his directorate the following instructions:

> "In consideration of the state of war *no* (sic!) agreement with other factories with respect to deliveries and prices of war materials for the German government. The determination of prices only on the basis of normal profit margins in times of peace."[100]

---

[97] These figures still contain the reserves. There is more detailed information on these below.

[98] See below Table 13. Additional information for the company AEG is contained in G. Hecker's highly interesting work: Walther Rathenau und sein Verhältnis zu Militär und Krieg. Boppard 1983, pp. 304ff., 347ff. and 420ff.

[99] Note W. v. Moellendorffs from 24.11.1916 (Bundesarchiv Koblenz, Nachlaß v. Moellendorff Nr. 117).

[100] Directive from Krupp v. Bohlen to the board of directors from about 30.10.1914 (HA Krupp, FAH IV. C 73a, pp. 25f.). Cf. also Krupp's similar notice from 18.9.1915 (below, note 102).

The Krupp company constituted a very strict hierarchy. Both legally and according to tradition the boss had a pronounced personal authority downwards. This alone refutes the theory that Krupp v. Bohlen was in this case "talking a lot of nonsense" (according to Manchester) without any practical importance. It is hardly imaginable that a Krupp director would have been able to ignore the orders mentioned above without difficulty. Later verbal mitigations from the boss of the company are even less likely. He was very fond of precise written instructions and trusted the spoken word only as a second best. There has also up until now been no proof of such a change in direction. Furthermore the previous data analysis supports the supposition that Gustav Krupp's instructions were followed at least in principle.

V. Use of Profits and Flow of Funds

Let us start by looking at the use of the pure profits! We shall begin by talking briefly about the dividends. In the last five years of peace the company had normally paid 10–12% on their share capital, then 180 million marks;[101] in the year before the war it was 12%. Although the sales figures of the first war years would have permitted an increase, the level originally remained the same. Privatly Krupp v. Bohlen noted as a rule of action:

> "No increase in dividends above the normal level, any sums which could be used for this are to be invested in general causes ... avoid the appearance of a high dividend level. Principally ... avoid any war profit.[102]

A few days later he defined more closely the amount and recipients of the sum destined for "general causes" as follows:

> "Of the sums destined for the distribution of profits 24 million marks are to be provided for the following causes as an extraordinary donation: The 'Nationalstiftung' p.p. with the aim of setting-up additional pensions for large families of those killed or permanently injured in the war 20 million marks; for East Prussia 4 million marks. The remaining sum of 24 million marks is to be supplied as a 12% dividend".[103]

A similar arrangement was made for the next year and the year after.[104] In the business year 1916/17 the dividends were cut back to 10% in order to allow higher depreciation of the war constructions.[105] In 1917/18 the board of directors recommended a 4% dividend but the supervisory board decided differently. In the mean time, the collapse and revolution had occured so that one had to expect high losses. Therefore it was considered wise to be extremely careful and to pay no dividends at all. This was the start of Krupp's "period without dividends" which was not to end until the years of the armament boom under the National Socialists.

---

101 The average for the years 1909/10–1913/14 was 11.6%.

102 Hand-written note from Krupp v. Bohlen dated about 18.9.1915 (HA Krupp, FAH IV. C 71b, p. 178).

103 Hand-written note from Krupp v. Bohlen dated 2.10.1915 (Ibid., p. 179).

104 Cf. the company reports for 1915/16, p. 8 and Boelcke, pp. 256f.

105 Cf. on this the hand-written note from Krupp dated 8.8.1917 (above in note 86).

Altogether almost 81 million marks were paid out in dividends during the war years, 15 million of which the shareholders immediately returned to the company as an interest free loan for 10 years. Spread over the years 1914/15–1917/18 these 81 million marks mean an average annual yield of 8.3%. If one includes the year 1918/19 then one reaches 6.7%, if one includes the previously mentioned credit then one only arrives at 6.8% or 5.4% respectively. These were hardly extremely high yields. It may be of interest to compare these Krupp dividends with the returns offered by other large enterprises which also profited from the armament boom. Table 13 gives such a summary.[106]

Table 13. Dividend payments of several large enterprises 1913/14–1918/19

	1913/14	1914/15	1915/16	1916/17	1917/18	1918/19	Average 1914/15–1917/18
Siemens-Halse	10	12	12	12	12	12	12
BASF	28	19	20	28	20	12	24.8
Daimler-Benz	4	16	28	35	30	6	27.3
MAN	8	8	16	18	18	10	15.0
GHH	10	15	20	20	20	6	18.8
Krupp	12	12	12	10	–	–	8.5

As the Table shows Krupp is almost always bottom. If we take the average of the last 4 war years 1914/15–1917/18 and compare them to the average dividend payments of the other firms, we find that the Krupp average is only 43% of this value.[107] This discrepancy is partly due to the careful calculation of the dividends which was mentioned above. Since more than 99% of the Fried. Krupp AG shares were in family hands there existed hardly any need to fear criticism of this policy from the shareholders. Basically very little had changed since Alfred Krupp had observed contentedly that in his firm "no shareholders were waiting for their dividends".[108]

Even our superficial review of the dividend payments of the entire company gives the impression of an extremely careful use of profits. This first impression is strengthend when we look at the use of the Fried. Krupp AG's financial reserves. There had already been a legal requirement to maintain certain reserves before the start of the war. In 1916 a further reserve requirement was introduced in the form of the war tax reserves which had to be kept in case there was a later war profit tax.[109]

[106] Based on the company reports. Cf. also the compilation by G. Mai, Kriegswirtschaft and Arbeiterbewegung in Württemberg 1914–1918. Stuttgart 1983, p. 72.

[107] The other 5 companies paid on average 19.6% dividends.

[108] Letter from Alfred Krupp to the executive secretary from 2.3.1867 in W. Berdrow (ed.), Alfred Krupp. 1826–1887. Berlin 1928.

[109] Legal basis was the law on the peparatory measures on taxing war profits from 24.12.1915 (RGBl., p. 837) and the war tax law from 21.6.1916 (RGBl., p. 561). For 1914/15 and 1915/16 the company were assessed for 23.6 million and Gustav Krupp v. Bohlen for 21.4 million marks war tax. Cf. on this the letter from the board of directors to the book-keeping department from 23.10.1917 (HA Krupp, WA IV. 2433).

However the company management was by no means satisfied with just this. Instead it built up, especially during the second half of the war, several other reserves in addition to the legal reserves. Table 14 summarizes this activity.

Table 14. The reserves built up by the Fried. Krupp AG between 1913/14 and 1918/19 in million marks[110]

	1913/14	1914/15	1915/16	1916/17	1917/18	1918/19
Legal reserves	11	13	17	20	22	25
Special reserves	18	20	23	25	30	10
Reserves for special depreciation and renewals	5	5	10	15	20	–
War tax reserves	–	–	28	28	28	–
For the depreciation of war constructions	–	–	30	30	50	–
War damage and losses	–	–	–	–	40	25
Total	34	38	108	118	190	60

As shown in Table 14 reserves were built up during the war to the amount of about 156 million marks. At least one third of these were legal reserves and were therefore not fully controlled by Krupp.[111] The remaining reserves, as one can tell from their titles, were meant to ease the effects of war damages and to smooth the path to a peacetime economy. In 1916/17, they amounted to about 105 million marks or 62 million gold marks. The company had never before possessed similar reserves. They could only be amassed under the particularly favourable profit conditions of the war years.[112] On the other hand the company in general and the cast steel factory in particular had never before been so completely and to such an extent engaged in the munitions business.

There were therefore even greater problems to be expected if and when business slackened off at the end of the war or even came to a complete stop. In other words, the company had entered into enormous risks under pressure from the state. These could only be contained by a careful financial policy, which strove to maintain independence and which had long been practiced at Krupp. Accordingly, the company built up reserves over and above the legal minimum requirements in order to secure itself against the harder times to be expected. Let us now look at the long and short term use of the available funds and at the procurement of these sums. Amongst the long-term effective means of use we should mention first the investments. Table 15 summarises the expansion of the Gußstahlfabrik during the war.

---

110 Compiled from the company reports.

111 This calculation is also valid for the years 1916/17 and 1917/18.

112 This was already noted by Fuchs, p. 58.

Table 15. The Expansion of the Gußstahlfabrik[113]

	Net additions in comparison to previous year (mill.)	This sum is shared by			
		Living accomodation %	Factory premises %	Machines and equipment %	other %
1914/15	33.3	10.5	15.3	60.3	13.9
1915/16	54.5	9.9	18.5	55.4	16.2
1916/17	72.6	4.7	18.5	63.6	13.2
1917/18	155.7	4.3	25.6	65.5	4.6
1918/19	46.0	15.4	24.8	59.8	–

As far as the scale of the expansion is concerned, this Table for the Gußstahlfabrik repeats approximately the picture shown in Table 10 for the entire factory. In addition to this it stresses the main points and changes in emphasis in the investment programme of the Gußstahlfabrik. Particularly remarkable are the increasing proportions in factory premises and the comparable reduction in the proportion of living accommodations.

The latter position declined so quickly, in spite of a rapidly rising number of employees, because the new employees mainly moved into joint accommodations whose construction costs were comparatively low. On the other hand the regular accommodation construction of the Gußstahlfabrik was greatly reduced. These savings were invested in the expansion of the factory itself. The sole purpose of this expansion was to increase the production capacity in the field of war materials. A glance at the most important investment objects will make this clear:[114]

1914/15	Preßbau III.	4.1 Mio.
	Geschoßdreherei VI.	3.5 Mio.
	Zünderwerkstätten	3.3 Mio.
1915/16	Kanonenwerkstatt III.	4.5 Mio.
	Preßbau IIIa.	3.6 Mio.
	Kanoenwerkstatt IV.	3.3 Mio.
1916/17	Preßbau III.b	8.9 Mio.
	Geschoßdreherei VII.	7.1 Mio.
	Kanonenwerkstatt V.	4.7 Mio.
1917/18	Martinwerk VII.	15.3 Mio.
	Kanonenwerkatatt VII.	14.2 Mio.
	Kanonenwerkstatt V.	12.0 Mio.

Apart from the Martinwerk VII which could also be used for the production of peace material, all these new shops were designed and suited for munitions production only. Once the demand for such goods fell then these capacities could at the best be converted with great effort. At any rate, production capacities here and in the

[113] Compiled according to papers in HA Krupp, WA IV. 2429–2434. The incomings listed in column 1 have already been accounted for through the deductions from demolition or sales.

[114] Our list only shows the 3 largest measures undertaken in each business year. More detailed lists are to be found in the balance sheets (HA Krupp, WA IV. 2429–2434). The corresponding supervisory board decisions are to be found in WA 41/2–185.

Gußstahlfabrik as a whole gradually reached a level which was far above anything imaginable during peace times.

Altogether the cast steel factory invested in the years 1914/15 to 1918/19 a nominal value of about 359 million marks, the entire company about 539 million; the corresponding values in goldmarks are about 234 and 352 million marks respectively.[115] With the aid of these investments the Gußstahlfabrik covered by the end of 1917 about 450.000 sq.m. which was an increase of about 170% in comparison to the area before the war. This was far more than for example the chemical giant BASF could lay claim to, even though their factories in Ludwigshafen, Oppau and Leuna-Merseburg were among the main supports of the German war economy.[116] There should at last be a brief mention of two foreign investments connected with this, even though their scale is not in any way comparable with the inland investments: In 1916 and 1917 Fried. Krupp AG invested 3.75 million Norwegian and 2.2 million Swedish crowns in an iron ore mine each in Norway and Sweden.[117] They were meant to insure the delivery of Scandinavian ore even in the event that a change of opinion occured in Scandinavia which made exporting more difficult. Another long-term effective method of using financial reserves was the acquisition of war-loans. Krupp being a quasi-national institution, the management felt that "the company .... had an obligation, which should also set an example, to provide the highest amounts possible as war-loans".[118] Since it was only able to do this under the given circumstances to a limited amount the following method was introduced: Whenever a new loan was started, the Krupp company demonstratively provided a sum, usually about 50 million marks.[119] Altogether more than 380 million marks were paid in this way.

However since even Krupp was in no position to financially accommodate this sum the war loan papers were continually being re-sold – of course in the most inconspicuous way possible.[120] Therefore the amount of the Krupp war-loans never exceeded a total of 50 million marks and even in the business year 1917/18 they were steadily reduced due to incipient cash flow problems. At the end of the business year the company only had 31 million and in December 1918 only 8 million marks in war-

---

[115] These figures are the totals of the incomings to the housing account shown in Tables 10 and 15. The total investments of 629 million marks mentioned by Boelcke, p. 226, include the year 1919/20. Slightly diverging gold mark values for the cast steel factory can be found in Dieter Lindenlaub's interesting study, Maschinenbauunternehmen in der deutschen Inflation 1919–1923. Berlin 1985, p. 226.

[116] On the previous comparison: Letter from Carl Bosch to Krupp v. Bohlen dated 28.12.1917 and Krupp v. Bohlen's answer from 30.12.1917 (HA Krupp, FAH IV. C 205). Cf. additionally note 10 above. The BASF built up during the war approx. 326,000 sq.m., equivalent to an increase of about 51%.

[117] Minutes of the supervisory board meeting from 27.11.1916 and 16.4.1917 (HA Krupp, WA 41/2–185).

[118] Cf. the retrospective paper in HA Krupp WA IV, f 1080, p. 11. The fact that this was also the opinion during the war is also proved by Haux's letter to Krupp v. Bohlen dated 2.9.1915 (HA Krupp, FAH IV. C 71b, p. 200).

[119] A list is contained in HA Krupp, WA VI. f 1080, p. 11.

[120] The fact that this was not a special Krupp reaction is shown in the example of the Kaiser-Wilhelm-Gesellschaft, which reacted similarly. Cf. on this L. Burchardt, "Die Kaiser-Wilhelm-Gesellschaft im 1. Weltkrieg" in R. Vierhaus (ed.), Forschung im Spannungsfeld von Politik und Gesellschaft. Stuttgart 1990.

loans.[121] However the company did have on average in the years 1915/16–1917/18 36 million marks continuously tied up in war-loans which were lacking in other places. Thus, Krupp was able to start the post-war period without the ballast of war-loans which were continuously decreasing in value.

In the short-term, part of the totally available finances were used in order to increase the floating capital: With the increased production volumes there arose the need to increase the supplies of raw materials, intermediate products, spare parts etc. In addition to this the fluid capital[122] rose constantly until the business year 1917/18. Whilst in the balances provided at the beginning of the war it had amounted only to about 116 million marks it had reached at least 170 million marks three years later but sank after that. Table 16: Fluid Finances, Current Credits and Current Debits according to the Balance Sheets (million marks)

Table 16. Fluid finances, current credits and current debits according to the balance sheets (million marks)

	Liquid funds	Current credits	Current debits
30.6.1914	115.9	105.6	58.8
30.6.1915	125.1	111.3	105.6
30.6.1916	139.1	192.1	132.7
30.6.1917	170.4	369.0	208.0
30.6.1918	130.4	403.7	296.3
30.6.1919	157.8	629.4	450.4

As shown in Table 16 the company's current credit also rose. There was usually a relatively long period between the actual production (including the costs which the production incurred) and/or the delivery on the one hand and the state payments on the other hand. Usually, the state paid promptly, but the increase in production was bound to lead to an increase in the payments which Krupp had to advance, in particular to the Prussian military administration, without attaining any mentionable advantage.

When we look at the source of the financial means which were necessary for the measures mentioned above, then we notice that they mainly came from four sources – deprecitation and write-offs, increase in the reserves, capital increases, credits and subsidies. Depreciation and write-offs have been discussed in depth above as have been the increases in the reserves, but the remaining two sources demand a short mention. An increase in capital occured in 1914/15 and 1915/16. At the time the share captial was increased in two steps of 35 million marks each from 180 to 250 million marks.[123] A short time later the Krupp family supplied the already mentioned 15 million marks from their 1915/16 dividends as an interest-free loan.

[121] Calculated according to the lists on the portfolio of the Krupp AG in the balance sheets (HA Krupp, WA IV. 2431–2433).

[122] In the following the liquid reserves will be considered to be the totals from the tills, change, fixed-interest papers and bank savings.

[123] Minutes of the supervisory board meeting from 16.11.1914 (HA Krupp, WA 41/2–185). A listing of the development of the share capital can be found in HA Krupp, FAH IV. C 71b, p. 156.

Finally a hefty subsidy from the Reich must be mentioned. Due to a contract with the Arms and Munitions Supply Office (henecforth shortened to Wumba ("Waffen- und Munitionsbeschaffungsamt") the Reich supplied in 1917 and 1918, through the Wumba, lost subsidies to the amount of 55 million marks. They were intended to cover a third of the construction costs of the Gußstahlfabrik's newly built "Hindenburg-Werkstätten".[124]

Although the plant had on completion cost a lot more than had originally been planned, the payments of the Wumba could be considered as an effective support. In addition to this they at last made an old dream come true: the at least implicit recognition that the largest Krupp customer by far was at least somewhat responsible for the prosperity of the company – and additionally for their own sake had to provide for this prosperity. Altogether the capital increase (after subtracting the resulting increase in dividends), the credit of 15 million marks from the Krupp family and the lost Reichs subsidies of 1917/18 provided the company with about 120 million marks.

In addition to these there were also several sources effective in the short run. As far as the company management was concerned it was particularly relevant to achieve a reduction in the length of the payment period as practiced by the state. For the area of ships equipment where the sums involved were particularly high, the procurement office had already started in peace times to make advanced payments[125] but the army had always railed against this practice. It was not until some time after the beginning of the war that the military administration succumbed to the urging of the company. However the advance payments coming from this source appear to have been not too high. The military also deducted interest for this money and refused for some time to enter into long-term delivery contracts which would have given Krupp more room for manoeuvering.

It was the more industry friendly 3rd OHL which started to terminate this practice since otherwise it would have proved more difficult to achieve the increase in capacity demanded of the enterprises. Following long negotiations in January and February 1917, Krupp and Wumba finally signed the contract mentioned above which amongst other things agreed on the following:[126] Wumba would from now on accept contracts lasting 18 months; it would pay within 6 months – retrospectively from 1.11.1916 – an interest-free advance payment to talling 124 million marks; the previously mentioned subsidies should follow directly after this.

In spite of this contract the position "current debits" continued to increase at almost the same rate as in the previous year. However the company compensated for this to a great extent by slow payment to their own suppliers. As shown in Table 16, the position "current credit" rose more slowly than the outstanding debts but by no means less in terms of absolute growth.

Krupp's financial director Haux was thus a few years later able to look back on a basically positive balance. He noted in retrospect that it had not been difficult "to keep the finances reasonably fluid until near the end of the war"; there had never been any need for serious concern.[127]

---

[124] W. Berdrow, Kriegsdenkschrift (HA Krupp, FAH IV. E 10.1), pp. 143f.

[125] On the following cf. ibid., p. 310.

[126] Cf. above note 124. and Haux's confidential notice of 5.7.1917 (HA Krupp WA IV. 2433).

[127] According to retrospective work by Haux (HA Krupp, WA IV. f 1078).

It was not until the last months of the war that, as a result of the continuous expansion measures, the financial situation became more strained. Finally in the summer of 1918, the company took out a short-term bank credit of about 34 million marks. The last external credit of 20 million marks had been taken up by the Fried. Krupp AG in 1911 but this had been a long-term loan and was not a bank payment: Short-term debts had always been avoided.[128] The credit of 1918 was thus a highly unusual measure for which there were few precedents in the company's history. Nevertheless the debt coefficient (which remained low even after this credit) showed that the situation was as yet not too precarious.[129]

Summarising our investigation into the long-term effective movements of finances in the accounts of the Gußstahlfabrik for the years 1914/15 to 1917/18 provide the following picture:

Use of finances (mill. M.)		Source of finances (mill. M)	
Investment in Essen	316	Depreciation	155
Investments and ore purchases in Scand.*	42	Write-offs	117
tied up in war loans*	31	Increase in capital*	59
		Credit from owners*	13
		Lost Reich subsidy	55
Total	389	Strengthening of reserves*	133

(The figures marked with * are only available for the entire company. In this case it was, as was explained earlier, presumed that about 85% of the figure was accountable to or earned by the cast steel factory. The summary provided above can therefore only have the character of a rough approximation).

As is shown in the list above, the investments in Essen could be financed largely by depreciation and write-offs. Altogether the money additionally available amounted to about 140 million marks more that the amount additionally required, As far as one can determine it was with this excess of long-term company capital that the fluid assets were mainly financed. (Whether they were also used illegally to invest in neutral foreign countries must be considered later). Similar short-term debts could therefore be totally avoided until the last months of the war and – as they finally became unavoidable – could be kept low.

VI. The Situation at the End of the War

What sceptics had long feared finally happened in November 1918 – the outbreak of the revolution in Kiel caused the entire political system to collapse within a short period of time. Krupp felt the results immediately. Within hours of the outbreak of the revolution in Berlin, the Reich and Prussia annulled all of their contracts. At the

128 A list of the loans taken up since 1893 can be found e.g. in the Findbuch WA 41 of the HA Krupp. The amount of the loan debt can be found in the respective accounts. As of 30.6.1918 they were 43.6 million marks.

129 The debt coefficient is the quotient between foreign capital and company capital. Cf. also Hofmann, p. 254.

same time the company was ordered not to dismiss anybody but to somehow or other continue employing their workers.[130]

This development put considerable strain on the company. From one day to the next the complex apparatus of the Gußstahlfabrik with its 110,000 employees and the daughter companies ground to a halt.[131] Certainly it was possible to carry out some left-over contracts after a while. However it could not be supposed that under the existing circumstances there would be any further state contracts worth mentioning; it even appears that the goods already produced could no longer be delivered in many cases.[132] Private orders could only be expected after the company had adjusted to peace time production.

Additional difficulties were caused by the fact that Prussia and the Reich at the end of the war had even stopped paying their outstanding debts. The state normally paid promptly. On average during 1914/15–1917/18 the open sums at the end of every business year were covered by about 83% 5 months later.[133] Even then the remaining sum was often large enough; in December 1918 there were almost 31 million marks outstanding from 1917/18. Further supplies had also been delivered right up to the last days of the war. They came to about 40 million marks and had by no means been totally paid off by the end of the war.[134] It is however not yet possible to give precise information on the extent of these outstanding debts.

Compared with the scale which had in the mean time become usual at Krupp these outstanding debts of course did not present astronomical sums; in the autumn of 1918, however, they were sorely missed. In order to be able to keep up its payments the company management and even the Krupp employee and soldier soviet "pulled all levers" in Berlin. It was thus that payments recommenced slowly towards the end of the year and continued to be correctly processed by the new rulers in the following period.[135]

There was however one snag: the speed of inflation had increased noticeably since the end of the war. Between January and April 1919, the mark lost against hard currencies such as the Dutch gulden or the Swedish krone one third of its value (already reduced to about half of the value before the war); in the second half of 1919 it fell again by considerably more than 50%.[136] The state payments continued however at face values, thus decreasing in real value continuously. In other words; a delivery from Krupp to the State in October 1918 brought in real terms hardly more than 60% of the original price even if it was paid for within the next six months. When

---

130 W. Berdrow, Kriegsdenkschrift, p. 284.

131 Cf. the monthly lists on the deliveries to the states in the business year 1918/19 (HA Krupp, WA IV. 2434).

132 The accounts for 1918/19 contain a list of "products which are accounted for in the product account without being able to pass them on before June 1919". (HA Krupp, WA IV. 2434). Together they total 114 million marks and consist to about 98.5% of war material.

133 Cf. eg. the current book-keeping in the Kontokorrentbuch Z (HA Krupp, WA I. 1574). Additional material is contained in the accounts (HA Krupp, WA IV. 2429–2433).

134 Calculated according to a list in the accounts for 1918/19 (HA Krupp, WA IV. 2434).

135 Cf. the list from Haux in HA Krupp, WA IV. f 1080, pp. 12f.

136 Cf. the figures in the Vierteljahreshefte zur Statistik des Deutschen Reiches, 1920 I, p. 7 and 1920 IV., p. 131.

payment of the state obligations from the war was finally completed in the spring of 1921[137], the mark had dropped to about one tenth of its value at the end of the war.

As stated above, it is not possible to make a clear statement about the extent of the state debts in November 1918 since Krupp's books have only partially survived. Therefore, we cannot quantify the losses due to inflation. During the first post-war week, the abrupt stop of all payments cut much deeper anyhow: The Krupp company had little cash on hand, but the Gußstahlfabrik alone had to meet fortnightly recuring wage demands (plus the salaries of more than 5000 white-collar employees) of more than 13 million marks.[138] Added to this there were the welfare expenses which rose steeply during this period. There were neither new orders or incomes nor the arrival of outstanding payments to compensate for this. It was not possible to envisage an end to this situation in November/December 1918.

Under these circumstances the company management had to reduce the workforce as quickly as the confused situation permitted, and this in particular in the Gußstahlfabrik. For this they were not totally unprepared, since in the middle of October Gustav Krupp v. Bohlen had entrusted the directorate with the development of suitable plans.[139] They had originally foreseen not only incentives for voluntarily leaving the company but also for dismissals. However, Krupp v. Bohlen warned the directorate that they were not to dismiss workers for reasons of cost efficiency alone:

> "It appears to me to be particularly necessary to avoid any sort of haste even when this could cause financial sacrifice. The Krupp company must remain aware of its particular position in German industry and take account of all relevant social aspects, putting them before financial considerations".[140]

The ban on dismissals from Berlin then produced a new situation. Under these circumstances the Gußstahlfabrik increased the incentives for voluntary leavers at the Gußstahlfabrik where the problem was particularly acute: Whoever left before November 19 would receive 2 weeks wages and a free train ticket home. Since large traffic restrictions were expected during the second half of November due to the demobilisation, this offer did not go unheeded. First the foreign civil workers left, then the prisoners of war and a large proportion of the German workers from farther away. By the 19th approximately 36 000 workers had left the Gußstahlfabrik; another 16 000 had followed by the end of the month.[141] This made the problem less acute but by no means solved it since the workforce at Essen still counted more than 60 000 employees for whom there was at the moment no work. In addition to this the company had agreed to re-employ the ex-Kruppians returning from active service. For the cast steel factory alone this meant about 21 000 men.[142] There was therefore no choice for the company but to dismiss workers. The first had to go in January 1919. Krupp tried to avoid hardship since the situation in the Ruhr area was

---

137 Minutes of the supervisory board meeting of 23.5.1921 (HA Krupp, WA 41/2–185).

138 Cf. above Table 4.

139 Notice from Krupp v. Bohlen dated 14.10.1918 (HA Krupp, FAH IV. C 178, p. 75).

140 This citation comes from a letter from Krupp v. Bohlen to the board of directors of 6.11.1918 (ibid., p. 71). Cf. additionally ibid., pp. 72–74.

141 A list of the voluntary leavers can be found ibid., p. 68. Cf. also Heinemann, pp. 176–179.

142 Heinemann, p. 176; Klass, pp. 358f.

explosive enough. During the following months the number of employees had nevertheless to be reduced more drastically than ever before until it finally reached its lowest level since 1913.[143]

Even these reductions were, according to strictly economic considerations, not enough.[144] But the company's social traditions and the political situation counseled against an even harder line. Thus, one had to live with the fact that the Gußstahlfabrik was still burdened by a ballast of thousands of superfluous employees.

Apart from the excessive number of employees and the overblown production apparatus the company also had to take other burdens from the war years into the post-war era. Most important was the so-called Swedish debt. During the war the German or rather German owned ore deposits did neither qualitatively nor quantitatively meet all requirements. The Gußstahlfabrik and the Friedrich-Alfred-Hütte were therefore forced to rely to a considerable extent on the only foreign soruces which had not been affected by the British blockade, Scandinavia. The Swedes were quite happy to deliver but demanded payment in foreign currency.[145] In the face of continuous losses in the buying power of the mark this could hardly be taken amiss, but their desire ran counter to the German foreign currency policy[146] which forbade the private export of foreign currency during the war.

Finally the suppliers agreed to accept bills of exchange which were to be paid after the end of the war. When the war ended, this Swedish debt amounted to at least 31 million Swedish krone – in itself not a great amount had there not been two factors which aggravated the situation: Firstly it was not possible under the particular circumstances of the early post-war period to pay this debt, which even rose to 34 million kroner due to additional deliveries. Secondly their mark equivalent grew continuously with the rise in inflation. At the end of the war the Swedish krone had a value of 1.90 M; the debt at this time was therefore barely 60 million marks. Due to the los in value of the mark, it had risen to 120 million marks by the summer of 1919. Later that year it reached 234 million marks and at the end of January 1920 it peaked at almost 600 million marks.[147]

Of course these were nominal amounts. However if one considers the company's extremely precarious income situation at the time, this sum takes on threatening proportions: The poor sales position in the first post-war years forced Krupp to use the reserves built up during the war. This was in itself not unusual since these reserves had been built up for this very event. However it had not been anticipated

---

143 Cf. the development of the membership figures for the Krupp company insurance which are almost identical to the figures for the size of the workforce (W. Vossiek, 100 Jahre Kruppsche Betriebskrankenkasse 1836–1936. Berlin 1937, p. 61 and 128).

144 W. Berdrow, Nachkriegsdenkschrift (HA Krupp, FAH IV. E 10.2) p. 118. As a result of this there was a second wave of redundancies which reduced the work force at the cast steel factory to about 25 000 (Vossiek, p. 128).

145 On the following cf. Berdrow, Kriegsdenkschrift, p. 311. A list of the Swedish debt as of 30.8.1918 is contained in HA Krupp, WA IV. 2433.

146 Cf. eg. the publication on the trade with foreign currency of 20.1.1916 (RGBl., p. 49) and the publication on the trade with foreign countries of 8.2.1917 (RGBl., p. 105). Additional information is also available in HA Krupp, WA VII. f 1080, p. 2.

147 Ibid., p. 9f. Detailed calculations for autumn 1919 are to be found in HA Krupp, WA IV. 2434. The total of 600 million SKr. mentioned by Heinemann, p. 181, has arisen due to a confusion between the krone and mark debt.

at the time that the mark would fall as quickly as it had done. If one adds up all of the reserves available in the business year 1917/18 and even includes the reserves required by law (although they could not be used by the company), one arrives at 190 million marks. This would been enough at the time to have paid the Swedish debt more than three times over. The debt, however, rose with the inflation while the reserves retained their nominal value. By November, 1919, they just covered three-quarters, a few months later only one third of the Swedish debt. The result was that it burdened the company during the early post-war years in a way that nobody could have foreseen. Another part of the burden of the war period was the repeatedly voiced accusation that Krupp had traded with enemy states during the war and therefore committed treason. This problem of course does not necessarily come within the framework of our more economical investigation, but it does require a short explaination since it is an important argument of those who accuse Krupp of having made excessive war profits and of having shrunk from nothing in doing this.[148]

Basically one must differentiate between three acts, namely:

- the fulfilment of obligations towards enemy states,
- deliveries to enemy countries, and
- the fulfilment of obligations from the pre-war period and from unlimited licence contracts with enemy companies.

The settlement of the demands from enemy creditors was suspended at first. It was not until April 1917 that the Reichsamt des Innern engaged a "trustee for enemy assets". He accepted the appropriate payments in order to take care of them until the war ended; transfers to the enemy states did not take place. The Krupp files do show that the company took note of this regulation but do not show either whether payments were made to the trustee or whether there was a direct transfer.[149]

In a few cases foreign military adminstrations had made pre-payments before the war on orders which then were not delivered due to the start of the war. In order to repay at the appropriate moment both these pre-payments and the interest which had accumulated in the mean time, the company amassed a "solid foreign currency reserve". This was given to a Dutch bank in which Krupp had shares. More accurate information about the amount has not yet come to light. It is also still unknown whether this fund was started during the war or after the end of the war. There are reasons for assuming that the latter was the case.

During the war the German iron and steel industry (with state approval) delivered sizable amounts under lucrative conditions to neutral states.[150] The cast steel factory could not participate in this since the German military and naval

---

[148] Cf. eg. H. Engelbrecht and F.C. Hanighen, Merchants of Death. New York 1934, pp. 155ff.; Weber, p. 31.

[149] Order from 19.4.1917 (RGBl., p. 363). An explanatory note can be found in HA Krupp, WA 41/2–327. On the following cf. the work "Finanzgebahrung 1922–1923" in HA Krupp, WA VII. f 1081.

[150] Cf. on this the material from the Verband Deutscher Eisen- und Stahlindustrieller in the Bundesarchiv Koblenz, R 13 I 185, pp. 66–99; Weber, p. 31; G. Feldman, Army, Industry and Labor in Germany, 1914–1918. Princeton 1966, pp. 52–54.

administrations practically held a monopoly on deliveries. Whilst they only bought up about 60% of the production in war materials in 1913/14 they regularly took 99–100% of the production of war materials and armour plate during the war. The small remainder went mainly to Germany's allies Austria and Turkey, with only 2–3% of this remainder going to Switzerland.[151]

Even before the war deliveries to the later enemy states had been rare.[152] At the beginning of the war these deliveries were stopped. Material which could no longer be delivered either went to the German military or was kept on the accounts at company cost. The author does not know of any indications for further deliveries to enemy states.[153] Even indirect deliveries – for example via Switzerland – could noly have occured to a very limited extent since Switzerland only received far less than one percent of the Krupp production.

Alleged proof of deliveries to enemy states came to light occasionally in the 20's but proved regularly to be unsupportable. When finally the Oberreichsanwalt followed up such accusations he came to the conclusion that "there is no reason for intervention".[154]

Krupp demands on enemy firms totaled a mere 122 000 Ffr at the beginning of the war.[155] Mr. Sorge of the board of directors soon gained the impression that "there was little hope for a realisation of our demands in the warring countries for the time being".[156] His guess proved to be correct. Accordingly all but a small part of the demands, except for one on the Belgian war ministry, were written off as losses.

The question of the payment of licence levies to the Gußstahlfabrik became somewhat famous. In the last years of peace the Gußstahlfabrik had received about 0.8 million marks in such payments. 70% of them came from German and Austrian companies. A further 12% came from the Russian firm of Putilow, the remainder from Krupp's English competition Vickers.[157] The Vickers payments had arisen on account of a licence contract for Krupp detonator patents from 1902.[158]

Shortly after the start of the war Krupp v. Bohlen and the directorate agreed to donate any payments from licencees in enemy states to charitable causes.[159] However they never received any such payments. Whilst the demands on Putilow were overshadowed by the Russian events, Vickers paid up in 1924 following legal proceedings, but the amount paid was far below that demanded by Krupp.[160]

---

151 Cf. the compilations in the balance sheets (HA Krupp, WA IV. 2429–2434).

152 A compilation of the foreign deliveries is to be found in the balance sheets for 1913/14 (HA Krupp, WA IV. 2429).

153 In December 1916 Fried. Krupp AG applied for permission to deliver some trial gun barrels to the U.S. Navy, but permission was only granted for one barrel which was then delivered in 1917 (Boelcke, p. 259).

154 Letter from the Oberreichsanwalt to the Krupp company dated 10.1.1931 (HA Krupp, WA 41/2–309).

155 List from the book-keeping department of 3.12.1915 (HA Krupp, WA 41/2–321).

156 Sorge to Hugenberg, 5.10.1914 (ibid.)

157 Cf. the list "Abgaben auf Kriegsmaterial" in the balance sheets 1913/14 (HA Krupp, WA IV. 2429).

158 Particulars in Boelcke, p. 160.

159 Cf. the exchange of letters between Krupp v. Bohlen and the board of directors in April/May 1915 (HA Krupp, FAH IV. C 73a, pp. 15–19).

160 Manchester, pp. 285f. and 330f. Krupp is said to have demanded £ 260,000, Vickers finally paid £ 40 000.

The problem of the export of capital must also be mentioned at this point. The fall in the value of the German currency led many enterprises from 1916 onwards to transfer money that they did not need to neutral foreign countries.[161] Legally such transfers were forbidden, but the German bureaucracy found themselves forced to tolerate them since they had no effective means of combatting them and also because they saw some positive sides in this export of capital.

Krupp, too, has been accused or moving capital to neutral foreign countries. In particular the Krupp AG was accused of selling a share package to the value of "approximately 100 million marks to the portfolio of a Dutch bank", with the somewhat foggy addendum that this was all part of "the Krupp war profits invested abroad".[162] What really happened was that, anticipating great burdens from the Reichsnotopfergesetz of 31.12.1919, the Krupp family sold 70 million marks worth of shares to a Dutch bank. On doing this it was agreed that the Krupp family had the right to buy back these shares at a later time at a value of 110. This occured during the next few years in several stages.[163] In other words, Krupp sold some shares long after the end of the war due to temporary liquidity problems and bought them back at a later stage. War profits had as little to do with this as the desire to move any Krupp assets abroad. The entire accusation turns out to be one of those a publicity moves based on half-truths and free speculation of which the writings on the Krupp company and family history abound. The Scandinavian investments mentioned above must also be remembered here. They neither represented an attempt to move company or family assets abroad but served clearly definable aims of provision. Further foreign investments do not appear to have occured during the war years. Altogether there has until now been no evidence that Krupp either directly or indirectly traded with enemy states during the war or that it moved capital into neutral foreign countries.

Basically the "condemning material" is reduced to the licence contract with Vickers. This contract was made at a time when German foreign policy – let alone German industry – did not view England as a future opponent and represents a licence contract as any other. The fact that Vickers paid the debts resulting from it was in keeping with correct international practice and also had to be enforced in a legal battle. Taken by itself, it would not have aroused any interest. What made it so odious to the critics (and since then so interesting for many historians) was not its existence but its content: munitions goods in the form of certain detonator models.

This way of looking at things indicates a lack of understanding of the mechanics of economic war. Even in the First World War there were in addition to armament and munitions innumerable goods which indirectly were of no smaller importance for the war: iron ore, used for producing grenade steel, non-ferrous metals, used to produce navigational equipment or the leather needed for the manufacture of cavalry saddles and infantry boots etc., wool, cotton and colours for uniform cloth,

---

[161] This point can only be touched upon here. Cf. e.g. the material in the files of the Verein Deutscher Eisen- und Stahlindustrieller (Bundesarchiv Koblenz, R 13 I 181, pp. 24–39 and R 13 I 182, p. 161), also the letter of the state secretary of the Reichsschatzamt to the home secretary from 23.3.1917 referring to the loss of capital to Holland (Politisches Archiv des Auswärtigen Amtes, Bonn, AA/IA: Niederlande 59 vol. 6, A. 10232). For the legal position cf. above note 146.

[162] Cf. eg. Engelmann, pp. 276f.

[163] Notice in the files dated 15.8.1961 (HA Krupp, WA IV. 2436). Cf. also the company report for 1920/21. The text of the Gesetz über das Reichsnotopfer in RGBl. 1919, p. 2189.

medicines and food for the soldiers and civilians – all of these were scarcely of less importance than detonators or grenades. The licences for detonators were therefore basically no different from the licences for the production of certain medicines, colours or tools. The fact that Krupp prosecuted for the fulfilment of Vickers' obligations was of no surprise: At the beginning of the 20's the company was locked in a fight for survival which was made worse by the catastrophical state of the German currency. Under these circumstances, there was no reason to relinquish claims to outstanding foreign currency payments which had been contractually agreed upon.

VII. The War Profits of the Gußstahlfabrik

The amount resulting from the licence contract with Vickers was in any case only a very small proportion of the profits gained during the war. As we have seen, these profits were high even if they remained well below the figures which have been prevalent in the literature since then. On the other hand the estimated pure profits even of the Gußstahlfabrik as estimated in Table 12 rose far above the 182 million marks that were reported in the company reports for the entire company.

Even if these profits were effected by inflation they remained impressive enough, but they were not excessive and represented a smaller percentage of the turnover each year.

Furthermore the Gußstahlfabrik (as the entire company) did not make full use of its opportunities to push prices up, for example by price agreements amongst the large munition manufacturers. Even the dividends remained below rather than above the pre-war level and were often lower than those of comparable large enterprises. Low dividends of course do not necessarily indicate a poor sales position. Even during boom periods it can be advisable to follow a financial policy aimed at building up reserves; the Krupp company management was particularly aware of this fact. Thus, substantial sums remained disposable even after dividend payments. They were partly used to build up of capital reserves but mainly re-invested.

These investments served mainly to increase the capacity of the cast steel factory for the production of war material – vast facilities of very limited use for which there would be little need after the war. Their conversion to non-military production was at the very least an expensive affair. If one dispensed with it for reasons of costs, these installations could not be used. Even if conversion could be achieved at acceptable costs, it remained to be seen whether Krupp would ever find customers for the goods to be produced there: the war had created an international surplus in the steel producing and machine construction areas. On top of all this the German suppliers were barred for the time being from the international markets. All in all, conditions for such a drastic conversion as the Gußstahlfabrik necessarily faced after the war were extremely difficult.

Since these circumstances could to a certain extent be foreseen, the Fried. Krupp AG had in good time amassed considerable financial reserves. They were to finance the production conversions and to cover the period until these conversion measures would begin to take effect. However, events worked out differently. Even in November and December 1918 the wage and welfare costs, for which there were no equivalent incomings, swallowed up much of the reserves. The delayed arrival of any payment meant that it had lost some of its value due to inflation. The remaining reserves were also subject to this devaluation process. All these factors operated to create a noticeable liquidity problem, which became more threatening on account of the Swedish debt.

Perhaps the clearest indication of the poor position of the Gußstahlfabrik, and also the entire company, is a letter from the member of the board of directors Wiedfeldt to Krupp v. Bohlen in the summer of 1920. In it, Wiedfeldt outlined the poor financial position of the company and warned against illusions about the sales possibilities for iron, steel and steel products. Since he assumed that there was only a small chance that they could themselves earn the money necessary for a conversion, Wiedfeldt finally recommended the sale of 100 million marks worth of Krupp shares to an interested American consortium.[164]

Whoever knows the history of Krupp also knows to what extent they had always shrunk away from this sort of step. The expansion of the cast steel factory under Alfred Krupp and his successors had caused acute lack of capital at various times. However they had always preferred other solutions to that of turning to the stock market. More than any other risk the company managers feared this loss of their independence. It was only in extremis that a member of the board would advise such a step.

Krupp AG had arrived at this precarious position not because of too low profits but mainly due to the fact that a large part of the profits had been invested in the construction of installations which now no longer turned a profit. The previously mentioned Kommerzienrat Böker had at the beginning of 1918 pointed to this problem with the comment that Krupp was unique in this amongst the large German companies.[165] This was true. Companies which had not become so exclusively involved in the production of munitions and/or had been able to convert to more marketable products were without question in a better postion than the Gußstahlfabrik with its armament production quota of more than 90%.

This becomes evident in a comparison between the cast steel factory and companies such as BASF or AEG. They also produced for armaments but had never become pure munitions factories. Their conversion problems were accordingly fewer. They, too, had to expect more competition on the international markets but they could at least depend on a back-log demand within the German civilian sector. It quickly became evident for example that the BASF's ammonia factories in Oppau and Leuna, whose production during the war had mainly served as a raw material for the production of explosives, had found a very willing market in agriculture.[166] As a result of this demand some of the existing facilities soon even became too small and had to be extended. If we compare the Krupp and the AEG accounts for 1918/19, we find a similar picture:[167] Whilst Krupp carried 672 million marks credit which

---

164 Letter from Wiedfeldt to Krupp v. Bohlen dated 8.7.1920 (HA Krupp, FAH IV. C 71a, pp. 147–153).

165 Cf. above Part IV.

166 Die BASF. Ludwigshafen n.d. (approx. 1922), pp. 148–150 and 212–214.

167 On the following cf. the "Analyse der Vermögensaufstellung von 8 Industrieunternehmungen" (HA Krupp, FAH IV. C 71a).

were not covered by fluid reserves, this position at AEG amounted to a more 72 million. Both companies differed little in assets, in total share capital, and financial reserves. Whilst however Krupp's accounts closed with a loss of 92 000 marks the AEG accounts showed a profit of more than 27 million marks. In reality the financial disparity between the two companies was even greater. If one looks at the internal rather than the published Krupp accounts one encounters even higher losses: Even if one includes all outstanding incomings and reserves then there is still a negative balance of 57.5 million marks.[168]

Where AEG and BASF both worked to full capacity and even in some cases expanded, Krupp at the end of the war had to sell the Bayerische Geschützwerke, which had only just been completed at a cost of 35 million marks, for half that price. If one takes into account the inflation which had taken place in the mean time the selling price proves to be even more unfavourable.[169] In Essen a large part of the cast steel factory was closed due to loss of orders. Wherever possible, the firm rented out buildings in question in order at least to cut losses. There is a certain symbolism in the fact that at that time the AEG showed lively interest in the leasing of some of the enormous Krupp halls.[170]

As shown above, the factors leading to this dead end had to some extent been foreseen. This holds true in particular for the threat of over-capacity of the cast steel factory. Nevertheless, the company management followed this path for the following reasons:

1. The company management hoped for state support in the form of long-term contracts. If it was possible to carry over the contract type as promised by Wumba in 1917/18 to the post-war period, then at least a partial use of the over-capacity could be expected, perhaps even a monopoly over and above the status quo for Fried. Krupp AG.

2. All this could only happen in the event of a German victory or at least a tie. The fact that the war would not only be lost but would end in collapse, revolution, and a dictated peace was not anticipated by the Krupp directors for a long time. When at last in the middle of October 1918 this was first considered the Krupp production capacities had been expanded long ago. Just as unexpected was the post-war inflation. The fall of the mark during the war years had of course not gone unnoticed, but the dramatic rise in the rate of inflation at the end of the war was all the more unexpected since one had not anticipated the defeat which caused it.

3. Finally the question should at least be asked even if it cannot be answered as to whether the boss of the company would have reacted very differently had there been no prospect of state support for the post-war period. Krupp v. Bohlen had an unlimited loyalty to the Kaiserreich, a loyalty which was only exceeded by this attachment to his company, a loyalty by the way, which should not just be attributed to the unconsidered representation of Pan-German thinking.[171] He saw Germany

---

168 Cf. the list "Verlust-Ausgleichs-Konto" (HA Krupp, WA IV. 2433).

169 Ibid.

170 Cf. E. Haux, Bei Krupp. Bilder der Erinnerung aus 45 Jahren 1890–1935. Manuscript Essen 1935, p. 124 (HA Krupp, FAH IV. E 16).

171 Cf. eg. Krupp v. Bohlens persistent refusal to force Bethmanns downfall. His exchange of letters with Haux in April 1917 relating to this can be found in HA Krupp, FAH IV. C 73b, pp. 160–183.

with her back to the wall and therefore perceived himself even less in a position to ignore the request of the third OHL for maximal cooperation since the OHL and Wumba for their part had accommodated some of the wishes of the company. It is known that this commitment was not easy for either himself or his directors but that it was entered into "only follwing the OHL's pressing pleas and with great reservations".[172] However, Krupp did not believe that he had any other choice.

In conclusion let us again consider the question asked at the beginning about the nature of war profits. Our investigation has shown that the Gußstahlfabrik in Essen made a profit during the war years which after deflation was more in line with the profits attained in good years of peace than were the size of the workforce, sales and other relevant data. Only a small part of these profits ended up in the accounts of the share holders; there can hardly be any talk of unlimited enrichment or excessive war profits in Krupp's case. This becomes particularly clear in a comparison with other large companies.

The largest part of the profits were partly reinvested, partly placed in financial reserves. All in all Krupp AG drew little benefit from this money. The machines which it financed could only be profitably used during the war, and the financial reserves turned out, under the inflationary conditions of the first post war years, to be barely enough to keep the burdened company afloat until it could regain its footing in the peacetime economy.

The company management was not prepared for this development. This becomes clear enough through the fact that at first nobody knew to which products the cast steel factory could possibly convert. A certain amount of clarity was only slowly brought about by an internal ideas competition[173] and several conferences of the company heads in the winter of 1918/19. Thus, the absolute amount of the war profits attained appears to be of less importance than the question as to whether the company was capable of converting to peace production easily or only with great difficulty. Only then could it be ascertained whether lasting profits had been made or whether the conversion would swallow up the profits and financial reserves as quickly as they had been built up during the war years. Whoever let himself, in the innumerable parliamentary discussions on a war profit tax, be blinded by Krupp's particularly high profit figures and picked on this enterprise as the actual scape-goat[174] had thus overlooked an important, perhaps the crucial point. At least one can exonerate him by saving that during the war it was not possible to gain a clear picture of all the points which have been mentioned. This is however not true for the authors writing later who, during their attacks on Krupp, obviously overlooked that in

Cf. also his increasing scepticism in Hugenberg, as is evident in his exchange of letters with Eberhard v. Bodenhausen in January 1918 (ibid., pp. 131–143).

172 Letter of the Fried. Krupp AG to the Prussian war ministry of 16.4.1917 (Boelcke, pp. 260–262). Cf. also the ibid. cited passage from a Krupp-Denkschrift of 1926.

173 Proclamation from the board of directors of 6.12.1918 in: Kruppsche Mitteilungen of 7.12.1918, pp. 305f. About 1300 suggestions were made. A number of them were short-listed and the winning suggestions are to be found in HA Krupp, WA 41/2–116. Cf. additionally Klass, pp. 379ff. and Manchester, p. 311.

174 Cf. Wette in: Militärgeschichtliche Mitteilungen 2/1984, pp. 42 and 45f.; R. Schiffers etc. (eds.), Der Hauptschuß des Deutschen Reichstages 1915–1918. Düsseldorf 1981, Vol. 1, p. 237. Cf. also Moellendorffs notice from 24.11.1916 mentioned in Note 99.

relation to the size of the workforce, the factories etc., the largest war profits were not made at the Gußstahlfabrik or at Fried. Krupp AG generally but rather at other companies. They also overlooked the fact that Krupp's particular position demanded the build-up of large reserves for the transition problems which were to be expected at the end of the war. Finally they over-looked the fact that during the first post-war years even these large financial reserves almost proved insufficient to help the company survive.

Indicators of Real Effective Exchange Rates of Major Trading Nations from 1922 to 1937

Volker Hentschel

In grateful memory of Werner Conze

I.

From the beginning of the First World War to the beginning of the Second World War trade was affected by frequent, varied and unusually extensive shifts in international price relations and exchange rate parities. The First World War and the varying degrees of inflation caused by the war economy in every country gave rise to the first wave of extensive change. The situation was further distorted by the success in combatting inflation in some countries and the progressive deterioriation in the currency in others during the immediate postwar years. The violent fluctuations took place during a period when exchange rates were free to move. In the mid-twenties relative calm was restored when most of the major international currencies returned to the gold standard and the price trends steadied somewhat. But, of course, the inherent deviations from the price and exchange rate relations of the 'halcyon' prewar days in world trade continued to have an effect. Moreover, the calm was of short duration, and the world slump set off a second wave of hectic fluctuations in price and exchange rates, which only gradually ebbed after 1934. This was a period of arbitrary changes in exchange rates that were on principle fixed[1], and it corrected or accentuated the results of the first wave.

The literature on the economic history of that period contains a large number of more or less fixed assumptions, ideas and statements on the effects of these many and varied changes in price and exchange rate relations on international trade in goods and services, and hence on the prosperity of nations. It is, for instance, largely assumed that the successive, uncoordinated return of the major currencies to the gold standard during the twenties led to considerable distortions in exchange rate relations which were ill adjusted to the changes in price relations, and brought the United States and France very considerable international competitive advantages, while Great Britain certainly and Germany with some probability suffered no less remarkable disadvantages. That is why Britain and Germany encountered hitherto unknown obstacles to exports, which hampered growth in their economies, while the United States accumulated extensive trade balance surpluses, although its newly acquired position as international creditor would really have required deficits to help keep the world economy functioning. It is also assumed that the controversial devaluation of the pound in September 1931 brought about a decisive and lasting improvement in British price competitiveness but burdened the world markets,

[1] To be more precise, these were arbitrary devaluations stretched over time, the extent of which the monetary authorities *on principle* left to the market. *De facto*, admittedly, they intervened on the markets to bring rates where they desired.

already shaken by crisis, with a very difficult adjustment requirement. That is why it is generally regarded as a key event in the world economic crisis.[2]

These are only a few rough indications. They could be multiplied, and, naturally, should be formulated with more differentiation to give a comprehensive survey of the comments in the relevant literature on our problem. But that is not our concern here. Whatever such comments may tell us, they have one thing in common: they are all at most analytical or intuitive conclusions drawn from fragmentary data. Such conclusions may be correct. They frequently are. But they are not based on very strong empirical statistical evidence, for there has not so far been any attempt to work out systematically the actual extent of the changes that are assumed, or said to have happened, in international price competitive positions in the period between the wars, and *that* is what we are concerned with here. It is the purpose of this article to quantify the changes in international price competitive positions of 15 of the most important world trading nations between 1913 and 1937[3], and give a brief comment on the results for the seven countries with the biggest shares of world trade.

The article makes no claim to give a full 'explanation' of the development in foreign trade and its effects on growth and prosperity during that period. There are factual, methodological and statistical reasons for not attempting to do this. Firstly, the direction and size of the international trade flows depended on more than price relations and price movements. But where they did depend on these, the degree of dependency was a question of price elasticities, and very little is known about these.[4] Secondly, the values that are presented and reflected are only 'correct' within the framework of the conditions of the arithmetical concept with the help of which they

---

[2] On these two areas see z.B. Gerd *Hardach* Weltmarktorientierung und relative Stagnation. Währungspolitik in Deutschland 1924–1931, Berlin ¡}76, p. 70ff., 149, 161, Knut Borchardt, Wirtschaftliche Ursachen des Scheiterns der Weimater Republik, in: K.D. *Erdmann* u. H. *Schulze*. Weimar. Selbstptreisgabe einer Demokratic, Düsseldorf 1980, p. 228 (against the view that the RM was overvalued right from the start A.J. *Youngyon*. Britain's Economic Growth 1920–1931. The Normann Conquest of Dollar 4,86. Cambridge 1972, p. 100ff., D.H. *Aldcroft* Britische Währungspolitik und Wirtschaftstätigkeit in den zwanziger Jahren, in: H. *Winkel*, ed. Finanz- und wirtschaftspolitische Fragen der Zwischenkriegszeit, Berlin 1973, p. 100, S. *Howson*, Domestic Monetary Management in Britain 1919–1938, Cambridge 1975, S. 47ff., H. v.B. *Clereland*, The International Monetary System in the Interwar Period, in: B.M. *Rowland*, Hrsg., Balance of Power versus Hegemony: The Interwar Monetary System, New York 1976, p. 32f., J. L. *Kooker*, French Financial Diplomacy. The Interwar Years, in: ibid, p. 96ff., Melchior *Palyi*, The Twilight of Gold 1914–1936. Myths and Realities, Chicago 1972, p. 185f. against the view that Poincaré had undervalued the franc in the twenties M. *Falkus*. US Economic Policy and the "Dollar Gap" of the 1920's in: EHR 24, 1971, p. 599–623, S. *Glynn* u. A.L. *Lougheed*. A Comment on US Economic Policy and the "Dollar Gap" of the 1920's, in: EHR 26, 1973, p. 693. A summary Ch. P. *Kindleberger*, Die Weltwirtschaftskrise. Geschichte der Weltwirtschaft im 20. Jh. Bd. 4, München 1973, p. 42ff. J.B. *Condliffe*. The Reconstruction of World Trade. A Survey of International Economic Relations, London 1941, p. 71ff., W.A. *Lewis*, Economic Survey, 1919–1939, London 1949, p. 82ff., S. *Howson*, Sterlings Managed Float. The Operation of the Exchange Accounts 1932–1939. Princeton 1980. D.H. *Aldcroft*, The Interwar Economy: Britain 1919–1939, London 1970, p. 281.

[3] 1913 is the base and reference year. The first year used for comparison is 1922, for that is the first year for which enough of the necessary data is available.

[4] Instead of a number of individual studies see the review by Hang Sheng Cheng: Statistical Estimates of Elasticities and Propensities in International Trade. A Survey of Published Studies, in: IMF Staff Papers, Vol. 7, 1959/60, pp. 107–158.

were produced. The concept is not beyond all doubt or criticism. Thirdly, and finally, the base data for the calculations are burdened with the uncertainties of historical economic statistics in general and the problems of indexes in particular.

So these extensive calculations and brief comments are presented in the more modest hope that they may help to widen what has been the rather narrow basis for assessment, and perhaps make it more informative as well.

Section II contains a brief discussion of the analytical concept and the reliability of the data. Sections III to V comment on the results of the calculations, which are contained in the tables and graphs in the Appendix.

II.

As an instrument of analysis we have used the concept of *real effective exchange rates*. The development of the real effective exchange rate shows whether the price competitive position of a country on international markets improved or deteriorated over time, and it consists of changes in the relations of the country's own prices to those of other countries[5], and of movements in exchange rates (changes in the price of the country's own currency, expressed in units of other currencies). The price and exchange rate relations of one country against those of many other countries are grouped into *one* indicator, and this requires weighting the many bilateral relations.

So the concept of real effective exchange rates contains four analytical problems, some of which are interrelated. Since the real effective exchange rate only tells us something as a flow over time, the first problem lies in selecting a suitable reference year. The second is to work out a meaningful price index. Thirdly, the question arises what countries should be included in the price and exchange rate comparison, and fourthly, it is difficult to decide how to weight the price and exchange rate relations with the countries included.

Admittedly, the four problems are of differing degrees. The first two are ultimately a matter of analytical intent and the interpretation of the results, and they can be solved on a pragmatic, case-to-case basis.

It is best to choose as reference year one which seems 'normal' taking a long view, or one in which a development began which is interesting scientifically or practically. In our case 1913 is the obvious choice.

It is less easy to find the most suitable price index than base year. The aim to show changes in international price competitiveness would at first seem to point very definitely to the index of the average value of exports, and, in fact, the calculations are based on this. But it has its analytical weaknesses. Exports compete in the countries to which they are imported both against the domestic prices in those countries and against the prices of third countries' exports. Competition from the

---

[5] Changes in *cost* relations would be analytically more desirable, because they would tell us more. Changes in price relations can reflect the greater or less earnings power of exports, as well as better or worse price competitiveness, and it would be helpful if this double significance could be excluded in assessing the trend over time of real effective exchange rates. But there is no adequate data for the calculation of real effective exchange rates on a cost basis. Even in calculating figures that apply to the present one has to use one element of costs, wage costs, for which adequate statistics are available, and for older periods not even sufficient data on wages is available.

domestic prices of import countries is not covered by the index of average export values, and that *can* lead to distortions, if a country's exports are concentrated on a few countries, and the movements in their domestic prices differ greatly from those in its export prices. Moreover, similarities and differences in the export ranges cause some problems. But since calculating a more suitable combined index gives rise to more uncertainties than it promises advantage of knowledge, we can only hope that the apparent presumed distortions will be slight. The hope is not unfounded, at least in the context of the broad spread of trade of the major industrial states.

The third and fourth analytical problems are of a more fundamental nature, and ultimately they cannot be solved, either pragmatically or in any other way. They are also closely related.

The question of what countries should be included in the comparison of prices and exchange rates can be answered in two ways. Firstly, all the countries with which the economy, with whose competitive position we are concerned, is competing. The second is: all the countries with which it trades. For the advanced industrial economies the two groups are usually largely identical, and that was true even between the wars. The intensity of the competition and trade with certain countries, however, differed from one economy to another, and that leads us to the problem of weighting, which ultimately cannot be solved.

Out of a range of alternatives two are particularly appropriate.[6] In one case the bilateral price and exchange rate relations are weighted with the shares of the buyer countries in the exports of the country with whose competitive position we are concerned, and in the other with the shares of the competitors in world trade. The first variant stresses the intensity of trade relations between certain countries and regions. This is the method used by the Deutsche Bundesbank and the German Council of Experts (Sachverständigenrat).[7] The second method puts more weight on the density and adjustment elasticity of the world trade network, and this is the method used, for instance, by the American Federal Reserve Board.

In both alternatives the question also arises whether one should weight with "current" shares, that is, changing from year to year, or with constant shares. Weighting with current shares could show, in the development of the real effective exchange rate, not only changes in price and/or exchange rate relations, but also shifts in shares that might have been caused by changes in relative prices and effective exchange rates. The use of constant weights excludes from the calculation such intercorrelation of changes in prices, exchange rates and shares, together with their repercussions on the course of the real effective exchange rate. There are sound, objective reasons for both methods. Control calculations with current shares from 1922 to 1937 on the one hand, and with constant shares from 1929 and 1936 on the other, helped the decision in this case between the two possibilities. The deviations proved to be slight. They are at most two, but usually less than one percent. In view of the general uncertainty of the data the choice between current and constant weighting is therefore virtually of no account.

---

[6] On effective exchange rates see Rudolf R. Rhomberg: Indices of Effective Exchange Rates, in: IMF Staff Papers XXIII, 1976, pp. 89ff.

[7] See Annual Report by the Council of Experts for 1976/77, p. 80f.

That does not apply to the decision between using export shares or world trade shares as weights. The regional composition of exports of all countries shows more or less high degrees of concentration and so differs notably from the regional composition of world trade. So if the calculations using the two sets of weights produced virtually identical results, this could only be by chance. Deciding between such clearly different figures is always tricky, and averaging the two sets of figures, which is sometimes proposed, is not basically different from using a third indicator, which can be closer to reality but can also deviate further from it than the two others.[8] It is therefore advisable not to decide for one or the other or to "average out", but to use both sets of figures. That is the method used here, with justifiable reservations. To prevent excessive arithmetic only real effective exchange rates were worked out on the basis of export shares for every year and 15 countries. The calculation of real effective exchange rates on the basis of world trade shares, on the other hand, is limited to five "key years" – more are only used when need required – and the seven countries with the highest shares in world trade, the United Kingdom, the United States, Germany, France, Canada, Japan and India.[9]

The key years were 1925, 1929, 1932, 1934 and 1937. In the spring of 1925 the pound returned to the gold standard, and the world economy seemed to have found its way back to normality. The semblance of normality lasted until 1929. Then the world slump broke out, throwing international competition and trade relations into total confusion. First came dramatic price shifts. Then in 1931 the devaluation of the pound, the Yen and a number of other currencies set new accents, which were reflected in the figures for 1932. In 1934 the violent fluctuations in prices returned to relative calm. In addition, at the beginning of the year, the exchange rate for the dollar was de facto re-stabilised at a lower level. 1937 is the last year before the Second World War for which sufficient data is available.

The calculation with export shares did not include all the exports of the countries concerned, nor did the calculation with world market shares include total world trade. That was not necessary for the analysis, nor was it statistically possible. In the calculation with – current – export shares all the trade partners were usually considered which had a share of at least one percent in the exports of the country whose real effective exchange rate was being considered[10], and this generally meant that between 65 and 90 percent of exports was covered. The degree to which this was representative dropped noticeably in the later 1930s.[11] Analogous to this, the

---

[8] Very much more complex procedures are possible and are practised. See especially Jaques R. Artus and Rudolf R. Rhomberg: A Multilateral Exchange Rate Model, in: IMF Staff Papers, Vol. 20, 1973, pp. 591–611. However, the IMF's MERM requires a knowledge of data that is not available for older periods.

[9] India was only one of the seven largest trading nations in the twenties, being replaced by Belgium in the thirties. Whether it is methodologically justifiable and meaningful to treat India the same as the four industrial countries and the two "threshold contries", Canada and Japan, in the analysis and interpretation, is very questionable. The data and notes are given with considerable reserve. Similar reservations apply to the unannotated data on China and Argentina. On the fundamental problem see Gérard Bélanger: An Indicator of Effective Exchange Rates for Primary Producing Countries, in: IMF Staff Papers XXIII, 1976, pp. 113ff.

[10] Minor exceptions had to be made to this owing to lack of data.

[11] It fell to under two thirds for Japan, Italy and China.

calculation using constant world trade shares (from 1929) covered the countries with at least one percent of world trade[12], which was rather more than three quarters of total world trade.

With these conditions and reservations the indices of relative prices, effective exchange rates and real effective exchange rates (price competitive positions) given in the Appendix were worked out as follows[13]:

1. Indices of relative prices =

$$\frac{P_{i(1922-1937)}}{(P_{j1(1922-1937)})^{g_{j1}} \times (P_{j2(1922-1937)})^{g_{j2}} \times \ldots (P_{jn(1922-1937)})^{g_{jn}}} \cdot 100$$

P_i = Index of average export values in the country whose competetive position is being calculated, from 1922 to 1937 using 1913 as the base year (= 100).

$P_{j1 \ldots n}$ = Indices of average export values of the trade partners included in the calculation, or world trading countries in the appropriate years, also 1913 as the base year

$G_{j1 \ldots n}$ = Export shares or world trade shares of countries j_1 to j_n

$\sum_{j=1-n} g_j = 1$ = The export or world trade shares not included were distributet proportionally between the shares that we included

An index figure over 100 indicates that the price relations have changed to the *dis*advantage of country i in comparison with conditions in 1913. Export from country i had become relatively more expensive, even if they were cheaper in absolute terms. A figure under 100 indicates the opposite. Accordingly, the increase (or reduction) in the index figure from one year to a later year shows that the relative export prices of i had risen (or fallen) in the meantime.

2. Indices of effective exchange rates =

$$(R_{ij1(1922-1937)})^{g_{j1}} \times (R_{ij2(1922-1937)})^{g_{j2}} \times \ldots (R_{ijn(1922-1937)})^{g_{jn}}$$

Rij = Index of the value of one unit of a currency of the country whose competitive position is being calculated, expressed in units of the currency of country j from 1922 to 1937, with 1913 as base year (= 100).

An index figure over 100 indicates that the currency of the country i had become more expensive on a weighted average of foreign currencies since 1913.[14] It had

---

[12] Spain, Brazil and British Malaya are exceptions, owing to lack of data.

[13] On the reason why the geometric link between weighted prices (and exchange rates) is preferable to the arithmetical link used at the beginning see the Monthly Report of the Deutsche Bundesbank, 1979, pp. 22–25.

[14] The development in relations between two currencies will show this:
1913: 1 US $ – 5.18 Ffrs. = 100; 1925: 1 US $ – 20.96 Ffrs. = 405; 1934: 1 US $ – 15.22 Ffrs. = 294
So the dollar quadrupled in value against the French franc from 1913 to 1925, and then lost a good quarter of this again by 1934.

upvalued. A figure under 100 indicates the opposite. Accordingly, the increase (reduction) in the index figure from one year to a later year shows that the currency of i had been upvalued (devalued) in the meantime.

3. Index of real effective exchange rates =

$$\frac{\text{Index of relative prices x index of effective exchange rates.}}{100}$$

An index figure over 100 indicates that the price competitive position of the country for which the real effective exchange rate applies had deteriorated since 1913. The deterioration could be for the following reasons: an increase in relative prices *and* an upvaluation in the currency; an increase in relative prices, which was only partly compensated by a devaluation in the currency; an upvaluation in the currency which went beyond the fall in relative prices.

A figure under 100, on the other hand, indicates an improvement in the price competitive position since 1913. This could result from a reduction in relative prices *and* a devaluation of the currency; a fall in prices only partly compensated by an upvaluation of the currency, or a devaluation of the currency beyond the rise in relative prices.

Accordingly, the increase (or reduction) in the index figure from one year to a later year shows that the price competitive position of the country had deteriorated (or improved) in the interim.

Once more: changes in the price competitive positions say nothing definite on whether and to what extent the export chances of the country affected had improved or deteriorated. That depended on the price-export elasticities and many other influences on international trade flows. But noticeable and lasting fluctuations in real effective exchange rates will certainly have had an effect on a country's international competitiveness and foreign sales.

Before finally coming to our calculations, a few sentences on the source and quality of the basic data. The figures are taken from the League of Nations international economic statistics, and the data is available in the desired quantity for the years 1922 to 1937. The original data for the individual countries was not collected absolutely identically. The usual doubts must be entertained on comparability, but this is not fundamentally in question. The annual data is composed of partly weighted, partly unweighted monthly figures, and the time flows were constructed by the League of Nations using a uniform procedure.[15]

The average export figures are of course arithmetical fictions and have the familiar problems of such usual fictions.

The exchange rates are usually shown as the rate for the dollar in New York, in exceptional cases in London, and for our purposes they were converted using the dollar rates for the currency whose real effective exchange rate we are concerned

[15] The question arose whether this should be supplemented or replaced by contemporary, estimated or calculated, "national" figures. In some cases that was unavoidable (see sources given on p. 62), but otherwise it was deliberately avoided to preserve the uniformity of the procedure and, as far as possible, the consistency of the data base.

with: $R_{\$j} / R_{\$i} = R_{ij}$.[16] That corresponds to the procedure now used by international monetary authorities. Control calculations of the effective rate for the pound using London quotations for the pound, and the effective rate for the Reichsmark using Berlin quotations for that currency yielded results which agreed with the figures worked out using the dollar rates.

It is, however, doubtful whether the official rates in the later thirties still accorded with the actual trade conditions in every case. In Nazi Germany they certainly did *not*, at the latest after the New Plan was passed in the summer of 1934.[17] It was a question whether there would be more distortion of the results by nevertheless including Germany in the calculations for the period after 1932, or by leaving it out. It was included after 1932, because the distortion *this* would cause seemed to be controllable. Since the official rate for the Reichsmark was higher than the actual value of the currency in the labyrinth of barter and offset agreements being made by German suppliers, the price competitive positions of the countries that were engaged in intensive trade with Germany, and competing with it, was slightly worse in the later 1930s than the results of the calculations show. So the German competitive position must have been somewhat better. But conventionally calculated real effective exchange rates make very little sense in any case for the Reichsmark at this period.

III.

The tables and illustrations 1 to 7 show the developments in relative prices, effective exchange rates and real effective exchange rates for the United States, the United Kingdom[18], Germany, France, Canada, Japan and India, and the following commentary is limited to this.[19] The tables contain both the figures calculated on the basis of export shares and those calculated using world trade shares. The illustrations only show the curves obtained using export shares. The commentary always refers first to the results obtained using export shares. Then, where necessary, reference is made

---

[16] In words: the price of the dollar expressed in units of the currency j divided by the price of the dollar in units of the currency i shows the price of the currency i in units of j. For example: if 1 \$ = 4.20 RM = LO.205, then L 1 = (4.20 : 0.205) = 20.40 RM.

[17] On the foreign exchange regulations in Germany and the "split" exchange rate see Howard Ellis: Exchange Control in Central Europe, Cambridge 1941, pp. 191–289, Frank C. Child: The Theory and Practices of Exchange Control in Germany, The Hague 1958, Knut Borchardt: Ein neues Urteil über die deutsche Währungs- und Handelspolitik von 1931 bis 1938, in: VSWG 1959, pp. 526–546.

[18] See John Redmond: An Indicator of the Effective Exchange Rate of the Pound in the Nineteen-Thirties, in: EHR 1980, pp. 83–91. The appropriate figures in Table 2 are lower than Redmond's, and this is mainly the systematic expression of a different method of calculation. Redmond links the bilateral exchange rates arithmetically, while here they are geometrically linked.

[19] The word "commentary" should be taken as simply as it is meant. The following remarks are in the main a verbal paraphrase of the results of the calculations, with occasional reference to possible historical causes and consequences. They are not intended to be a thorough-going interpretation, and I have deliberately refrained from references to the very extensive literature on the history of international trade between the wars. I regard it as appropriate to present the method of calculating and the results for *discussion* first, and not just assume that the data is viable by making extensive interpretations.

to deviations resulting from weighting with world trade shares. This method is facilitated (and at the same time justified in many respects) in that the different weightings usually only affect the extent of improvements or deteriorations in international competitive positions, but do not distort the flows.

Tables 8 to 15 and illustrations 8 to 10 give reduced data, on which no further comment is given, for Belgium and the Netherlands, Sweden, Italy and Switzerland, as well as for China, Argentina and Australia. The tables are limited to show the figures calculated from export shares, and the illustrations only show the curves of real effective exchange rates.

The subject itself, and the need for clarity, made it appropriate to subdivide the period considered when commenting on the results into three shorter phases. The first covers the restabilisation and relatively calm development in the twenties, the second the extremely violent fluctuations from 1930 to 1934 and the third the repercussions of the crises up to 1937.

In the twenties the seven countries with the largest world trade shares fell into two groups. The first includes the United Kingdom and Japan. The price competitive positions of these two countries had deteriorated notably during the course of the First World War and the transition from the war economy to a peacetime economy, and until the great slump they remained in a worse position than they had been in 1913. The second group includes the USA, Germany, France and Canada. The price competitive positions of these countries were better, at least for most of the twenties, than before the war. India moved between the two groups, taking a less clear course.

But apart from such immediate similarities there were singular characteristics in the development in all the countries:

For the *United Kingdom* we must say first that the competitive disadvantage fixed up to 1929 by retying the pound to gold was very much greater, according to evidence from the real effective exchange rate, than is generally supposed. Keynes had warned against returning to the old gold parity in 1924/25, because British prices were still about 10% above US prices. And many economic historians have become accustomed to seeing this price differential as an indication of the continued loss of competitiveness which Churchill imposed on British exports when he disregarded Keynes' warning, albeit with a heavy heart. It is possible that the economic historians have become used to what is in fact an error. For it was not only the price and exchange rate relation to the USA that mattered. Our calculations show that Britain's relative prices had returned to their prewar level, and actually fallen slightly below it, by the time of the stabilisation of the pound, while the effective exchange rate at the old gold parity moved to nearly 20% above its prewar level. Necessarily, therefore, the real effective exchange rate was between 15 and 20% higher. This more marked deterioration in the price competitive position was conserved by Britain's return to the gold standard. A calculation using world trade shares shows the deterioration to be actually even more marked.

In *Japan* the situation was just the reverse. Here the war and a powerful postwar inflation had driven prices up far beyond the average price level on international markets. Unlike the British and American governments the Japanese government prevented a thorough-going deflationary correction to the upward drive in the early twenties. That widened the gap further, and between 1922 and 1925 Japan's relative export prices were around half as high again as their prewar level. Nevertheless, the

Bank of Japan and the Finance Ministry were trying to return to the old gold parity of the Yen as soon as possible. The currency was supported with all means to keep it near the prewar level. After the catastrophic earthquake of 1923 strength failed for a time, but as soon as possible the support actions were resumed. Although at the same time prices for Japan's main export commodity, silk, began to fall drastically, continuously and with extremely difficult economic, social and finally political consequences as well, the competitiveness of Japanese exports remained severely affected throughout the whole of the nineteen-twenties.[20]

The developments in the four countries whose competitive positions improved also differed in many ways. American and French exports only gained noticeable advantages of price competitiveness at the time of the stabilisation of the pound and the Mark[21], while German and Canadian exports enjoyed such advantages before that. But the French and the Americans were able to increase, or at least maintain, their advantages in the next few years, while the improvement in the German competitive position was continuously eroded.

The *United States* could afford a powerful increase in the rate for the dollar, because its export prices were falling far below the average price level of their trade partners and competitors, thanks to the superior productivity of US labour. The contrary movements are even more evident in a calculation with world market shares, but the result is the same using real effective exchange rates.[22]

France, on the other hand, balanced the rise in its relative prices, which was hardly checked until Poincare's de facto stabilisation in 1926, with a fall in the effective rate for the franc, and made sure that none of the competitive advantages thus gained was lost when the franc was officially tied to gold in 1928. The improvement in the real effective exchange rate in the second half of the twenties

[20] If the calculations were weighted with world trade shares the effect would be the same. The developments in relative prices and the effective rate for the Yen would, however, be different. Since with this alternative way of calculating trade with the United States and China, which together took about two thirds of Japanese exports, would be playing an inappropriately low part, the method would not appear to be so advisable.

[21] It is of course very tempting to conclude that they gaind those advantages *as a result of* the stabilisation. Nor would it presumably be entirely wrong, but it cannot be definitely proved, and for that reason caution is advised.

[22] The United States has frequently been accused of burdening the world economy with a problem that was heavy, could not be resolved over the longer term and so was ultimately disastrous, through the improvement of its international price competitiveness (usually branded as the 'undervaluation' of the dollar) in connection with its newly acquired position as creditor to the world economy. This certainly brought America high trade balance surpluses, even if other factors than the better real effective exchange rate made a major contribution to this. It was also argued that the continued trade balance surpluses prevented America's debtors from earning the dollars they needed for the interest and redemption payments on their loans. That is also largely true. But it is highly questionable and probably not correct to conclude that an upvaluation of the dollar would have been a way out of the dilemma. There is much to suggest that the price-demand elasticities of American foreign trade in the twenties were extremely low. Under that condition an upvaluation of the dollar would hardly have reduced American exports, but would have made the goods more expensive in other currencies, nor could it hardly have improved American imports, but would have made them cheaper in dollars. America's trade balance surplus might well have increased and the dilemma been greater for the debtors.

was between 15 and 25%. When calculated with world trade shares – though this is the less illuminating method[23] – it is larger than when calculated with export shares.

Germany's return to the prewar gold parity for the Mark was clearly justified by international price relations. It maintained for German exports at least some of the price competitive advantage they had enjoyed during the period of inflation, according to contemporary accusations and more recent calculations.[24] However, this advantage dwindled rapidly in the ensuing years, and after 1927 it had gone altogether. The reasons for this differ according to the weighting used. In weighting with export shares the rise in the real effective exchange rate is mainly due to a noticeable upvaluation of the Reichsmark, but in calculating with world trade shares it is mainly due to a marked rise in relative prices. Weighting with world trade shares gives the USA and Britain a larger role, with their falling prices and fixed rates, while France and Belgium play a smaller part, with their rising prices and falling rates, than when weighting with export shares. In view of the intensive international competition between German, American and British industries weighting with world trade shares should, no doubt, be seen as more realistic, and the loss of the German price advantage as due mainly to the rise in relative prices. But however one calculates, the result certainly contradicts the widespread view that the Reichsmark was "overvalued" at the time and Germany's exports simply too expensive. Germany's price competitive position in the twenties was generally better and never worse than before the First World War. That German goods nevertheless had a much more difficult time on international markets must be mainly due to other reasons.

In *India* finally the development was on principle similar, though it differed in time, moved in different dimensions and was very much less even. But there too relative prices had fallen clearly below their prewar level in 1922, while the Rupee was slightly upvalued. The result was a noticeable improvement in the Indian competitive position. The fall in prices and upvaluation went on until 1926. The upvaluation, however, was the result of political decisions, and it moved faster than the fall in prices. That destroyed the price competitive advantage within a short space of time. After 1924 the real effective exchange rate oscillated around its prewar level.

IV.

The world slump came almost like a severe shock, completely confusing the price and exchange rate relations that had been readjusted in a so lengthy and difficult process, and were hardly consolidated. From the autumn of 1929 to the autumn of

[23] The difference results mainly from the fact that in the calculation with world trade shares America plays a very much bigger part and Belgium a similarly smaller part. In relation to the dollar the franc was strongly devalued, but it was noticeably upvalued in relation to the Belgian franc or the Belga, apart from 1925/26. So the effective exchange rate, and with it the real effective exchange rate, is lower right through when calculating with world trade shares. But virtually everything suggests that Belgium should be given greater weight as a trading partner *and* competitor of France than the United States, and for that reason the higher real effective exchange rates seem more realistic.

[24] Carl-Ludwig Holtfrerich: Die deutsche Inflation 1914–1923, Berlin 1980, pp. 22f.

1931 dramatic price shifts predominated, after which often described and much decried changes in exchange rates set the signals, namely the devaluation in the pound, the Yen and the dollar between September 1931 and January 1934.[25] The Rupee followed the devaluation of the pound. The Canadian dollar followed it only partly, but later it followed the devaluation in the dollar far enough to restore the old relation between the two currencies. Germany and France kept to the gold parities for the Reichsmark and the franc fixed in 1924 and 1928 respectively.

The price and exchange rate changes turned the price competitive disadvantages Japan and India were suffering – still measured by the 1913 level – into considerable advantages. The upwards movement in the real effective exchange rate for the Reichsmark accelerated above the critical borderline. The competitive advantages enjoyed by France and the United States shrank and at times disappeared altogether. The competitive disadvantages to the United Kingdom increased remarkably. The real effective exchange rate for the Canadian dollar remained fixed, with the exception of a brief improvement in 1931.

The great improvement in the *Indian* competitive position was due to a successive fall of about ten percent in relative prices in 1930, and an effective devaluation of just on 15% the following year. Together these resulted in a plunge in the real effective exchange rate by a good 20%.

Japan, on the other hand, did not derive any competitive advantages from the even deeper fall in its export prices in 1930. In January the Yen was at last brought back to its old gold parity and then upvalued by 20% in the two following years. That neutralised the downward plunge in prices. Contrary to an opinion still widely held, the ill-timed stabilisation did not worsen Japan's competitiveness, but it did prevent the urgently needed improvement in it. In December Finance Minister Takahashi drew the long overdue conclusions, in extremely unfavourable political conditions, and uncoupled the currency from gold. The effective rate for the Yen dropped, with the help of the Japanese monetary authorities, down to half of its gold standard level within two years. The fall created scope for considerable price increases, which helped the (silk) farmers back on to at least a subsistence level income and increased the chances of profit for commercial firms. But by far the main effect of the unique devaluation was to improve Japan's international position in trade. Since 1932 the real effective exchange rate for the Yen had been 30 to 40% lower than in the crisis years from 1928 to 1931, and the admittedly more questionable method of calculating with world trade shares actually accentuated the fall further.

The deterioration in the *German* price competitive position in the two first crisis years was mainly due to an increase of about 10% in relative prices. Brüning's deflationary policy was to force German prices down below the world market level, but this was foiled by the actual development, and it was not until 1932 that relative prices began to move downwards, hesitantly at first, and then forced down by the National Socialists' price policy, until they went into a downslide that continued until the outbreak of the war. Admittedly, from the same year onwards the effects of first the devaluation in the pound and then that in the dollar were felt. The Mark moved upwards effectively in 1932 and 1933 more than relative prices fell. The real

[25] To prevent misunderstanding: in January 1934 the dollar was restabilised and its downward slide *ended*.

effective exchange rate for the Reichsmark rose by 20 to 30% from 1929 to 1933, and remained unchanged in the following year. The higher figure results from calculating with world trade shares, and it is the more likely, for the reasons already explained. The disastrous effects on German exports, which were further accentuated by worldwide protectionism, are well known.

The *United States* were able to maintain their international competitive position, more or less, up to the devaluation of the pound, the Yen and the Canadian dollar, as relative prices fell slightly on the whole and the effective exchange rate rose slightly. A noticeably sharper fall in prices then had no further effect against the devaluation in the three countries – which after all took 40% of American exports. The real effective rate for the dollar rose by 10% in 1932, but the loss in position was corrected in the following year by a powerful devaluation of the dollar, although this was not the primary aim. Roosevelt's main concern was to raise the level of prices, since he believed that too low prices were the main cause of the American crisis, and that a politically arbitrary increase in the gold price would necessarily pull commodities prices, that are regulated by the market, up in turn. At first sight it does look as if events confirmed the President's strange theory, but a closer examination will show that the powerful increase in prices in 1933 and 1934 was due to other causes.[26] The devaluation simply ensured that the marked rise in prices did not damage the competitiveness of American exports further. Whether conversely the price increases prevented the competitive advantages accumulated up to the outbreak of the crisis from being regained through the devaluation is uncertain. If calculating with export shares is more realistic, they did; but if calculating with world trade shares is more realistic, then they did not. But however one sees it, at the end of the period of violent fluctuations in prices and exchange rates America was certainly in the best position compared with the three major European industrial states, but only as far as its international price competitiveness was concerned, and not in its recovery from the crisis as well. For in the United States there was remarkably little interrelation between the two.

France's competitive position deteriorated steadily and strongly, especially after 1931. Although the effective upvaluation of the franc by 25 to 45% was partly compensated by an extraordinarily drastic policy of deflation, the real effective exchange rate in 1934 was 20 to 30% above its prewar level, depending on the method of calculation used. In many respects France acted in the early thirties completely contrary to its action in the midtwenties. Then an inflationary price upward movement had been compensated by a deliberately over-proportional devaluation, and now a price deflation, mainly induced for political reasons, softened the effects of a strong upvaluation, which the monetary authorities, for mistaken ideological reasons, did not want to change, and which at first they probably could hardly have changed for more tangible political reasons.

The real effective exchange rate for the pound took what was presumably the most surprising development during this period. It is generally assumed that the devaluation of the pound brought a basic improvement in the *British* competitive position, at least for a time, but according to our calculations that was not the case.

---

[26] Volker Hentschel: Wege aus der Arbeitslosigkeit – USA, Frankreich, Japan, in: Vierteljahrshefte des Deutschen Instituts für Wirtschaftsforschung 1, 1984, pp. 70ff.

As is well known, Britain was relatively mildly affected by the slump, and mainly in its foreign markets. The two were related. Since the domestic economic situation suffered less in Britain than elsewhere prices did not fall so far. Britain's relative export prices rose from 1929 to 1932 by 25%. Moreover, by the autumn of 1931 the pound had moved upwards by around 10%. The two together caused a deterioration in the price competitiveness of British exports, which was in any case weakening, to a hitherto unknown degree, and together with the reduced purchasing power of buyers this led to a collapse in exports by 30% in two years, which brought about a crisis. In 1931 the real effective exchange rate was about 20% higher than in 1929. The effective devaluation of the pound by a good 15% – not by the oft-named third, which results from measuring the rate for the pound only against the dollar – was just enough, as the rise in relative prices continued for a time, to reverse part of the unwelcome upward movements. On a calculation with export shares this was the smaller part, and on a calculation with world trade shares it was the larger part. But however one looks at it, the British competitive position was even worse in the thirties, despite the devaluation, than it had been in the twenties. At most the devaluation helped to ensure that the deterioration was less than in Germany and France. But taking 1913 as the standard, Britain was still the industrial country with the most price competitive disadvantages.

Canada's international competitiveness was not lastingly changed by the fluctuations in prices and exchange rates. The fall in relative prices which began in 1926 continued until 1932, and up to 1931 the real effective exchange rate continued to fall, while the currency remained stable. In the two following years the Canadian dollar first moved up by a good 10%, and then down by rather less. The upvaluation concealed the continued decline in relative prices and took the real effective exchange rate back to the level of 1929. As in America and Japan the devaluation was used to achieve a powerful increase in prices. So relative prices rose to the same extent as the effective exchange rate fell, leaving the competitive position unchanged.

V.

After 1934 the fluctuations in prices and exchange rates moderated somewhat. Prices moved upward again worldwide. The only important exception were German prices. Exchange rates remained for the most part firm, and the most important exception to *this* was the French franc.

The real effective exchange rates for the US dollar, the pound, the Yen and the rupee reflected the fluctuations, which in any case had moderated, only in a more weakened form. Relative price reductions compensated for the moderate rise in effective exchange rates which resulted from the successive devaluations of the gold block currencies, with minor deviations in the extent and time patterns of the movements. There were no more significant changes in competitive positions up to 1937.

But the exception countries, Germany and France, and Canada, which had played a rather modest role up to then, showed greater fluctuations. Germany and France experienced a noticeable improvement in their price competitive positions for very different reasons, while Canada lost competitive advantages.

As the National Socialist price and foreign trade policy depressed German export prices beyond 1934/35, while prices elsewhere started moving upwards again more or less strongly, Germany's relative prices fell by a further 20 to 25%. Admittedly, on the other hand the Reichsmark moved up further, but not so much as prices fell, so a considerable part of the cumulative loss of international competitiveness between 1929 and 1934 was reversed. The calculation with world trade shares shows this as less remarkable than the calculation with export shares. For the rest, it should be pointed out again that all this is on the arithmetical basis of the "official" prices and exchange rates, which were not de facto prices or rates.

France's competitiveness continued to fall at first, because the other gold block currencies began to devalue *before* the franc.

After a short interruption continued relative price reductions did neutralise the resultant upvaluation of the franc, but at the same time they caused a major deterioration in the domestic situation and the social climate, which was in any case wretched. Finally, in September 1936 the Popular Front government could no longer resist the pressure to devalue, and the result was a deep fall in the effective exchange rate. However, some of the hoped-for effect failed to materialize, because other components of the "Blum experiment", which was largely motivated by the desire for social reform, drove prices steeply up again. And so the effective exchange rate moved back to its pre-crisis level in 1937, while at the same time relative prices shot up far beyond this. So French exports remained less competitive than they had been in the later twenties.

After 1932 *Canada* experienced a rise in prices that was both powerful and continued, and this drove its relative export prices up by about 15% from 1934 to 1937. Since the exchange rate remained firm, Canadian price competitiveness fell to the same extent. On the eve of the Second World War the real effective exchange rate for the Canadian dollar was back on the same level as on the eve of the First World War, and so higher than at any time in the intervening years.

We can now move away from the subdivision into periods and trace these movements in a way that is less awkward and confusing, if at the same time less differentiated and more immediate:

Britain's international competitive position was worse right through the inter-war period than it had been before the First World War. The deterioration was worsened by the slump, despite the devaluation of the pound.

North American exports generally enjoyed a better competitive position than before the war, thanks to a clear change to their favour in international price relations and despite higher rates for their currencies. Their price competitive advantage increased during the twenties and shrank or disappeared again in the thirties. This was first due to temporary effective upvaluations, and then continued relative price rises.

Germany emerged from the postwar inflation with visibly better price competitiveness, but soon lost these advantages again, mainly through relative cost and price increases, and also through a moderate upvaluation. From the beginning of the world slump a lasting deterioration in Germany's international competitive position, which varied only in its – admittedly uncertain – size, replaced the now eroded improvement.

Exactly the reverse happened in *Japan*, which found itself in a very much worse price competitive position at the beginning of the twenties than before the war, with excessively high relative prices. The disadvantage was largely eliminated by 1930 but not completely neutralised. From 1932 onwards an effective devaluation of hitherto unknown proportions turned the shrunken disadvantage into a definite advantage.

Similar movements took place in *India*, with a time differential, in a more even movement and on a rather smaller scale.

France, finally, created for itself a notable price advantage in the mid-twenties with a deliberately excessive devaluation of the franc. It retained this until the beginning of the slump and then gradually lost it again through clinging too long to the gold value of the franc as established by Poincare.

Appendix

Tables 1–7; diagrams 1–7; tables 8–15; diagrams 8–10

Sources: The figures were calculated using base data from the following works:

Price indices: League of Nations: Review of World Trade 1930, Geneva 1931, pp. 63–65

Société des Nations: Memorandum sur le Commerce et sur les Balances de Paiements 1938, Vol. 1: Apercu General du Commerce Mondial 1938, Geneva 1939, pp. 84–87

Charles P. Kindleberger: Industrial Europe's Terms of Trade on Current Account 1870–1953, in: E.M. Carus-Wilson, Essays in Economic History, Vol. 3, London 1966, p. 304 (Belgium and Netherlands)

Kazushi Ohkawa et al.: Patterns of Japanese Economic Development, A Quantitative Appraisal, New Haven 1979, pp. 331 (Japan)

Exchange Rates: League of Nations, Memorandum on International Trade and Balances of Payments, 1927–1929, Vol. I, Geneva 1930, pp. 110–119

Société des Nations: Memorandum sur le Commerce et sur les Balances de Paiements 1938, Vol. 1: Apercu General du Commerce Mondial 1938, Geneva 1939, pp. 84–87

Charles P. Kindleberger: Industrial Europe's Terms of Trade on Current Account 1870–1953, in: E.M. Carus-Wilson, Essays in Economic History, Vol. 3, London 1966, p. 304 (Belgium and Netherlands)

Kazushi Ohkawa et al.: Patterns of Japanese Economic Development, A Quantitative Appraisal, New Haven 1979, pp. 331 (Japan)

Exchange Rates: League of Nations, Memorandum on International Trade and Balances of Payments, 1927–1929, Vol. I, Geneva 1930, pp. 110–119

Société des Nations, Memorandum sur le Commerce et les Balances de Paiements 1934 Vol. 1: apercu General du Commerce Mondial 1934, pp. 90f., ibid 1938, pp. 88f.

World Trade Shares: League of Nations, Review of World trade 1930, Geneva 1931, pp. 19

Export shares: League of Nations, Memorandum on the Balances of Payments and Foreign Trade Balances 1911–1925, Vol. 1, Geneva 1926, pp. 218–235

League of Nations, Memorandum on International Trade and Balances of Payments 1927–1929, Vol. III, Geneva 1931, pp. 328–345

Société des Naitons, Memorandum sur le Commerce et sur les Balances de Paiements 1933, Vol. 3, Statistiques du Commerce International 1933, pp. 323–245, ibid 1935, pp. 324–241, ibid 1937, pp. 396–414

Tables 1–7. Relative prices, effective exchange rates, real effective exchange rates 1922–1937 – Indices 1913 = 100

1. United States

Year	Relative prices	effective ex. rates	real effective ex rates	Rel. prices	eff. ex rates	real eff. ex rates
	on the basis of current export shares			on the basis of world trade shares in 1929		
1922	83.42	125.07	104.33			
1923	79.66	127.92	101.90			
1924	74.41	132.53	98.62			
1925	72.98	128.59	93.84	68.28	138.47	94.54
1926	71.06	128.86	91.57			
1927	72.17	123.12	88.86			
1928	70.86	124.03	87.88			
1929	74.30	126.00	93.61	65.76	141.96	93.36
1930	75.14	129.16	97.05			
1931	69.89	135.45	94.67			
1932	62.59	166.32	104.11	58.66	171.80	100.77
1933	63.15	146.41	92.46			
1934	76.91	121.95	93.80	74.64	116.64	87.06
1935	79.54	124.20	98.77	82.20	117.69	96.74
1936	76.88	128.18	98.55			
1937	73.32	132.90	97.44	72.16	134.78	97.26

2. United Kingdom

Year	Relative prices	effective ex. rates	real effective ex rates	Rel. prices	eff. ex rates	real eff. ex rates
	on the basis of current export shares			on the basis of world trade shares in 1929		
1922	126.05	112.91	142.30			
1923	108.49	120.59	130.80			
1924	102.34	116.85	119.59			
1925	98.34	118.17	116.20	92.07	136.20	125.40
1926	104.82	116.47	122.09			
1927	101.12	116.92	118.23			
1928	99.56	118.23	117.71			
1929	97.84	112.26	119.62	88.25	141.22	124.63
1930	107.60	126.95	136.60	95.68	143.32	137.13
1931	116.05	129.89	150.74	105.13	139.88	147.09
1932	124.93	111.94	139.86	111.98	114.94	128.71
1933	124.01	115.60	143.35			
1934	120.59	116.19	140.12	110.54	120.64	133.39
1935	125.03	113.26	141.61			
1936	117.81	116.30	137.02			
1937	114.74	121.10	138.95	101.61	135.88	138.08

3. Germany

Year	Relative prices	effective ex. rates	real effective ex rates	Rel. prices	eff. ex rates	real eff. ex rates
	on the basis of current export shares			on the basis of world trade shares in 1929		
1923	55.54	142.64	79.22			
1924	57.94	151.85	87.97			
1925	59.76	152.47	91.11	64.01	135.28	86.59
1926	58.60	162.15	95.02			
1927	63.01	156.45	98.58			
1928	60.75	163.16	99.12			
1929	60.83	165.69	100.70	72.03	138.53	99.79
1930	63.54	172.21	109.42			
1931	67.93	168.75	114.63			
1932	66.46	182.45	121.20	77.91	165.67	129.08
1933	62.86	194.96	122.55			
1934	55.59	217.88	121.10	62.47	206.09	128.74
1935	51.12	222.73	113.86			
1936	48.23	242.90	117.15			
1937	42.14	253.79	106.90	48.83	240.73	117.54

4. France

Year	Relative prices	effective ex. rates	real effective ex rates	Rel. prices	eff. ex rates	real eff. ex rates
	on the basis of current export shares			on the basis of world trade shares in 1929		
1922	152.16	64.21	97.71			
1923	182.04	54.55	99.31			
1924	209.33	47.40	99.21			
1925	212.95	42.42	90.30	276.10	29.21	80.64
1926	239.30	32.51	77.79			
1927	221.36	37.03	81.96			
1928	208.25	39.47	82.19			
1929	204.60	39.78	81.39	299.60	24.19	72.47
1930	217.83	39.12	85.21			
1931	208.51	40.56	84.56			
1932	188.20	46.90	88.29	312.42	28.71	89.69
1933	181.61	49.29	89.51			
1934	194.78	50.26	97.89	273.57	35.65	97.51
1935	187.53	56.00	105.02	267.82	36.28	97.17
1936	173.12	53.95	93.41			
1937	222.25	39.91	88.66	346.43	23.51	81.69

5. Canada

Year	Relative prices	effective ex. rates	real effective ex rates	Rel. prices	eff. ex rates	real eff. ex rates
	on the basis of current export shares			on the basis of world trade shares in 1929		
1922	79.46	108.60	86.28			
1923	73.34	108.51	79.58			
1924	80.55	110.43	88.95			
1925	84.25	107.24	90.35	77.49	132.12	95.77
1926	87.26	109.37	95.44			
1927	85.73	107.84	92.45			
1928	82.98	110.41	91.62			
1929	78.94	108.35	85.53	72.63	133.67	97.09
1930	76.94	110.70	85.17			
1931	72.64	109.93	79.85			
1932	68.83	122.71	84.46	64.11	138.95	89.09
1933	81.55	101.82	83.04			
1934	81.75	105.19	85.99	79.13	114.17	90.34
1935	86.57	105.14	91.02			
1936	89.96	106.52	95.82			
1937	93.64	105.90	99.16	83.96	129.31	108.57

6. Japan

Year	Relative prices	effective ex. rates	real effective ex rates	Rel. prices	eff. ex rates	real eff. ex rates
	on the basis of current export shares			on the basis of world trade shares in 1929		
1922	149.18	100.51	149.94			
1923	149.33	99.47	148.54			
1924	140.12	88.58	124.12			
1925	147.63	82.66	122.03	116.45	108.10	125.88
1926	134.50	97.61	131.29			
1927	121.57	101.44	123.32			
1928	114.97	99.20	114.05			
1929	117.86	98.74	116.37	92.25	125.47	115.75
1930	95.62	114.20	109.20			
1931	96.99	120.14	116.53			
1932	116.57	68.50	79.86	82.05	83.60	71.11
1933	138.30	59.39	82.14			
1934	123.69	60.04	74.26	93.73	66.82	62.63
1935	114.64	59.15	67.81			
1936	110.25	62.45	68.85			
1937	118.24	63.88	75.53	95.09	73.79	70.17

7. India

Year	Relative prices	effective ex. rates	real effective ex rates	Rel. prices	eff. ex rates	real eff. ex rates
	on the basis of current export shares			on the basis of world trade shares in 1929		
1922	79.99	107.36	85.88			
1923	71.20	123.14	87.68			
1924	72.24	138.58	100.11			
1925	70.05	152.16	106.59	76.33	147.22	112.37
1926	64.18	153.81	98.72			
1927	67.99	151.12	102.75			
1928	68.42	148.08	101.31			
1929	65.08	148.09	96.37	65.86	150.43	99.08
1930	57.60	149.86	86.32			
1931	56.45	130.99	73.94			
1932	57.43	134.38	77.17	61.68	124.76	76.95
1933	56.82	135.14	76.79			
1934	57.78	136.36	78.79	59.66	130.16	77.65
1935	61.24	141.20	86.48			
1936	59.41	140.49	83.46			
1937	55.35	147.43	81.60	57.20	147.36	84.29

Diagrams 1–7. Relative prices, effective exchange rates, real effective exchange rates 1922–1937 on the basis of current export shares (1913 – 100)

relative prices effective exchage rates real effective exchage rates

1. United States

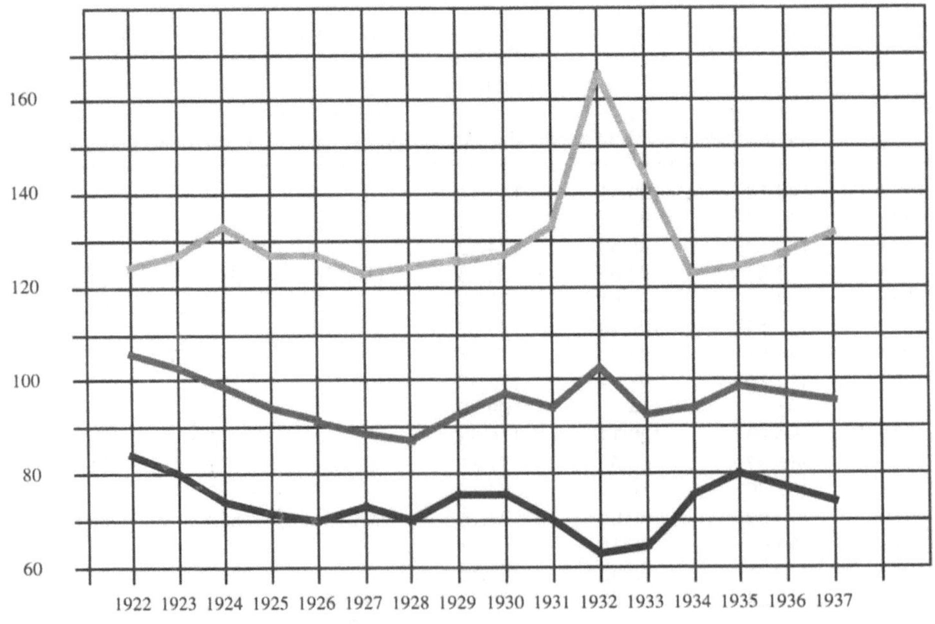

2. United Kingdom

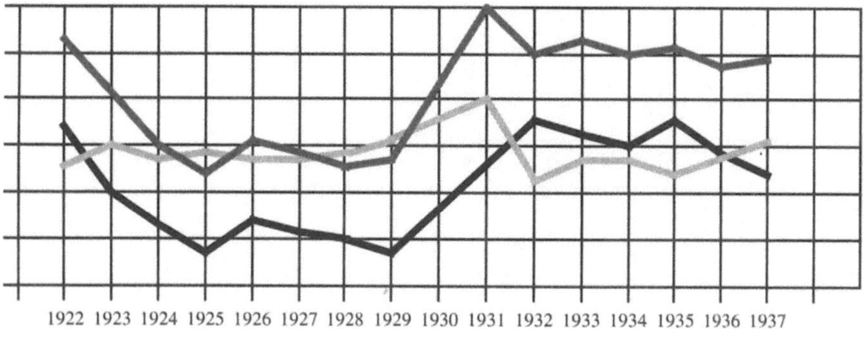

3. Germany

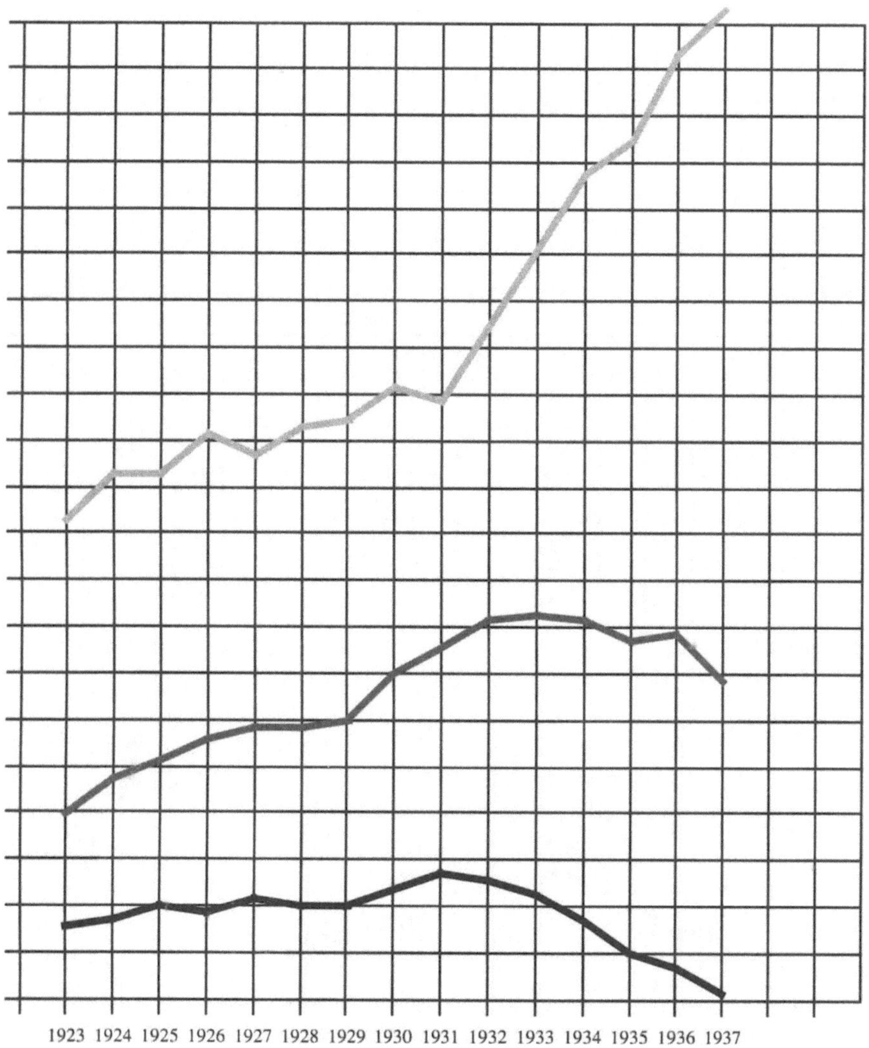

4. France

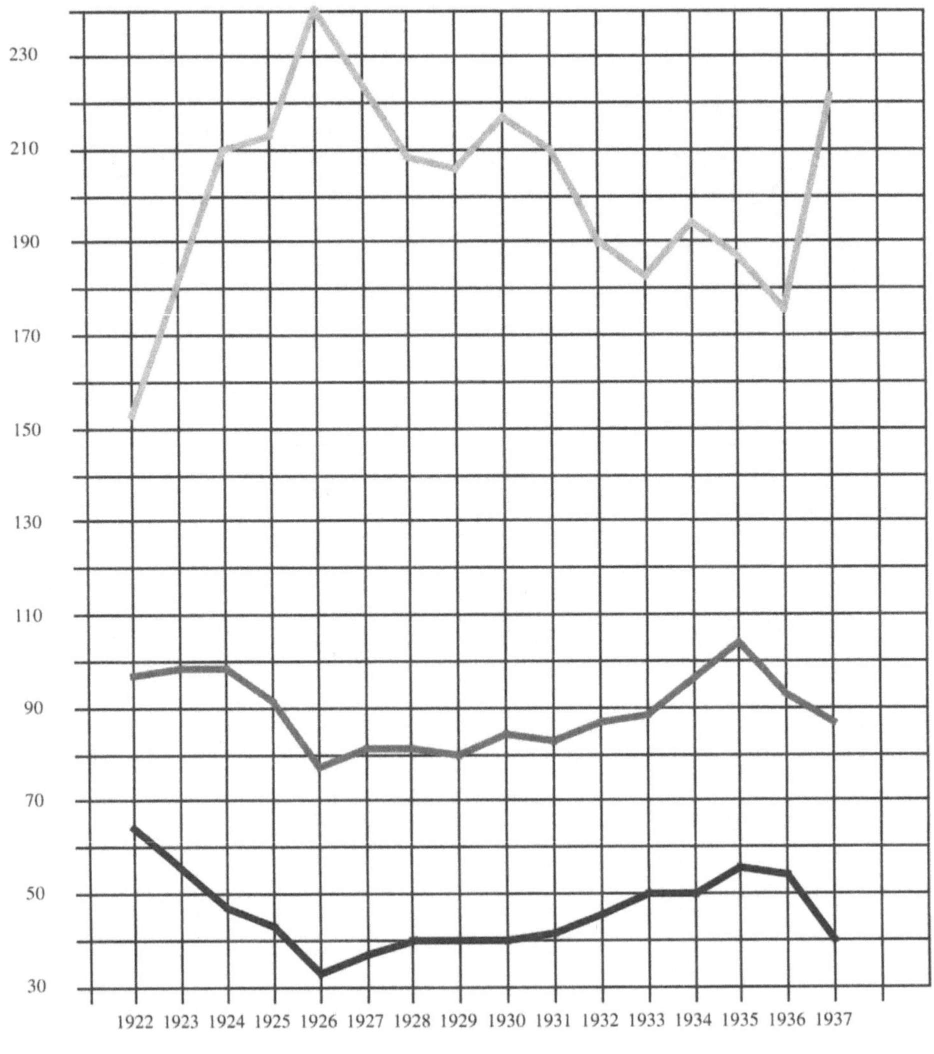

5. Canada

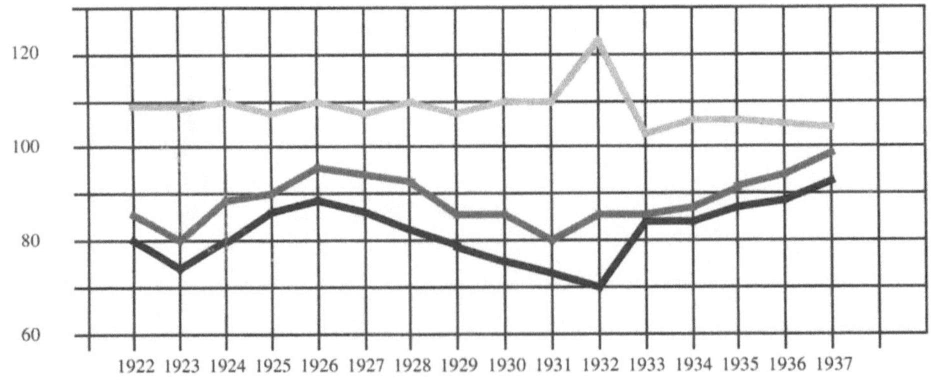

6. Japan

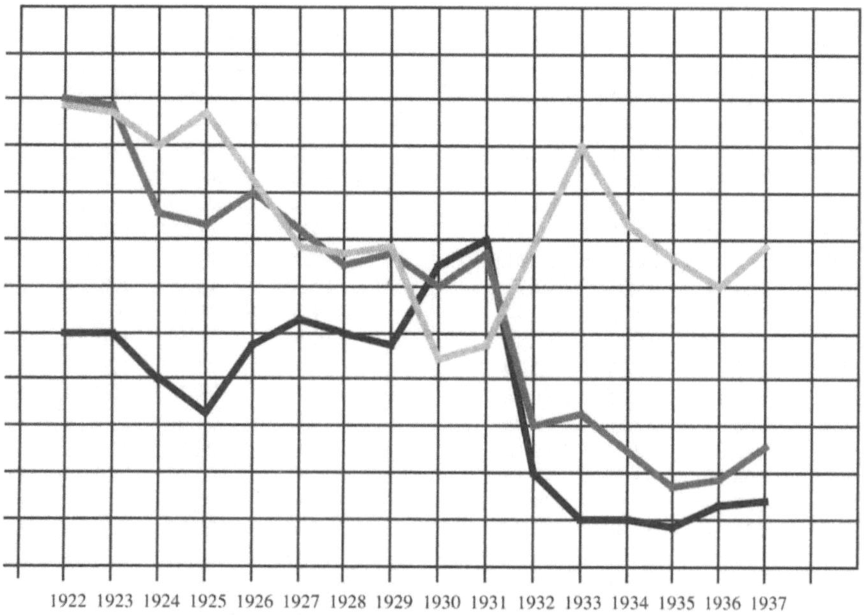

7. India

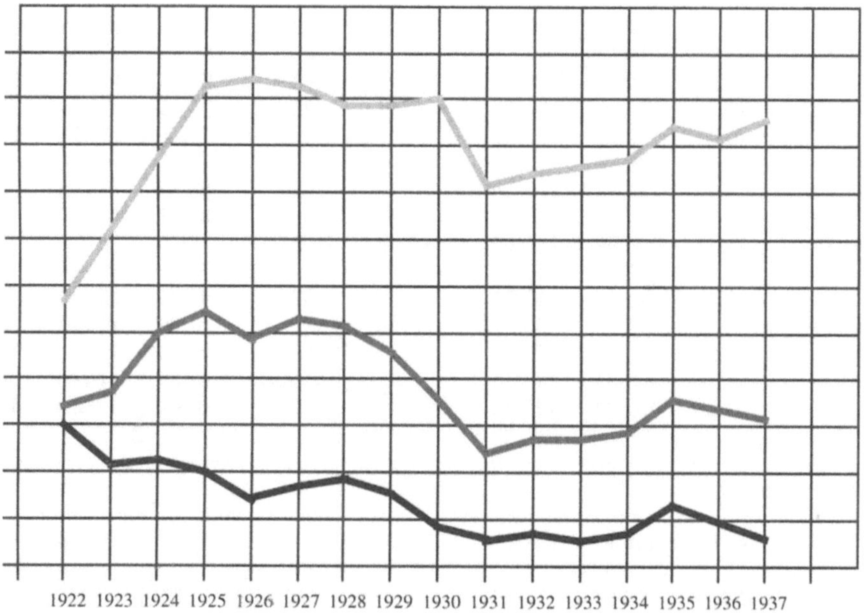

Source: Tables 1–7

Tables 8–15. Relative prices, effective exchange rates, real effective exchange rates on the basis of current export shares 1922–1937 – Indices 1913 = 100

8. Italy

Year	rel. Pr	eff. ER	r. e. ER
1922	291.10	37.71	92.31
1923	255.30	33.86	86.42
1924	243.47	32.65	79.49
1925	271.20	28.38	76.97
1926	311.40	29.87	93.01
1927	280.54	35.57	99.78
1928	247.28	37.34	92.34
1929	238.50	36.84	87.85
1930	207.41	38.71	80.29
1931	207.14	39.55	81.93
1932	206.07	37.88	78.05
1933	182.06	42.91	78.12
1934	168.58	43.39	73.15
1935	177.94	41.79	74.35
1936	221.11	31.42	69.46
1937	227.42	28.45	64.70

9. Sweden

Year	rel. Pr.	eff. ER	r. e. ER
1922	99.63	126.81	126.34
1923	88.35	132.40	116.97
1924	80.39	138.43	111.29
1925	82.48	130.65	107.77
1926	89.22	133.05	118.71
1927	96.65	124.79	120.60
1928	91.17	131.67	120.05
1929	91.49	130.43	119.33
1930	93.47	129.51	121.05
1931	98.78	125.85	124.31
1932	104.29	111.34	116.11
1933	98.62	112.98	111.42
1934	102.42	109.25	111.88
1935	100.29	110.23	110.55
1936	100.99	112.46	113.57
1937	101.01	120.23	121.45

10. Switzerland

Year	rel. Pr	eff. ER	r. e. ER
1922	98.34	136.40	134.13
1923	79.07	137.37	108.61
1924	80.32	136.42	109.57
1925	77.54	140.19	108.69
1926	72.34	151.00	109.23
1927	76.96	140.10	107.82
1928	76.45	146.94	112.33
1929	74.49	154.89	115.37
1930	75.13	160.90	120.88
1931	75.75	173.09	131.12
1932	69.68	212.68	148.19
1933	68.89	216.41	149.08
1934	70.27	213.95	150.33
1935	69.56	223.74	155.64
1936	70.17	209.93	147.30
1937	74.36	182.24	135.52

11. Netherlands

Year	rel. Pr.	eff. ER	r. e. ER
1922	83.98	131.96	110.82
1923	72.53	143.36	103.98
1924	80.35	135.50	108.88
1925	81.16	125.83	102.12
1926	72.68	136.28	99.05
1927	72.01	139.15	100.21
1928	71.06	140.68	99.97
1929	68.74	145.95	100.33
1930	65.37	153.30	100.21
1931	59.25	165.21	97.98
1932	51.52	190.19	97.99
1933	49.25	151.67	95.76
1934	51.89	113.01	97.73
1935	51.44	118.47	103.29
1936	52.87	126.44	107.82
1937	60.40	133.26	110.26

12. Belgium

Year	rel. Pr	eff. ER	r. e. ER
1922	179.97	54.96	98.92
1923	201.19	38.70	77.90
1924	240.39	33.46	80.43
1925	267.26	33.24	88.83

13. China

Year	rel. Pr.	eff. ER	r. e. ER
1922	73.79	128.96	95.16
1923	71.73	125.54	90.05
1924	71.11	139.60	99.27
1925	72.15	149.06	107.55

Year	rel. Pr	eff. ER	r. e. ER
1926	363.67	23.86	86.77
1927	414.95	19.21	79.71
1928	431.35	19.20	82.81
1929	450.07	19.43	87.44
1930	444.91	20.42	90.83
1931	439.37	21.93	96.37
1932	417.99	24.40	102.00
1933	389.29	26.84	104.50
1934	383.76	27.53	105.66
1935	403.89	21.82	88.13
1936	438.86	20.27	88.95
1937	424.02	23.18	98.30

Year	rel. Pr.	eff. ER	r. e. ER
1926	80.08	133.82	107.14
1927	95.68	117.57	112.49
1928	96.84	120.84	117.02
1929	102.47	107.17	109.82
1930	131.10	72.73	95.34
1931	165.53	50.88	84.22
1932	147.96	67.33	99.62
1933	127.93	76.65	98.06
1934	112.15	83.30	93.42
1935	119.93	89.54	107.38
1936	146.84	73.94	108.58
1937	156.00	71.62	111.73

14. Argentina

Year	rel. Pr	eff. ER	r. e. ER
1922	65.28	112.42	73.38
1923	61.66	113.57	69.41
1924	62.71	120.32	75.09
1925	67.34	137.86	92.83
1926	51.38	147.60	75.83
1927	55.14	150.01	82.71
1928	62.76	150.34	94.36
1929	57.80	151.31	87.45
1930	57.21	125.48	71.79
1931	49.26	105.96	52.19
1932	51.98	110.37	57.37
1933	55.09	104.93	57.81
1934	67.94	78.42	53.28
1935	71.12	81.36	57.87
1936	82.03	89.96	74.70
1937	83.88	101.18	84.87

15. Australia

Year	rel. Pr.	eff. ER	r. e. ER
1922	65.30	119.93	78.32
1923	72.25	129.05	93.24
1924	82.03	142.02	116.50
1925	102.66	105.44	154.44
1926	71.59	157.34	112.66
1927	74.87	151.38	113.34
1928	82.11	149.22	122.52
1929	78.05	148.24	115.70
1930	68.79	124.81	85.86
1931	55.80	97.77	54.55
1932	62.92	95.91	60.35
1933	61.45	97.92	60.17
1934	81.11	82.91	67.24
1935	65.13	100.13	65.22
1936	82.60	103.44	85.44
1937	87.16	106.93	93.20

Diagrams 8–10. Real effective exchange rate 1922–1937 on the basis of current export shares

8. Italy, Sweden, Switzerland

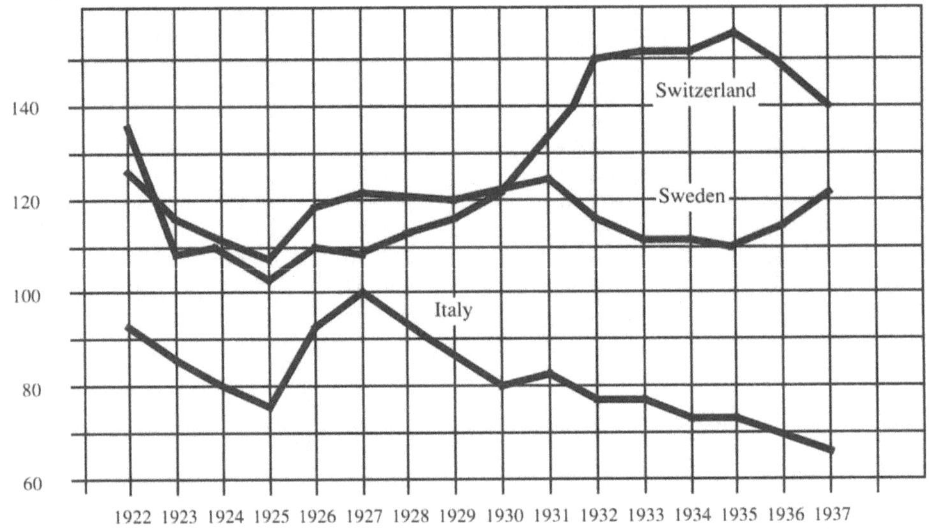

9. Belgium, Netherlands

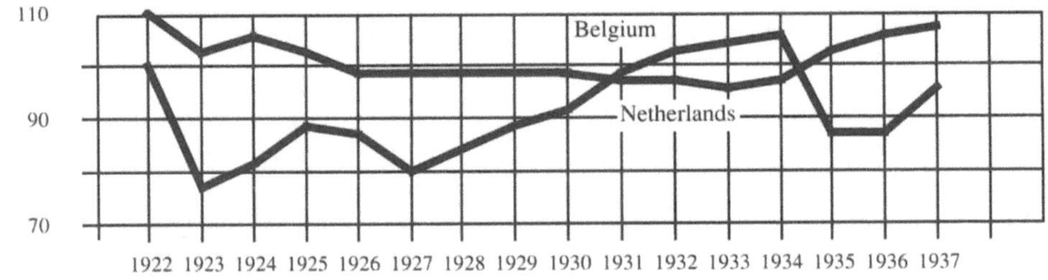

10. China, Argentina, Australia

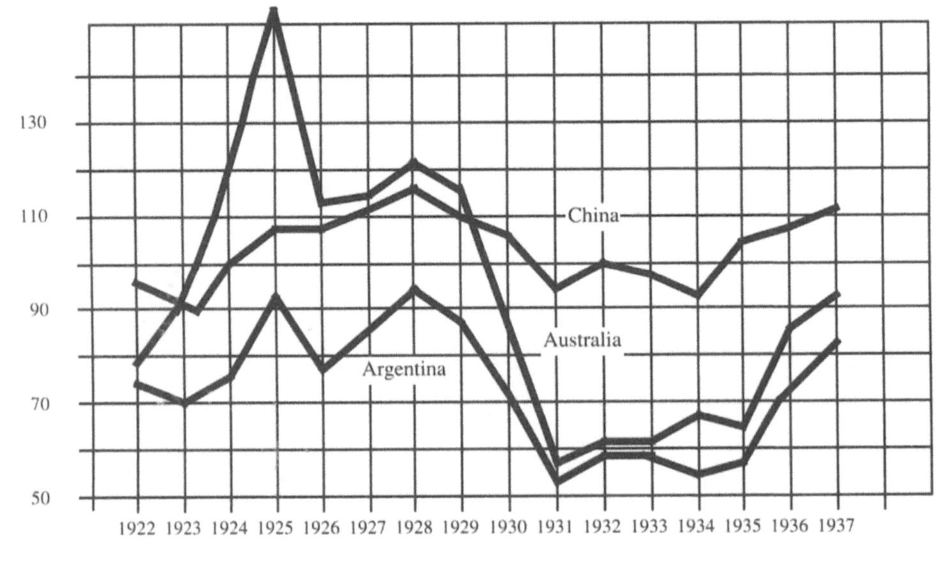

Reichsbank President Hjalmar Schacht and the Reparation Payments (1924–1930)*

Johannes Houwink ten Cate

Introduction

In the prime period of the Weimar Republic the name and personality of the President of the Reichsbank, Dr. Hjalmar Schacht, were a guarantee of monetary stability. Certainly, the generation traumatized by the inflation considered him as such. After the collapse of the Third Reich, in which he had been the leading figure in economic policy until 1937, Schacht was discredited and put on trial. Subsequently, he endowed the public with self-eulogies in his own defence[1], the only result of which has been that the guardian of the Weimar currency, who was one of the earliest to support Hitler, has been characterized as a dilettante in foreign policy[2], an intriguer[3], an opportunist[4], and even a quasi-pathological case.[5] The ritual of discrediting Schacht has been performed so often that recently only an occasional hagiography[6] or factual analysis[7] has recently appeared, and there is noticeable *ennui*[8] at the prospect of more critical studies of him.[9] That Schacht's resignation on 7 March 1930 and his support of Hitler were connected with his conflict with the Müller cabinet over financial and reparation policy is generally known. Schacht himself whipped up public controversy when he published his unbridled polemic account of

* The following article was written in connection with the publication of the source volume "De Berlijnse Dagboeken van Prof. dr. mr. G.W.J. Bruins", for the Nederlands Historisch Genootschap [The Hague, The Netherlands], see Note 12. I am grateful to Prof. Dr. K. Borchardt (Munich) for his help and support.

1 H. Schacht, Abrechnung mit Hitler, Hamburg 1948, and 76 Jahre meines Lebens, Bad Wörishofen 1953.

2 P. Krüger, Die Aussenpolitik der Republik von Weimar, Darmstadt 1985, p. 481.

3 K.D. Bracher, Die Auflösung der Weimarer Republik. Eine Studie zum Problem des Machtverfalls in der Demokratie, Villingen, 5th edition 1971, pp. 263f.

4 O. Braun, Von Weimar zu Hitler, New York 1940, p. 256 and H. Heiber, Die Republik von Weimar, Munich 1974, pp. 205f.

5 H. Müller, Die Zentralbank – eine Nebenregierung, Reichsbankpräsident Hjalmar Schacht als Politiker der Weimarer Republik, Opladen 1973, pp. 14ff.

6 One exception is the recent work by H. Pentzlin, Hjalmar Schacht, Leben und Wirken einer umstrittenen Persönlichkeit, Berlin 1980. The main early hagiographies are F. Reuter, Hjalmar Schacht, Berlin 1937 and H.F. Berger, Die Etappen der Reparationspolitik, in: Probleme des deutschen Wirtschaftslebens, Berlin 1937 and H. Bertrand, Le Docteur Schacht, Paris 1939.

7 H. James, The Reichsbank and Public Finance in Germany 1924–1933: A Study of the Politics of Economics during the Great Depression, Frankfurt am Main 1985.

8 P.D. Stachura, The Weimar Era and Hitler. A Critical Bibliography, Oxford 1977, pp. 14, 132.

9 E.N. Peterson, Hjalmar Schacht. For and Against Hitler: A Study in the Problem of Political Guilt, Boston 1954; E.A. Beck, Verdict on Schacht, Tallahassee 1955; A.E. Simpson, Hjalmar Schacht in Perspective, The Hague 1969.

his reparation policy optimistically titled 'Das Ende der Reparationen' (The End of the Reparation Payments) in 1931 and attacked the politicians of Weimar in his malicious speech at the notorious Bad Harzburg rally of the nationalist opposition to the republic a few months later.[10]

Even if views differ on Schachts role in Hitler's rise to power in general, and in particular on the significance of the 'Schacht Bureau' in the summer of 1932 and the genesis and the importance of the industrialists' petition to Reich President Hindenburg in November that year [11], Schacht's name was foremost. *Prima facie* it could be concluded from this that judgments on Schacht like the above seem more or less justified. That, on the other hand, the way taken by the former President of the Reichsbank in 1931–1932 was not predetermined by his political principles or his personality, is asserted in this comprehensive (and lengthy) account of his reparation policy during his first term as central banker and its relation to Stresemann's foreign policy of reconciliation and compromise, which is partly based on new sources.[12]

I. First Attempts

Since the Dawes Plan was regarded as the first step to economic and internal stability for Germany after 1924 and as such formed the precondition for the Treaty of Locarno, fulfilling the Plan, at least for the time being, was the official motto of Foreign Minister Gustav Stresemann's policy of understanding and reconciliation. The plan was the price Weimar had to pay after 1924 for the French defeat in 1923. Under the Plan, the duration of which was unlimited in time, the annual payments after four trial years, that is, from 1928/29, were to rise to the very high annuity of 2.5 billion RM per annum. Foreign supervision of German finances under the Agent-

---

[10] "I have personally experienced what it is like fighting against foreign countries at the negotiating table with a government at home that has no national support. And so I wish that the hurricane of nationalism that is sweeping Germany may not diminish until the way to self-assertion and ultimate success is open again", as Schacht said on 11 October 1931 in Bad Harzburg. See Schacht, 76 Jahre, p. 368 and Bracher, Auflösung, pp. 366f. In "Das Ende der Reparationen" (Oldenburg 1931) Schacht attacked the reparation politicians of the Republic. On the view from the opposite side by the Foreign Minister see J. Curtius, Der Young-Plan, Entstellung und Wahrheit, Stuttgart 1950, and for the view of the Reich Government M. Vogt (ed.), Die Entstehung des Young-Planes dargestellt vom Reichsarchiv 1931–1933, Boppard 1970.

[11] E. Kolb, Die Weimarer Republik, Munich, Vienna 1984, p. 214. See also H.A. Turner, Faschismus und Kapitalismus in Deutschland. Studien zum Verhältnis zwischen Nationalsozialismus und Wirtschaft, Göttingen 1972 and D. Stegmann, Zum Verhältnis von Grossindustrie und Nationalsozialismus, in: Archiv für Sozialgeschichte 13 (1973), pp. 399–482 and R. Neebe, Grossindustrie, Staat und NSDAP 1930–1933. Paul Silverberg und der Reichsverband der Deutschen Industrie in der Krise der Weimarer Republik, Göttingen 1981 and James, Reichsbank pp. 335ff. See also H. James, The German Slump, Politics and Economics 1924–1936, New York 1987, p. 187.

[12] Mainly the diaries by Dr. Hans Schäffer, Secretary of State in the Reich Ministry of Finance and Prof. Dr. Mr. G.W.J. Bruins, Commissioner for the issue of banknotes at the Reichsbank. See Note 95 and E. Wandel, Dr. Hans Schäffer, Steuermann in wirtschaftlichen und politischen Krisen, Stuttgart 1974 and J. Houwink ten Cate (ed.), De Berlijnse Dagboeken van Prof. dr. mr. G.W.J. Bruins (1924–1930), Serie kleine Bronnen van het N.H.G., The Hague 1989, See Note 22.

General Parker Gilbert and the Central Bank Commissioner Bruins restricted the financial authority of the Government and limited the autonomy of the Reichsbank.[13] The United States were the creditor for the inter-allied debts from the First World War, and since 1924 those of the Republic as well. Thanks to foreign loans, mainly from the United States, the German economy was working and Germany could make reparation payments. In a realistic assessment of the position of the United States as the true victor in the First World War Stresemann (of the right liberal German People's Party) saw economic cooperation with America as a way to strengthen the German position in Europe, since it would be bound to weaken the French hegemony.[14] The second basic component in his policy was to take account of the need for security on the part of the old "arch enemy". There were therefore two aspects to Stresemann's Locarno policy, Atlantic and European.[15] Although Stresemann thought it necessary to temporarily fulfil the Dawes Plan, he also supported revisionist tendencies. Confronted with the Dawes arrangement, he said later he had been in the position of a condemned man who is offered a year of life if he will teach the king's horse to fly. One does not turn down such an offer; after all, "before the year is out, the king, or I, or the horse may die. Anyway, who knows, perhaps the horse will really learn to fly". But as early as September 1925, a year after the Reich government had formally accepted the Dawes Plan and the German horse had, in fact, learnt to fly faster than had been thought possible, he wrote to the (former) Crown Prince that "the solution of the reparation question" was one of the three "great tasks" of his policy.[16] "As a German statesman, he felt that it was his obligation to concern himself with urgent national requirements, and the goal he set himself was to regain full sovereignty and independence for his country so that it was no longer at the mercy of others and could protect itself against attack or dictation or indirect pressure. This would be possible only after more specific goals had been attained: the diminution and eventual removal of the financial burdens imposed by the Versailles Treaty; the evacuation of German soil by foreign troops; the attainment of military parity with other Powers; and, finally, the rectification of its eastern frontier and, perhaps, the regulation of its relationship with Austria by 'Anschluss' or fusion" – to quote Gordon A. Craig. Quite apart from economic considerations, Stresemann regarded a revision of the Dawes Plan and a new, less exhausting, arrangement as the basis of his medium-term foreign policy objectives.[17]

---

[13] G. Hardach, Weltmarktorientierung und relative Stagnation, Währungspolitik in Deutschland 1924–1931, Berlin 1976, pp. 44ff; H. Schacht, Ende der Reparationen, p. 47; see James, Reichsbank, pp. 19ff.

[14] M.O. Maxelon, Stresemann und Frankreich, Politik der Ost-West-Balance, in: W. Michalka/ M.M. Lee (ed.), Gustav Stresemann, Darmstadt 1982, pp. 149ff; Michalka, loc. cit., p. XIII.

[15] P. Krüger, Deutschland und das internationale System der 20er Jahre, in: Gesch. in Wiss. u. Unterr. (GWU) 33 (1982), pp. 405f. and A. Rosenberg, Geschichte der Weimarer Republik, Frankfurt am Main 1962, pp. 162f. and A. Thimme, Gustav Stresemann, Legende und Wirklichkeit, in: Histor. Zs. 181 (1956), p. 328.

[16] Michalka, Stresemann, p. XXIV. For the anecdote about the horse, see G.A. Craig, Germany 1866–1945, Oxford 1981, 8th ed., p. 515. Stresemann's letter to the Crown Prince is quoted by Michalka, Stresemann, p. XXIV.

[17] Craig, Germany, p. 512 and Michalka, loc. cit., p. XXIV; see also W. Weidenfeld, Stresemanns Englandpolitik im Spannungsfeld zwischen Kooperation und Konfrontation, in: Michalka/Lee, Stresemann, p. 166.

Like the Foreign Minister, thanks to whose support Schacht, then a member of the Management Board of the Darmstädter-Nationalbank, had been appointed President of the Reichsbank in 1924[18], Schacht was a former national-liberal businessman who, again like Stresemann, had been co-founder of a liberal political party, the left of center DDP (German Democratic Party), in 1919. Since the negotiations on the Dawes Plan in the spring of 1924 the Reichsbank President had seen a rational American policy vis à vis Germany as identical with the efforts by the American financial world to support the reconstruction of Central Europe.[19] Because Wall Street was supplying the Republic with credits, Schacht, who had converted the Rentenmark into a gold currency with American assistance, saw cooperation with the United States as the basis of the central bank's policy.[20] Even in the company of the high-ranking financiers who formed the General Council of the Reichsbank under the Dawes Plan and had to supervise its policy, it was not the representative of the United States, Gates W. McGarrah, but Schacht who seemed to be "the true American" (Bruins). In the opinion of the Reichsbank Commissioner he was vociferous, sensitive to public criticism, egocentric and dictatorial. Schacht's oldest friend in central bank circles, Governor Norman of the Bank of England[21], also said that he really was "a man with a heart."[22] Since Schacht's Atlantic sympathies were both for currency policy reasons and, as some thought, personal and psychological, his Americanist leanings went much deeper than the general admiration for American money, goods and mass culture current in Germany at the time. That Schacht had political ambitions had become evident to all who knew the scene in Berlin, including the United States Ambassador, Houghton, soon after he took office.[23] Of course Reichsbank President Schacht was fully aware of the military weakness of the Republic, and so he also realised that, as Stresemann put it, the only objective for German foreign policy in 1925 could be to make policy "with the only thing in which we are still a Great Power, our economy."[24] As a financier he was inclined to equate financial with political power. France had not even succeeded in stabilising its currency at the end of 1925, and for this reason, Schacht thought France of less importance as a potential power. Against that background it was inevitable that he would agree with Stresemann after Locarno that, excluding any foreign policy of coercion, the German economic potential should be used as a means to enable Germany to pursue a Great Power policy, particularly within the framework of close economic cooperation with the United States.[25] Schacht's overall concept thus agreed with the basic Atlantic-economic orientation of the

---

[18] Müller, Zentralbank, pp. 27ff. For the background see K.B. Netzband/H.P. Widmaier, Währungs- und Finanzpolitik der Ära Luther 1923–1925, Basle, Tübingen 1954.

[19] H. Schacht, Die Stabilisierung der Mark, Berlin, Leipzig 1927, pp. 143f.

[20] See Note 13.

[21] James, Reichsbank, pp. 21, 80.

[22] Bruins' diary, Algemeen Rijksarchief The Hague, 2.21.191, no. 79–84 (hereinafter Bruins diary), 13.7.1925, conversation with Norman (hereinafter Norman), translation by the author, see Note 12 and James, Reichsbank, pp. 26f.

[23] Bruins diary, 19.11.1924 (Houghton).

[24] Minutes of the meeting of the Central Board of the German People's Party on 22 November 1925, quoted by W. Weidenfeld, Gustav Stresemann – der Mythos vom engagierten Europäer, in: GWU 24 (1973), p. 741.

[25] See Note 14.

Foreign Minister's concept. But since Schacht was not particularly interested in France, his concept and that of the Foreign Minister were only partially identical.

Schacht saw possibilities for a revisionist reparation policy in the phenomenon of the American loans. After the foreign flow of credit had become a flood in the course of 1925, and Stresemann had approached the Crown Prince, the Reichsbank President went to see the princes of American high finance. During his visit he was able to establish with satisfaction that no-one in American financial circles believed that the Dawes Plan could be fulfilled and, secondly, that this was not regretted. On the contrary, it was held to be quite natural. But precisely for that reason Schacht thought that any suggestion of German sabotage of the Plan and the reparation payments it called for had to be avoided.[26] With an openness that was later to become a feature of his relations with Reichsbank Commissioner Bruins, Schacht immediately after his return from the United States asked the Dutch university professor whether "the British are such children that they believe that, while Germany is burdening her property with mortgages, the Americans will pay the reparations".[27] The Americans realised this as well, he, Schacht, was convinced.[28] There was hope in these observations; but since the Dawes Plan would be revised in the near future anyway, this view of the American position hardly encouraged the pursuit of an active revisionist policy.

For that reason Schacht for the time concentrated on the Eupen-Malmédy question. With Stresemann's agreement and in constant contact with the German Foreign Office he made unofficial soundings in the winter of 1925 among Belgian financiers, with the aim of obtaining agreement on a settlement, under which the Belgians were to renounce Eupen-Malmédy in return for compensation in the question of German occupation money. The attempt failed, because France refused to accept a Belgian settlement with Germany.[29]

So Schacht turned back to the reparation policy. In January 1926 he made his views on the impossibility of fulfilling the plan more plain. The transfer of the reparation payments, in which he had to cooperate under the terms of the Plan, was to him the main issue. He regarded it as merely a pretence.[30] By that he did not mean that there were no payments. What he meant was that the foreign exchange for the transfer was not earned from a surplus on the trade balance. The foreign exchange needed to make the payments flew in as Germany borrowed money from abroad, and then flow out again as reparation payments. Because Germany was importing capital after 1924 and this was reflected in the currency reserves of the Reichsbank, the Reichsbank had foreign exchange, despite the trade deficit, which it was obliged to sell to the reparation agency. The Agent-General for the Reparation Payments was

---

[26] Schacht to the Reich Government, 5 December 1925, Akten zur deutschen auswärtigen Politik, Serie B (1925–1933) (hereinafter ADAP B), 1,1, pp. 18ff.

[27] James, Reichsbank, p. 39.

[28] Bruins diary, 28 November 1925 (Schacht).

[29] Bruins diary, 30 August 1926 (Delacroix); M.J. Enssle, Germany, Belgium and the Eupen-Malmédy Question 1919–1929, Wiesbaden 1980, pp. 131ff.; Krüger, Aussenpolitik, pp. 356f.; W. Link, Die amerikanische Stabilisierungspolitik in Deutschland 1921–1932, Düsseldorf 1970, pp. 348ff.; Vogt, Entstehung, pp. 133f.

[30] Schacht to the Reich Government, 24 January 1926, ADAP B 1.1, p. 146; see James, Reichsbank, p. 60.

S. Parker Gilbert, a man of thirty-three and a former Under Secretary of State in the US Treasury, "a man of unlimited possibilities" (Norman).[31] He based his decision as to whether funds could be transferred or not, not on the trade balance but on the balance of payments and the Reichsbank foreign exchange holdings. As long as the foreign loans flooded in, Parker Gilbert could go on transferring foreign exchange. Only when the outflow of foreign exchange began to jeopardise the stability of the currency, was he to cease making transfers. That was the socalled transfer protection clause in the Dawes Plan.[32] Although Schacht held the view that Germany could only make reparation payments under the Plan if the economy could earn enough foreign exchange by way of exports of goods and services, Parker Gilbert went on transferring as long as the foreign exchange holdings in the Reichsbank sufficed and the currency remained stable. This constellation inspired the Reichsbank President to an active reparation policy which he pursued until his resignation, four years later.

After an excursion into policy on Poland in February and March 1926 – Schacht wanted to make broad financial aid to Poland, isolated since Locarno, dependent on a revision of the borders with Germany, a view which Stresemann supported[33], – the Reichsbank President ventured his first, cautious step on to the slippery floor of reparation policy in April 1926. He proposed to discuss the possibility of a revision of the Dawes Plan with Governor Norman of the Bank of England during a visit to London.[34] As Parker Gilbert had forecast to Bruins[35], Norman flatly refused. The disappointed Reichsbank President then commented tersely to Bruins that his journey had "not been a pleasurable experience".

In his efforts to improve his position before taking up the revision issue again, Schacht concluded from this first defeat that he would have to build up new alliances. Immediately after his return from England he therefore invited the Reichsbank Commissioner to discussions, in which he explicitly asked for his confidence, a gesture which Bruins noted with gratitude in his diary.[36] Schacht also changed his direction in domestic policy. Although he had been appointed to his office by Stresemann not last because of his activity as a founding member of the German Democratic Party, he took the occasion of the party's statement on the referendum on the financial compensation of the aristocracy for their losses during the revolutionary phase of the Republic in May 1926 as a reason to leave it.[37] Clearly Schacht was among the considerable number of those who had joined the German Democratic Party or voted for it after the revolution because they were opponents of socialism, and felt betrayed by the party leaders when they made a pact with the Social democratic Party of Germany.[38] After he left the DDP, the enthusiasm for

[31] See Note 22.
[32] Hardach, Weltmarktorientierung, pp. 44f.
[33] K.D. Erdmann, Das Problem der Ost- oder Westorientierung in der Locarnopolitik Stresemanns, in: GWU 6 (1955), p. 147; M. Walsdorff, Der Berliner Vertrag und Stresemanns Ostpolitik in der Locarno-Aera, in: Michalka/Lee, Stresemann, p. 125; G. Niedhart, Stresemanns Aussenpolitik, Locarno und die Grenze der Entspannung, in: Michalka/Lee, Stresemann, p. 419. See also Krüger, Aussenpolitik, pp. 308f.
[34] Bruins diary, 30 April 1926 (Schacht).
[35] Loc. cit., 27 May 1926 (Parker Gilbert).
[36] Loc. cit., 31 May 1926 (Schacht) and 1 June 1926 (ibid.).
[37] Reuter, Schacht, p. 96, see W. Lacqueur, Weimar, A Cultural History, London 1974, p. 10.
[38] Between 1919 and 1924 the GDP share of the votes had already dropped from 19% to 6%, see R.F. Hamilton, Who Voted for Hitler? Princeton 1982, pp. 247ff.

Schacht diminished in the left-wing liberal press, and the support for him grew in the more conservative circles.

II. Renewed Efforts

Indications that Parker Gilbert did not regard a revision of the Dawes Plan as feasible[39] encouraged Schacht, who had succeeded in relatively strengthening his position, to a more energetic approach in revision policy. From July 1926 he gradually changed from being a central bank president who was aiming to find a solution to the reparation question, to a reparation politician who was pursuing reparation policy as Stresemann had put it, "with the only major weapon we have, our economic position as a major debtor country to other nations".[40] To slow down the transfers and accelerate negotiation on revision he set about trying to reduce the Reichsbank's holdings of foreign exchange. This was bound to bring him into conflict with Parker Gilbert.

In August 1926 the Reichsbank repealed the fixed dollar rate. This meant that it would no longer guarantee the full link between the dollar and the Reichsmark within the gold points, and after that the German borrower, in considering whether he would be able to repay a dollar loan, would have to take a possible increase in the rate for the dollar during the term of the loan into account in his calculations. So terminating the fixed rate for the dollar did slow down the inflow of credit, even if only for a short time.[41] Secondly, this measure was the precondition for the emergence of a domestic gold market which would enable the Reichsbank to buy gold at home as well.[42] And in fact the central bank bought gold for 250 million RM on the domestic market during the autumn of 1926.[43] Reichsbank Commissioner Bruins soon began to suspect what this could amount to: since the stock of cover reserves[44] had risen to no more than RM 500 million[45], Schacht would be able to tell

[39] Note by von Schubert, 7 July 1926, ADAP B 1,1, pp. 634f.

[40] Speech by Stresemann to the 'Arbeitsgemeinschaft Deutscher Landsmannschaften' (compatriots organization) on 14 December 1925, ADAP B 1.1, Appendix II, pp. 727f.

[41] Bruins to McGarrah, 3 August 1926, Bruins papers, Algemeen Rijksarchief The Hague, 2.21.191 (hereinafter BP), 117; Hardach, Weltmarktorientierung, p. 75f.

[42] G.W.J. Bruins, Memorandum on the Movement of Gold into and out of Germany since 1924 (October) 1930, Archiv De Nederlandsche Bank N.V., Amsterdam, Directie-Archief Vissering, doos 67, Volkerenbond.

[43] Currency reserves table, 31 December 1926, BP 144.

[44] Under Art. 28a of the Banking Act only those reserves were eligible as cover that were deposited as money at call with the Reichsbank's foreign correspondent banks. Under this law at least 40% of the money in circulation had to be covered by gold or these foreign exchange reserves. None of the other foreign exchange held by the central bank was eligible as cover. More than 80% of the foreign exchange reserve that was not eligible for cover consisted of foreign bills. The Bruins papers contain, as do the Luther papers (Federal Archives, Koblenz) a table showing the main items in the Reichsbank balance sheet. This includes the non-cover reserves, and so can be regarded as more informative on the level of the currency reserves than the published weekly statements of the Reichsbank, which only shows the cover reserves. To prevent any misunderstanding the distinction between reserves eligible as cover and other reserves has always been observed here (see Hardach, pp. 84 and 104 and James, Reichsbank, Appendix 1, Table 1b).

[45] See Note 43.

Parker Gilbert in future that he did not have enough foreign exchange in hand for the "unnational" transfer (Bruins).[46] Although the Reichsbank still had ample foreign exchange in the autumn of 1926, Schacht made it plain to the Commissioner, and in all probability to Parker Gilbert as well, that he was not prepared to take up unlimited amounts of foreign exchange only to see the funds transferred out of the country again.

Stresemann then took the initiative again in reparation policy. In mid-September he went to Thoiry to negotiate with the French Foreign Minister Aristide Briand on a general settlement in Franco-German relations, offering financial compensation if the French troops which occupied the Rhineland were to evacuate it. However, Stresemann made his reckoning without the support of the United States[47], which wanted to see French finances stabilised and the Franco-American debt agreements ratified first.[48] For the present, as the Agent-General pointed out, nothing could be done in regard to revision. One must "wait and see, because revision is bound up with the question of reducing inter-allied debt. There is no support for a reduction of this debt at present, at least in America".[49]

So the optimistic interpretation of the American position, which Schacht had evolved during his visit to American in 1925, had proved mistaken. Thereupon Stresemann took the line that "reparation policy should be taken out of domestic and foreign policy discussion. This will give time for the political scene to calm down and enable us to direct the reparation issue away from the former political discussion and more into economic and financial channels".[50] In practice this meant abandoning an active revisionist policy for the time being. Although after Thoiry Stresemann saw revision as offering the possibility for a medium-term relaxation of German-American relations[51], he did not, at first, want to demand more than the Allies would be able to concede. Thus the German Foreign Office waited, as Parker Gilbert wished, for a swing round in American public opinion. How long they might have to wait for an American inclination towards revision, however, was not apparent. Before April 1928, when Germany was included in the negotiations on the Briand-Kellogg Pact[52], certainly, Stresemann saw no opportunity to create an atmosphere favourable to Germany in the United States.[53]

---

46 Bruins to Vissering, 28 December 1926, Archiv De Nederlandsche Bank N.V., Amsterdam, Directie-Archief Vissering, doos 2, Corr. Bruins.

47 W. Link, Grundzüge des deutsch-amerikanischen Verhältnisses in der Stabilisierungsphase 1925–1929, in: Michalka/Lee, Stresemann, p. 104. See Krüger, Aussenpolitik, p. 360.

48 Krüger, Aussenpolitik, p. 360; Link, Stabilisierungspolitik, pp. 348ff.; E. Wandel, Die Bedeutung der Vereinigten Staaten für das deutsche Reparationsproblem, Tübingen 1954, pp. 58ff.; Vogt, Entstehung, pp. 99f., R.E. Lüke, Von der Stabilisierung bis zur Krise, Zurich 1958, pp. 135ff.

49 Note by von Schubert, 9 October 1926, ADAP B, 1, 2, p. 315.

50 Circular from Stresemann, 30 January 1928, ADAP B, VIII, pp. 108f.; note by Ritter, 18 April 1927, ADAP B, V, pp. 194ff.; note by von Maltzan, 18 April 1927, ADAP B, V, pp. 199f.; Wandel, Bedeutung, pp. 168f.

51 Maxelon, Stresemann, pp. 158f.

52 P. Krüger, Friedenssicherung und deutsche Revisionspolitik, Die deutsche Aussenpolitik und die Verhandlungen über den Kellogg-Pakt, in: VfZ 22 (1974), pp. 244ff. and ibid, Aussenpolitik, pp. 386f.

53 Krüger, Aussenpolitik, pp. 415f.; Link, Grundzüge, pp. 108ff.

Schacht, however, did not want to wait for the mood in America to change. Is it surprising, that this "true American" concluded from Gilbert's reaction to Thoiry that reparation policy could only be pursued with the agreement of America, and that he would first have to create support in the United States, and firstly in Parker Gilbert, for the idea of revision? It certainly is understandable that Schacht regarded the period of cautious tactical manoeuvering as over by October 1926. He then embarked upon the intensification of his policy by making a public attack on the transfers. Before the Commission of Enquiry into the German Economic Situation he stated that the capital imports were "creating a pretence of solvency" which did not exist in reality.[54] According to Bruins, Schacht had stated more or less openly what he wanted: to reduce the possibility for Gilbert to make transfers. Since it became clear at the same time that Schacht was prepared to go as far as forcing a repeal of the exemption from capital yield tax, the concern of Schacht's close friend, the Dutch university professor Bruins, grew. For this would mean double taxation on interest earnings on a foreign loan, so causing the net yield to fall and making these bonds less attractive to foreign investors; again this would reduce the foreign exchange holdings and so the possibility of making transfers.[55]

But Parker Gilbert was not to be dismayed by Schacht's public criticism, and he reported on 30 November 1926 that there was no basis for a definitive solution to the reparation question.[56] As the cover ratio was 63% in December 1926, with gold and currency reserves RM 700 million 57 above the minimum cover level of 40% required by law, Gilbert had no reason to press for revision.[57] On the contrary, the Reichsbank had altogether RM 1 billion in foreign exchange reserves (including non-cover reserves). In the second year of the Plan, up to September 1926, Parker Gilbert had transferred about RM 400 million in cash. So in his opinion the transfer mechanism was working perfectly well. The transfer question, the only lever with which the Germans could raise the revision question, would presumably not become an acute issue for another one or two years, that is, in 1928/29, after the end of the trial period, and by then Germany would have proved its solvency.[58]

Because time seemed to be working for Parker Gilbert and the creditor nations, and the German Foreign Office had adopted a waiting policy after the failure of Thoiry, Schacht set about solving his main problem, the Reichsbank's surplus foreign exchange reserves, in a drastic way, through discount policy. While the inflow of long-term foreign credits slowed down to RM 200 million in the first half of 1927 after the repeal of the exemption from capital yield tax[59], the Reichsbank

---

[54] Bruins diary, 11 November 1926 (Schacht); Wandel, Bedeutung, pp. 103f.; I. Maurer, Reichsfinanzen und Grosse Koalition, Zur Geschichte des Reichskabinetts Müller 1928–1930, Frankfurt am Main 1973, p. 29; Hardach, Weltmarktorientierung, p. 71.; Link, Stabilisierungspolitik, p. 406.

[55] Bruins to McGarrah, 14 December 1926, BP 117.; Bruins to Vissering, 28 December 1926, Archiv De Nederlandsche Bank N.V., Amsterdam, Directie-Archief Vissering, doos 2, Corr. Bruins.

[56] Note by Simons, 10 January 1927, ADAP B, IV, pp. 35ff.

[57] Report on the cover reserves, 31 December 1926, Anlage F (as per 23 December 1926), BP 132.

[58] See p. 74 above.

[59] Hardach, Weltmarktorientierung, p. 77.

managed to achieve an outflow of short-term credit as well by lowering the discount rate. As German borrowers bought foreign exchange from the central bank to repay their loans, the foreign exchange holdings shrank rapidly, as the published weekly statements from the Reichsbank showed. In January the Reichsbank lost RM 100 million, in February 200 million, and by the end of that month it could only show RM 200 million cover reserves in hand. But the bank also had to sell non-cover reserves[60], 60 million in January and 100 million in February.[61] So within eight weeks the bank had lost half of the RM 1 billion it had held in foreign exchange reserves, and Schacht had so to speak solved half his problem.

But Parker Gilbert was still not prepared to give in. As in July and October 1926, he repeated in February 1927 that the issue of solving the German reparation question could only be tackled after the coming presidential elections in the United States, from September 1928.[62] In response to this passive attitude on the part of the Agent-General, Schacht stated provocatively that he was "no longer prepared to go along with" the vicious circle of surplus foreign exchange, transfers, shortage of foreign exchange, increases in the discount rate, surplus foreign exchange, transfers and so on.[63] Regardless of the foreign exchange losses, the Reichsbank did not increase the discount rate. But it was only now that Schacht decided to embark on an open trial of strength with Parker Gilbert. At a meeting of the Reichsbank directors[64] and to Professor Bruins personally he complained at the level of short-term debt in the banking sector: this was too high in relation to the central bank reserves, and should foreign loans be withdrawn the Reichsbank would not be able to provide enough foreign exchange. For that reason, as he informed Bruins on 9 May 1927, he intended to confront Parker Gilbert with the fundamental question whether it was allowed to transfer foreign exchange that was being lent, to make reparation payments from borrowed funds, in other words. "The transfer has to be stopped".[65] Long before the currency could be endangered, Schacht intended to propose to Parker Gilbert that the transfers cease. He could not induce a crisis in the form of an interruption to the transfers for the reasons of competence explained above; but he belived he could force Parker Gilbert in that direction. This was not without risk.[66]

Schacht took that risk. On the grounds that the unsound stock market speculation must be stopped and the short-term indebtedness in the banking sector be reduced, he forced the banks on 13 May to cut back their carry-over money. This draconian measure caused a sensational fall in share prices on the stock exchange and an acute loss of confidence among foreign banks, which withdrew short-term loans.[67] The Reichsbank had lost RM 700 million in foreign exchange since January, and the

---

60 See Note 44.

61 Currency reserves table, 28 February 1927, BP 144.

62 Note by von Schubert, 25 February 1927, ADAP B, IV, p. 413.

63 Note by La Valette, 24 May 1927, ADAP B, V, pp. 392ff.; James, Reichsbank, p. 61.

64 Notes by Bruins, on the meetings of the Reichsbank directorate 25 February 1927, von 140.

65 Bruins diary, 9 May 1927 (Schacht).

66 Krüger, Aussenpolitik, p. 423.

67 Hardach, Weltmarktorientierung, p. 79; Müller, Zentralbank, p. 57; Link, Stabilisierungspolitik, p. 406; Wandel, Bedeutung, p. 103; Lüke, Stabilisierung, p. 235; James, Reichsbank, pp. 39, 61.

losses were now rising to RM 30 million a day;[68] three days after this step the bank only had RM 195 million in foreign exchange left. Only after the cover ratio had dropped to about 50% did the Reichsbank President decide to raise the discount rate. Probably Parker Gilbert and the Governor of the Gederal Reserve Bank of New York, Benjamin Strong, insisted that he should do so.[69] Strong regretted the loss of foreign exchange, because it jeopardised the transfer and "prosperity abroad".[70] He invited Schacht to New York for a secret conference of central bank presidents to give him a lesson in monetary policy.

III.Success

A few weeks after his return from New York, however, Schacht told the Secretary of State in the Foreign Office, von Schubert, and Bruins, that he had reached an agreement with Strong under which the head of the American banking world had promised a revision of the Dawes Plan after the United States presidential election in September 1928, if Schacht agreed to go on playing the "Bizarre game" of transferring borrowed funds for another eighteen months.[71] Strong had indeed written to Gilbert immediately after his discussions with Schacht that the Plan should be revised "as soon as possible".[72] Thanks to his prestige, his persistence and the passion with which he could impress his convictions on others, Schacht had succeeded in turning Gilbert's non-binding statement that something could only be done after September 1928 into a promise from the Governor of the Federal Reserve Bank in person that the Plan must be revised immediately after the election of the next president.[73] Schacht's revisionist policy, which the German Foreign Office was admittedly bound to regard as jeopardising the conduct of a uniform foreign policy[74], had proved extremely successful. But Schacht was not content with this initial

---

[68] The Reichsbank had already lost much foreign exchange, "much more than is published in the weekly statements", and it "still has to deliver somewhat considerable sums which amounted to as much as RM 30,000,000 per day during the last few days", as Bruins wrote to Addis on 11 May 1927, BP 110.

[69] Wandel, Bedeutung, pp. 103f.; Hardach, Weltmarktorientierung, p. 86; Krüger, Aussenpolitik, pp. 419f.

[70] "It was therefore most satisfactory that Dr. Schacht could arrange to go away to make us a visit next month, and we are looking forward to a discussion of all these matters and to a better understanding as to the facts in the situation and as to future policies...If anything in the nature of a crisis in connection with the reparation transfers can be avoided...we would then feel that the foundation had been laid for a gradual restoration of prosperity abroad (barring political accidents) which indeed should be the objective of all central banks", Strong to Bruins, 20 June 1927, BP 76. See also McGarrah to Bruins, 2 June 1927, NB BP and Addis to Bruins, 13 June 1927, BP 110. Owen Young also criticised Schacht, Bruins diary, 26 July 1927 (Schacht). See James, Reichsbank, p. 61. According to Parker Gilbert Schacht had "a change of heart in June and went to America in a better frame of mind"; Parker Gilbert to Strong, 8 September 1927, quoted from Wandel, Bedeutung, p. 104.

[71] Note by von Schubert, 1 August 1927, ADAP B, VI, pp. 157ff. and James, Reichsbank, p. 62.

[72] Strong to Parker Gilbert, 21 July 1927, quoted by Link, Stabilisierungspolitik, p. 413.

[73] See above, Section II.

[74] Krüger, Aussenpolitik, pp. 419f.

success. He insisted that Parker Gilbert should make his doubts on the future of the Plan publicly known, for "... if Mr. Gilbert says often enough that it is breaking down, he will cause it to break down and thus force the pace of revision".[75] In order to achieve this Schacht stepped up his opposition.

Strangely, the Reichsbank's foreign exchange holdings rose again only very, very slowly after the discount rate was raised in June 1927; from 15 June to 22 October they went up only by RM 194 million, while the long-term lending by foreign creditors amounted to as much as RM 750 million.[76] Apparently, the mechanism Schacht had criticised so often, by which the borrowed foreign exchange earnings quasi automatically flowed into the cellars of the central bank, was no longer working. In fact, the central bank had taken the simplest alternative to the transfers: it has stopped buying foreign exchange. After raising the discount rate again on 4 October, the bank held to this passive tactic, and the foreign exchange holdings stagnated at RM 340 million.[77] Schacht was rather blunt about this and told Shepard Morgan, a member of Gilbert's staff, that his central bank was "not a conversion ofice".[78] Parker Gilbert was perfectly aware that Schacht had deliberately refrained from using the opportunity to make up all the foreign exchange losses of the first half of the year. When Bruins proposed a compromise Schacht replied in irritation that increasing the foreign exchange holdings would "open up the transfer question again, and inevitably lead either to inflation, an increase in the discount rate or credit restrictions...As long as he was President of the Reichsbank Gilbert could criticise the finance policy of the Reich Government, but he could not intervene in the policy of the Reichsbank. Anyhow, since the Dawes Plan had entered its final phase, Parker Gilbert would have to demand in writing that he should buy the foreign exchange".[79]

Schacht "was out to smash the Plan".[80] Parker Gilbert avoided a second conflict with Schacht; he bought foreign exchange on his own account for the transfer and went on transferring.[81] After that he managed his own reserve fund, at least now and then.[82] Since he had made his refusal to cooperate in the transfer plain, Schacht expressed the utmost satisfaction at this.[83] At the same time Stresemann indicated to Bruins that "Germany has no obligation in regard to the transfer. It is being performed with borrowed funds, and for that reason the foreign credits must be completely stopped. In that case Parker Gilbert would have to invest the money here and one would see how quickly France would change its views on the desirability

---

75 Leith-Ross to Sargent, 21 December 1927, quoted by James, Reichsbank, p. 66.

76 Bruins diary, 27 October 1927 (Schacht).

77 Currency reserves table, 31 October 1927, BP 144.

78 Bruins diary, 19 October 1927 (Schacht/Morgan).

79 Loc. cit., 28 October 1927 (Schacht/Parker Gilbert).

80 File note J.V. Perowne, 11 November 1927, quoted by James, Reichsbank, p. 63.

81 See Note 79.

82 According to statements by vice president Dreyse, Parker Gilbert had a foreign exchange reserve of RM 200 million in May 1929; loc. cit., 10 May 1929 (Dreyse) and 24 May 1929 (idem); see also Note 183.

83 See Note 79.

of changing the Plan".[84] Moreover, the prospects for the Plan were negatively affected by a memorandum from Parker Gilbert in which he sharply criticised the state's finance policy. He made this censure in the hope of throttling public expenditure, and so raising German credit abroad. The intended publication of the memorandum, which Stresemann, Schacht and Bruins all wanted and promoted[85], however, had as consequence that American bankers contemplated a withdrawal of their short-term loans[86], while the prospects for long-term loans were bad anyway thanks to the repeal of the exemption from capital yield tax.

This combination of German flight from responsibility for the transfer and the threat of tremors to the credit structure gave rise to a feeling of disappointment and doubt among the financiers who were supervising the plan. The Chairman of the General Council, the British banker Sir Charles Addis, complained to Bruins of Schacht's foreign exchange policy[87], forecasting immense difficulties if the credits were not to be forthcoming for an extended period.[88] On 10 November 1927 Benjamin Strong of the Federal Reserve Bank told Parker Gilbert that he ought to open up the question of revision.[89] Parker Gilbert, who had been working for this for a couple of months, agreed with enthusiasm. With his staff members, Shepard Morgan and Pierre Jay, he immediately started preparing for revision. He did not mention this to Schacht, however.

When Parker Gilbert finally, in mid-December, wrote in his halfyearly report the words Schacht had so long been waiting for, namely, that Germany was to be given "a definite task to perform on her own responsibility"[90], the president of the Reichsbank could rightly see this as due to his policy. He was certainly satisfied, and he was not alone in his jubilation.Stresemann called Gilbert's statement "the most important act of reparation policy" since the Dawes Plan.[91] However, the enthusiasm was based on the assumption that the United States would reduce the inter-allied debts from the First World War, so that France and Britain would be able to do without the major part of the German reparation payments.[92] The general expectation was that the annual payments could thus be drastically reduced. Schacht mentioned a sum of one billion Reichsmark per year to Parker Gilbert, that is, two fifths of the normal annuity under the Dawes Plan. Gilbert regarded that proposal as

---

[84] Loc. cit., 1 November 1927 (Stresemann). According to the provisions of the Plan, once the stability of the currency was jeopardised because of lack of cover in gold or foreign exchange and transfers were interrupted, the Agent-General had the duty to invest the reparations in Reichsmark in Germany.

[85] See Note 84 and loc. cit., 28 and 29 October 1927 (Parker Gilbert).

[86] In a letter to Governor Strong of 14 November 1927 Parker Gilbert said that he regarded it as very short-sighted of the American bankers to talk of recalling their loans and withdrawing their money at the first sign (reference from Professor Dr. K. Borchardt, Munich, source Federal Reserve Bank of New York).

[87] Addis to Bruins, 7 November 1927, BP 110.

[88] Addis to Bruins, 14 November 1927, BP 110.

[89] Hardach, Weltmarktorientierung, p. 92; Link, Stabilisierungspolitik, pp. 414, 418.

[90] Lüke, Stabilisierung, p. 146; Maurer, Reichsfinanzen, p. 28.

[91] Circular from Stresemann, 30 January 1928, ADAP B, VIII, p. 108f.

[92] Bruins diary, 23 January 1928 (Parker Gilbert) and 2 February 1928 (idem); James, Reichsbank, pp. 64f.; Lüke, Stabilisierung, p. 149.

"not unreasonable" for a first offer. But he thought that only a yearly sum of RM 1.5 to 1.8 billion would be acceptable.[93]

The euphoria over the coming revision, however, was only shortlived. In his conversations with Secretary of State von Schubert, representing Stresemann, who was ill, Gilbert was already expressing himself very cautiously in February 1928 regarding the possibility of solving the two debt complexes together.[94] The Reich Economics Ministry, more sceptical, had the impression that "America does not want a link with the debt system".[95] The reserve on the part of the Americans increased the relative importance of the French Premier, Raymond Poincaré, for the German reparation problem. Although he allowed Parker Gilbert to convince him of the danger of a coming crisis in the Dawes Plan, Poincaré was only prepared to agree to revision at the price of linking this with the pending question of the evacuation of the Rhineland, in return for which Stresemann had promised him Financial compensation during the conference of Thoiry. Secondly, he wanted a German request for revision in the form of a diplomatic initiative.[96] These demands further weakened the German position.[97]

His success at single-handed operations to date strengthened Schacht in his ambitions. In his view the record trade deficit in 1927 made the transfer less justifiable than ever.[98] So the Reichsbank began buying gold again, for the first time since the autumn of 1926.[99] Parker Gilbert intervened. The gold purchases induced him to warn the Germans that, should there be a crisis in the Dawes Plan, they would be running the risk of a collapse of the revision plans. For a transfer crisis would inevitably also mean a crisis in German credit, and this was needed to float the new reparation loan, the proceeds of which would enable Germany to make reparation payments after an agreement about the revision of the Dawes Plan would have been reached.[100] As the President of the Reichsbank was again playing with the idea of opening up the fundamental question of a transfer from borrowed foreign exchange in the summer of 1928,[101] he stuck to his view that the foreign exchange situation and German solvency were not as they should be: in a more intimate circle, at a meeting of academics in Bad Pyrmont in June 1928, he said quite openly that because there was no moral basis for the reparation payments he was not prepared to pay, and for that reason would not accept any academic theory proving that he would have to pay.[102]

---

93 Bruins diary, 9 February 1928 (Parker Gilbert); loc. cit., 7 February 1928 (Snouck Hurgronje) and 8 February 1928 (Bernhard/Dreyse).

94 Note by von Schubert, 22 February 1928, ADAP B, VIII, pp. 226ff., and idem, 28 February 1928, ADAP B, VIII, pp. 263ff.

95 Schäffer diary, Institut für Zeitgeschichte, Munich, ED 93/4 (hereinafter Schäffer diary ED 93/4), 29 March 1928, p. 17.

96 Vogt, Entstehung, p. 25.

97 Schäffer diary, ED 93/4, 19 March 1928, p. 49.

98 Bruins to MacGarrah, 2 February 1928, BP 117.

99 See above, p. 79.

100 Maurer, Reichsfinanzen, pp. 46, 162, 171.

101 Bruins diary, 9 May 1928 (Schacht).

102 H. Brügelmann, Politische Ökonomie in kritischen Jahren, Tübingen 1956, pp. 83ff. Parker Gilbert's attention was drawn to these remarks by Schacht and he remembered them: Bruins diary, 19 January 1929 (Schacht).

Naturally, the Agent-General did not share this view. He tried to persuade the Great Coalition cabinet under the Social Democrat Hermann Müller to drop its passive attitude to the coming revision, and he was able to point to the consensus that had formed in the German Foreign Office in April that revision must be a definite objective. In these efforts Parker Gilbert tried to play down the problem of the sum which he had already discussed with Schacht in February, maintaining that what mattered was not the new annuity but "honest discussion".[103] Schacht did not accept this. In July he quarrelled for the second time with Gilbert over the amount, in the presence of Benjamin Strong, indicating the possibility of a transfer crisis.[104] As Gilbert had good grounds to regret Schacht's stubbornness over this issue, he tried from now on to exclude him from the political scene. It would be best, as he told von Schubert, for the cabinet not to allow Schacht to take "a leading position" in the revision question, since he suspected that Schacht intended to make his doubts about transfers from borrowed funds public. Moreover, according to Gilbert Schacht was extremely jealous of Stresemann and was working far too much "with figures and numbers".[105]

The cabinet ignored this proposal. However, it could hardly reject Gilbert's and Poincaré's efforts at revision for domestic policy reasons. As there was now agreement within the coalition as well on the need for revision, the *tangible* advantages of a new arrangement – the prospect of a lower sum, premature avacuation of the Rhineland and the departure of the foreign controllers – seemed to the cabinet more important than the disadvantages, namely the lack of a firm commitment from the United States on an impending reduction in inter-allied debt and the fact that Germany would be the petitioner. Although it was well known that the American presidential candidate who seemed to have the best prospects of winning, Hoover, would take a hard line over the interallied debt question[106], the cabinet hoped, and Schacht probably did as well, that the two debt complexes could be linked following a solution to the reparation question. Even the cautious Economics Ministry thought it might be possible in that case to reduce the annual payment to two fifths of its normal Dawes annuity[107], a sum Schacht had already envisaged in February. In the hope of this, the cabinet, acting on a second recommendation from Gilbert[108], sent a delegation to Geneva to take up the revision question through the traditional diplomatic channels.

After Schacht, who was well aware of Gilbert's personal criticism of him, had joined him in calling once more upon the cabinet to take a diplomatic initiative[109], it was announced on 16 September after negotiations with Britain and France that "agreement has been reached on the need to settle the reparation problem fully and finally, and for this purpose a Commission of financial experts is to be appointed".[110] Now the Dawes Plan really entered its liqïdation phase. Stresemann "had not

---

[103] Note by Kiep, 6 July 1928, ADAP B, IX, pp. 288f.
[104] Vogt, Entstehung, p. 30.
[105] Note by von Schubert, 27 July 1928, ADAP B, IX, p. 450, Note 1.
[106] Schäffer diary, ED 93/4, 18 June 1928, p. 75.
[107] Loc. cit., ED 93/28, 20 August 1928, p. 102.
[108] See Note 103 and a note by von Schubert, 18 August 1928, ADAP B, IX, pp. 585ff.
[109] Schacht to Müller, 6 September 1928, ADAP B X, p. 1, Note 4.
[110] Quoted by Krüger, Aussenpolitik, p. 415.

expected so much". Gilbert was "highly satisfied at the results from Geneva"[111] and Schacht told the cabinet that "the result is generally delightful".[112] To Bruins he expressed himself rather more effusively, saving "they should put up a statue to Parker Gilbert in Germany".[113]

IV. Self-Deception

In the five months between the Geneva decisions and the first meeting of the International Commission of Experts in Paris the governments of the creditor nations tried to narrow the scope for the experts to negotiate. While seemingly endless diplomatic skirmishings went on over the composition of the commission and the mandate for the experts, the governments were already putting forward their demands in regard to the new annuity. As the Locarno policy sagged for this reason into a depressing petty struggle over formal questions[114], Schacht's chances of being appointed leader of the delegation increased, both as a result of his support for the German initiative in Geneva and through the formulation of the communiqué of September 16th. "Since care must be taken to see that German policy would be conducted in the right way", Schacht spoke to the Reich Chancellor Müller and Finance Minister Hilferding (SPD) on 19 September.[115] The following day he stated in writing his agreement with the foreign policy goals of the cabinet, namely the revision of the Dawes Plan and the evacuation of the Rhineland.[116]

Schacht elaborated on his ideas on the commission to Curtius, the Economics Minister, and Bruins on 20 September. The smaller commission should include the main representatives of the Dawes Committee, and above all Owen Young. "The commission must certainly be so composed that Poincaré cannot send the members home again with a word of thanks after giving them advice; what he (Schacht) would have to say would have to be taken in hand immediately by the main government branches, especially the bankers...and in such a way that America too would be forced to take risks and tackle the problem of interallied debts. A final settlement would have to concern both issues at the same time".[117] Over this too, Schacht expressed himself more clearly to Bruins: "On my remarking that I (Bruins) could not understand the whole affair, should there be no commitment from the United States, Schacht answered: But there are American commitments".[118] On the new annual payment, Schacht told Curtius that "one certainly should not participate into discussions on figures like 1.8 billion". Schäffer concluded from this that Schacht, because he believed that a solution was impending on both debt problems, the

[111] Loc cit., 456f.
[112] Schacht to Stresemann, 20 September 1928, ADAP B, X, p. 119.
[113] Bruins diary, 20 September 1928 (Schacht).
[114] Krüger, Aussenpolitik, pp. 457ff.
[115] See Note 113.
[116] See Note 112.
[117] Note by Schäffer, ED 93/28, 20 September 1928, p. 141.
[118] See Note 113.

German and the inter-allied, was reckoning on annual payments of scarcely more than 1.2 billion.[119]

When the entire press, including the SPD paper "Vorwärts", acclaimed Schacht's re-election as Reichsbank President in the General Council meeting of 29 September[120], his chances still seemed to be rising. On the one hand he wanted to be appointed as the head of the German delegation to the forthcoming international conference, and was deliberately working for it. On the other hand, he admitted to Bruins that recently he had had frequent meetings with politicians of the right-wing DNVP (German National People's Party) (which had opposed both the Dawes Plan and the Locarno Treaty in 1924–25). He also feared for his repute at home should he have to return from the Paris conference with a disappointing result in the matter of the annual payments.[121] But if a satisfactory new arrangement could not be reached, as he said to Bruins, the proposal could always be put to Parker Gilbert to cease transferring borrowed foreign exchange.[122] Threatening with a transfer crisis, which was an empty threat since he had no formal power to cause such a crisis (other than ruining the currency in the process), apparently had become a fixed idea. Clearly the potential leader of the delegation had been unable to evolve new tactics.

After "Die Weltbühne" had revealed that Schacht had said in Bad Pyrmont that he did not want to pay, the first criticism was voiced of his appointment as leader of the delegation.[123] In a later edition of this weekly of the international left its chief editor, Carl von Ossietzky, called Schacht "an opponent of economic cooperation and political reconciliation" (with Western Europe and the United States) and a "pseudo Helfferich" (a right wing politician who had been the candidate of the banking community for the post of President of the Reichsbank in 1924).[124] These comments were repeated, not without purpose, in the London "Times", so indirectly confirming that Governor Norman was opposed to Schacht's appointment.[125] But Parker Gilbert refrained from trying to exclude Schacht from the revision policy, as the cabinet had ignored his earlier request. However, the Agent-General also doubted that Schacht was the right man to head the German delegation, as did the chairman of the General Council, Addis.[126]

As in July, Gilbert's doubts were nourished by a conversation with Schacht on the new annual payment. At the beginning of October Gilbert was no longer talking

---

[119] See Note 117.

[120] Bruins diary, 15 October 1928 (Schacht).

[121] "He has good relations with the DNVP, better actually than the Government believes to be the case...Schacht is perfectly aware of the Committee's difficulty in deciding. He was not very optimistic that the sum could be greatly reduced. It could be very difficult if concessions had to be made at the last moment, while those who made the concessions would burden themselves with a stigma", loc. cit., 19 October 1928 (Schacht).

[122] See Note 120.

[123] Die Weltbühne (24), No. 41, 9 October 1928, see also Bruins diary, 15 November 1928 (Parker Gilbert).

[124] Carl von Ossietzky, Ist Schacht geeignet? in: Die Weltbühne (24), No. 43, 23 October 1928.

[125] "Gilbert actually received a letter from Norman a few days before, in which he said that it might perhaps be better if Schacht did not represent Germany", Bruins diary, 15 November 1928 (Parker Gilbert).

[126] See Note 125 and note by von Schubert, 14 November 1928, ADAP B, X, p. 320; James, Reichsbank, p. 73, Note 49.

of RM 1.5 to 1.8 billion, and on 25 October he told the Government and Schacht that there were "practical limits" which the experts would have to acknowledge; the limit was, it could not be helped, 2 billion.[127] Schacht, who had appointed himself interpreter in the absence of Stresemann, undermined this by handing on to the Reich Finance Minister Rudolf Hilferding (SPD) an allied demand for 5 billion.[128] No doubt this did not seem particularly constructive to Parker Gilbert, and as this was now the third time that Schacht had refused a high sum, the two avoided each other from now on.[129] But Reich Chancellor Müller was now in favour of a closer relationship with Schacht, and two days after the conversation with Gilbert he gave Schacht a promise in writing to consult him before important cabinet decisions were to be made.[130] This tactic on the part of the cabinet was also reflected in the Foreign Office's press policy, when press reports of tension between Schacht and Stresemann were expressly denied in October.[131] Thus only six weeks after the Geneva decision an informal understanding and coresponsibility had been formed with Schacht, which he himself could interpret as a prior decision over the choice of delegates.

Schacht expressed considerable disappointment on all the issues on which Parker Gilbert had laid down the Allied demands. Bruins was informed that Schacht did not feel bound by the demands handed on by Gilbert, although work on the revision question would have to continue.[132] As in 1927, it became clear that Schacht would not give in to pressure from Parker Gilbert. His demands only became more radical: a week later he told the Reichsbank Commissioner that Germany could only agree to payment of one billion RM, that Parker Gilbert should not interfere so much, that the conference should not take place and finally that he still regarded a transfer crisis as quite possible.[133] Naturally, Schacht was too cautious to express himself with such boldness to cabinet members, but in a private letter to the German ambassador in Paris, who was negotiating on the organisation of the Committee with Poincaré, he wrote in a semi-official capacity, that the German ability to pay was "not signed and sealed", on the contrary, the greatest significance should be attached to the experts' assessment of the situation. If the Allies could be persuaded that German credit was about to break down, they would not let the conference fail, and for that reason the German delegation could always threaten to break off the negotiations and return to the Dawes Plan.[134]

As the policy of reconciliation degenerated into a petty struggle over the commission, and as the demands inside Germany for concrete results became ever louder, moreover as Parker Gilbert had robbed the German politicians of their illusions, Schacht became increasingly irritated. So did Stresemann, whose mood,

---

127 Record from Parker Gilbert's office, not dated, ADAP B, X, pp. 209ff., see above.

128 Bruins dairy, 10 November 1928 (Parker Gilbert); Lüke, Stabilisierung, pp. 156f.

129 Bruins diary, 10 November 1928 (Parker Gilbert); Schacht, Ende der Reparationen, pp. 61f.; Vogt, Entstehung, pp. 230f.

130 Vogt, Entstehung, pp. 132f.

131 M. Vogt, Letzte Erfolge? Stresemanns Aussenpolitik in den Jahren 1928 und 1929, in: Michalka/Lee, Stresemann, p. 455.

132 Bruins diary, 25 October 1928 (Schacht).

133 Loc. cit., 1 November 1928 (Schacht).

134 Schacht to von Hoesch, 2 November 1928, ADAP B, X, pp. 255ff.

after Parker Gilbert had informed him that the sum would be high[135] gradually changed to one of disappointment and bitterness.[136] Tension mounted between the cabinet and the official Government advisor. When maintained that, to his dismay, a top official had discussed high figures with Parker Gilbert – it was none other than Stresemann who had at the time maintained that he was speaking in private –, Schäffer (of the Reich Economics Ministry)answered rather cynically that "we would never do that, in order not to relieve the experts of their responsibility for a possible failure".[137] Gilbert's efforts to enlighten the Germans and statements such as these made Schacht extremely nervous. He admitted to Bruins that he "could not sleep any more because he did not know how world opinion might react to a deadlock". He set all his hopes in the other experts and Owen Young, the most important United States representative[138], who had already expressed the view during the discussions in the Dawes Committee that reparation payments amounting to billions of Marks could only be transferred if Germany had a trade balance surplus.[139]

From the end of November, long before Schacht was finally appointed leader of the delegation, it became clear, from his attempts to overplay his nervousness, that he was suffering from self-deception. One of his suggestions, for instance, was that the amount should be made dependent on concessions in trade policy.[140] He even made these tactics plain to the opposite side by announcing at a Berlin evening engagement that he did not feel morally bound by either the Versailles Treaty or the Dawes Plan, and was only prepared to offer RM 500 million under the condition of continental free trade. Upon which Pierre Jay, a member of Gilbert's staff, answered "You will be pretty soon at zero, Mr. President!"[141]

After the German Foreign Office and Poincaré had decided upon the structure of the commission in keeping with German interests and Schacht's wishes, the cabinet had to decide on the question of the choice of delegates. Schacht put himself forward for the last time, writing to Stresemann that at the conference he would leave "outworn tracks" and cooperate "with generous proposals" in opening up a new "era of reconstruction".[142] In fact, his appointment was more or less inevitable on account of his fame in Germany as the creator of a stable currency. On the other hand Parker Gilbert, Addis[143] and Norman[144] had expressed doubts. Nevertheless, Schacht's appointment seemed desirable on account of the high regard in which he was held

[135] Note by Fuhr, 13 November 1928, ADAP B, X, pp. 376ff.

[136] Krüger, Aussenpolitik, pp. 461f.

[137] Schäffer diary, ED 93/4, 26 November 1928, p. 132. Two days before the meeting of the cabinet, which he had suggested, Schacht had expressed extreme dismay to von Schubert at the talk between Parker Gilbert and Stresemann on 13 November 1928, during which Stresemann, speaking in a private capacity, had mentioned a figure of 1.5 billion. "It was very incautious to mention even one billion", as Schacht commented. Note by von Schubert, ADAP B, X, p. 379, Note 4. See ADAP, B, XI, p. 467 and Vogt, Entstehung, pp. 162f.; Schacht, Ende der Reparationen, pp. 64f.

[138] Bruins diary, 16 November 1928 (Schacht); James, Reichsbank, p. 67.

[139] See Note 19.

[140] See Note 134.

[141] Bruins diary, 12 December 1928 (Poole/Morgan).

[142] Schacht to Stresemann, 11 December 1928, ADAP B, X, pp. 490f.

[143] Bruins diary, 3 December 1928 (Addis) and 7 December 1928 (Parker Gilbert).

[144] See Note 125.

in the United States as a finance policy expert.[145] Should the United States declare itself ready to reduce the inter-allied debts, the annual payment could be reduced to RM 1400 million; should the delegation not succeed in bringing this about, it would have to be assumed that the sum would be closer to the Dawes annuity.[146] Because he regarded Schacht as indispensable in dealing with the Americans, Stresemann appointed Schacht, thus formalising the joint responsibility of the cabinet and the President of the Reichsbank.

But even after his appointment Schacht failed to take a more realistic view of things. On the contrary, in Paris (as he said to von Schubert of the Foreign office) "we should tell the other side that we are not going to pay at all, if the world situation does not change completely", by which he meant, among other things, colonies being handed over to Germany.[147] The combination of pressure from the opposite side, nervousness and self-deception was particularly evident in his central bank policy. Allthough Schacht had refused to lower the discount rate in the meeting of the General Council of December 1928 because this would certainly be followed by an outflow of credit[148], he suddenly lowered the discount rate ten days after his appointment and three weeks before the conference was due to begin. He did this in the intention of proving by a concrete example his argument that the cover ratio was not an indication of Germany's ability to pay because the cover was, so to speak, borrowed. From mid-January, as the Reichsbank had hardly any foreign exchange left, the loss of large amounts of gold hung like the sword of Damocles over the central bank.[149]

The mood Schacht was in on the day the discount rate was lowered suddenly became clear to Reichsbank Commissioner Bruins in the last conversation he had with the Reichsbank President before Schacht left for Paris. When Bruins remarked in regard to the negotiations that were about to start that one should always remain "aequo animo", Schacht quoted from the third of Horace's Roman Odes the passage on the moral heroism of Aeneas, containing the statement that heroism will conquer the world because neither nature nor the fury of citizens, demanding evil deeds, nor the tyrant could shake a just man guided by his principles from his fixity of purpose. When Schacht declaimed the line "were the world to crack and collapse, the ruins will fall upon the fearless!" Bruins interrupted him by calling out, "Yes, ruins!" Upon which Schacht cried "Is not all in ruins already here?"[150]

As an independent expert, Schacht wanted to fight for a low annuity and he was hoping for a favourable solution. For the rest, he went to Paris without a definite plan but in a mood for destructive heroism.[151] He put his chances of success at about fifty-fifty.[152]

---

[145] Bruins diary, 18 May 1926 (Strong); James, Reichsbank, pp. 21, 62, and below.

[146] Schäffer diary, ED 93/5, 20 January 1929, pp. 38ff.

[147] "Moreover, Herr Schacht went very much further in that regard", note by von Schubert, 24 January 1929, ADAP B, XI, p. 25 and ADAP B, XI, p. 55.

[148] Bruins to McGarrah, 4 December 1928, BP 117.

[149] Schacht told the cabinet that in view of the reserves a loss of a billion did not matter; see Link, Stabilisierungspolitik, p. 440; James, Reichsbank, pp. 77f.

[150] Bruins diary, 19 January 1929 (Schacht).

[151] Schäffer diary, ED 93/5, 4 February 1929, p. 51.

[152] Bruins diary, 7 February 1929 (Schacht); see Vogt, Entstehung, pp. 175f.

V. Defeat

Schacht's task in Paris was to make the most of the policy of understanding and negotiate a reduction in the annuity. As Parker Gilbert had informed both him and Stresemann, the scope for negotiation was, however, extremely small. After Schacht had refused to name an initial sum right at the start, he lamed the conference with long monologues on Germany's inability to pay.[153] This was not convincing, because the transfer had never broken down and because the experts in the creditor nations had worked out how much they needed for their payments to the United States. After a week Schacht made an offer behind the scenes to the American financier J.P. Morgan of RM 800 million, one third of the Dawes annuity; however, his price was continental free trade, the return of some colonies and the return of the Polish Corridor.[154] When the British expert Stamp commented a few days later that he had heard larger sums mentioned by the German side before, Schacht said that Reich Finance Minister Hilferding had no idea and Stresemann was "a perfect fool".[155] Since Schacht's offer was anything but generous, some of the American delegates planned to break up the conference, but the Chairman, Owen Young, took charge of the tactics and attempted to "let Schacht peter out" (Parker Gilbert)[156] But as Young went on negotiating with the knowledge of this offer, Schacht believed that he had succeeded in creating a situation where he could not be blamed if the conference ended in faillure.[157]

Robbed in February of the illusion that he would be able to achieve much, Schacht raised his offer by 400 million to 1200 million.[158] Since he was aware of the risk of being defeated, he also asked the cabinet for authorisation to negotiate officially on the question of the colonies and Eupen-Malmédy, which was granted. But it was also agreed that the experts were "not to engage in politics". "The four gentlemen [of the German delegation – HtC] are to disappear afterwards and leave all the rest to the politicians", as Schäffer noted in his diary.[159] But Schacht's request startled Economics Minister Curtius, who wondered whether the government would not have to intervene after all if the experts failed to reach agreement with the creditor nations.[160] Schacht continued the negotiations, raising his offer by a further 250 million to 1450 million, upon which the Allies demanded 2.3 billion.[161] If agreement were finally to be reached in the middle, the new annuity would be 2 billion, a reduction by 500 million.

But in Schacht's view that was far too much. To his Reichsbank Commissioner Bruins, the Agent-General and the cabinet he had refused to accept a sum of that order at least eight times. To accept it now would not only mean that he had achieved

---

[153] Vogt, Entstehung, pp. 179ff.
[154] Schäffer diary, ED 93/5, 12 March 1929, p. 82.
[155] Bruins diary, 4 March 1929 (Parker Gilbert).
[156] Loc. cit.; Link, Stabilisierungspolitik, pp. 459f.; see also Bruins diary, 23 March 1929 (Addis).
[157] See Note 154.
[158] Bruins diary, 28 February 1929 (Dreyse); Vogt, Entstehung, p. 197.
[159] See Note 154.
[160] Loc. cit., p. 88.
[161] Vogt, Entstehung, pp. 200ff.

nothing whatever in Paris, a new annuity in that order also would have called in question his entire reparation policy. Was Schacht wrong to sum up the policy he had been pursuing since October 1926 to himself at this moment as that he had attacked the transfer of borrowed funds in public and that the Reichsbank in the last two years "had collaborated in reparation transfers out of borrowed money, and it (the Reichsbank) had done so in the hope of an early and definitive settlement of the reparation problem. The happenings of the last week had shown the grave dangers of this policy".[162] Would he now have to see the collapse of his concept?

It was a new experience for Schacht to be a loser, and it was one he could not take. He therefore set about putting an end to his co-responsibility with the cabinet. After all, the government had taken the initiative in Geneva, Stresemann and Hilferding had taken note of Parker Gilbert's comments on the new annual payment and the cabinet had appointed him head of the delegation although it knew what tactics he would pursue. He therefore decided only to sign a new arrangement if the cabinet instructed him to do so. As the Ambassador to Paris, von Hoesch, reported on 14 April, Schacht lacked "the necessary incentive" to go on negotiating.[163] The cabinet itself would of course have to insist on a new arrangement, since otherwise the coalition would be in danger of collapsing, and that would probably mean the end of the policy of reconciliation.[164] It was clear that not Schacht but the cabinet was in a straitjacket, both for domestic and foreign policy reasons. Therefore it was perfectly clear that Schacht would succeed in shifting the responsibility back where it in a more formal sense belonged anyway: on to the cabinet.

That Schacht, moreover, hoped to rescue as much as possible of his fame in Germany as an expert on reparations, is evident particularly from the formulations in his memorandum of 17 April, in which he offered RM 1650 million a year, under the above conditions (free trade, the colonies, the Polish Corridor). That was an infringement of the agreement not to engage in politics. Schacht however had only changed his tactics. As a financier he was ultimately convinced that the fulfilment of his conditions would increase Germany's ability to pay, and the cabinet had known of this standpoint since December 1928. After publication of Schach's memorandum the cabinet, utterly disappointed, expected the negotiations to be broken off. In despair an interim solution was discussed in government circles.[165] Schacht, who held the view that a definitive arrangement was more likely to be reached by returning to the Dawes Plan than with a provisional agreement, also refused to compromise.[166] The sudden death of one of the British experts meant that it was possible to avoid formally breaking off the negotiations in Paris, giving the cabinet time to disociate itself from the memorandum from the German delegation.[167] But Schacht had succeeded in giving the German public the impression that he had really tried all he could in Paris, while behind the scenes the government had taken responsibility for the defeat that was inevitably going to come.

---

162 Bruins to McGarrah, 1 May 1929, BP 118.

163 Von Hoesch to the German Foreign Office, 14 April 1929, ADAP B, XI, p. 397.

164 Bracher, Auflösung, pp. 248f.; Krüger, Aussenpolitik, p. 479f.

165 Schäffer diary, ED 93/5, 17 April 1929, pp. 137f.

166 Loc. cit., p. 149; James, Reichsbank, p. 82.

167 Note by von Schubert, 20 April 1929, ADAP B; XI, p. 420.

However, Schacht had also caused the worst monetary crisis since the stabilisation of the currency in 1924. Under the pressure of the reduction in the discount rate and the uncertainty in Paris, the difficulties had begun in February with a loss of RM 200 million in foreign exchange. In March the situation worsened, and the central bank had to sell RM 180 million in foreign exchange and RM 50 million in gold. Since this only left RM 30 million cover reserves[168], it seemed absolutely imperative to raise the discount rate. Although that step was championed in the General Council, Schacht flatly refused to do so before the Paris conference had ended.[169] After the publication of his memorandum, the losses gathered momentum rapidly, and the bank lost the next RM 234 million within a week.[170] Never, not even in May 1927, had the central bank lost so much foreign currency so quickly, and since the weapon of raising the discount rate had still not been used, further losses were inevitable.

Schacht's opponent at the conference, the Governor of the Banque de France, Emile Moreau, "that squareheaded French peasant", as Addis called him[171], sensed a possibility of turning this situation to good account and deciding the outcome of the negotiations quickly in France's interests. Indirectly, by raising the interest rate charged on acceptance credits to German borrowers, the French central bank gave expression to its doubts in the viability of the German reserve position and the policy pursued by the Reichsbank.[172] This, and the panic buying of foreign exchange, both by customers and by the managements of top banks[173], cost the Reichsbank another 240 million of its currency reserves in the last week in April, despite increase in the discount rate.[174] During that week the cover ratio dropped to 43%, 3% more than the legal minimum.[175] It was hardly astonishing that the publication of these depressing figures raised new doubts in the currency, and with the monetary crisis the threat of a transfer crisis now became real, which could have unforeseeable consequences.

Against that background the cabinet had to decide whether it should call Schacht's rebellious delegation to order. Parker Gilbert had left no doubt that the government would have to "put pressure on" him.[176] Although Schacht had already informally agreed to a solution proposed by Young[177], he stressed on his visit to Berlin on 1 May that he was prepared to make that "sacrifice of the intellect...for the

---

168 Currency reserves table, 28 March 1929, BP 144. Cf. Bruins to McGarrah, 23 March 1929, NB 118.

169 At the meeting of the General Council on 1 May Schacht stated bluntly that "another consideration which guided the Reichsbank – though not the decisive one – was its unwillingness to raise the discount rate during the Conference in Paris", Bruins to McGarrah, 1 May 1929, BP 118.

170 Currency reserves table, 23 April 1929, BP 144.

171 Bruins diary, 23 March 1929 (Addis).

172 Link, Stabilisierungspolitik, pp. 464f.; Vogt, Entstehung, pp. 229f.; see also Note 169.

173 Dreyse said to Bruins that certain banks, such as Sal. Oppenheim & Cie., [Cologne], were loading themselves with foreign exchange. "The inflation hyenas are scenting fresh morning air again", Bruins diary, 20 April 1929 (Dreyse); James, Reichsbank, pp. 78f.

174 Currency reserves table, 30 April 1929, BP 144. On 27 April the crisis seemed to have broken when RM 190 million was lost in one day; Bruins to Addis, 11 May 1929, BP 110.

175 Report on the Cover Situation, 31 May 1929 (as per 30 May 1929), BP 132.

176 Von Hoesch to the German Foreign Office, 28 April 1929, ADAP B; XI, pp. 454ff.; see also Vogt, Entstehung, p. 33.

177 Loc. cit., pp. 244f.

sake of the Fatherland" and to sign, but only at the price of a formal decision by the government.[178] But the cabinet still hesiated. After renewed losses of foreign exchange on 2 May[179], and when Parker Gilbert had again insisted on a reconciliation with Schacht as head of the delegation[180], the cabinet acceded to Schacht's and Gilbert's demands and took the responsibility for the new settlement.[181] From that moment at the latest the relations between the cabinet and the President of the Reichsbank were damaged beyond repair.

The same applied to Schacht's relation to the General Council, which had re-elected him unanimously as recently as September 1928. In pursuit of his reparation policy Schacht had first lowered the discount rate and then refused to raise it. Now he threatened to continue the tactics of passive resistance. On his future discount policy he stated in the General Council, in some despair over the failure of his policy, that he "would not take the responsibility for still further increasing those short-term credits for the sole purpose of reparation transfers". He left the responsibility for the transfers, so he said, to Gilbert.[182] That could only mean that he was not going to raise the discount rate a second time, and he would not buy any more foreign exchange. This declaration was intended as a provocation to Gilbert, whom Schacht suspected of working with Moreau in Paris. At any rate, Gilbert took it as a defiance.[183]

After the cabinet had taken the responsibility, Schacht went on negotiating. When he signed the new arrangement on 7 June, the government appeared to have found a solution that was politically acceptable at home. The annual payment would be lowered by 500 million to RM 2 billion, and the French would evacuate the Rhineland prematurely. The foreign financial controls were also soon to be lifted.[184] But since the American officials had not been prepared to accept a solution to the inter-allied debt question at the same time, Schacht's reparation policy concept had failed utterly. Nevertheless, he promised the cabinet to work "fully and completely" to implement the report by the experts.[185] Admittedly, mustering support for the plan at home was still first and foremost the task of the government.

178 Loc cit., p. 249.
179 Bruins to Addis, 11 May 1929, BP 110.
180 Note by Von Schubert, 1 May 1929, ADAP B, XI, pp. 467ff.
181 Telegram from Stresemann to von Hoesch, 3 May 1929, 22.00 hours, ADAP B, XI, p. 486; see ADAP B, XI, p. 493 and Vogt, Entstehung, p. 76 and ibid, Letzte Erfolge, p. 458.
182 Bruins to McGarrah, 1 May 1929, BP 118. Bruins diary, 27 May 1929 (Parker Gilbert), loc. cit., 31 July 1929 (Addis).
183 Parker Gilbert to Bruins, 24 May 1929, BP 93. In reaction to these statements by Schacht and his remark to Bruins that he was again playing with the idea of facing the reparation agent with the qëstion of the principle of the transfer from borrowed funds, Gilbert had smaller sums transferred on 7 and 27 May 1929, Bruins diary, 27 May 1929 (Schacht/Parker Gilbert). See above, Note 82.
184 For a survey of the state of research on this see Krüger, Aussenpolitik, pp. 483f.
185 Vogt, Entstehung, pp. 90, 270f.

VI. Obstruction

Although Schacht stated publicly in June that he was in favour of the Young Plan he never inwardly accepted it.[186] Immediately after his return from a vacation in Marienbad, which he had commenced when the conference closed, he made no secret of his dissatisfaction to his closer acquaintances. As before his departure, he again recited poetry to Bruins, though this time not a eulogy on the Reichsbank President but a satire he had written himself on the Paris conference, and which he read out "in high spirits", as Bruins recorded. Somewhat frivolously he commented that he regarded it as his most important achievement to have discredited the Young Plan right from the start by his remarks on Germany's inability to pay, so that the Plan was bound to be seen abroad as a provisional arrangement.[187]

Even before the right-wing opposition to the New Plan mounted and resulted in the joint formation of a Reich Committee to petition for a referendum against the Plan, there were further signs that Schacht rejected it. Firstly, his relations to the General Council and to Parker Gilbert remained wretched. After Gilbert commented to Bruins in writing that remarks like those made by Schacht on 1 May in the General Council were intolerable[188], Schacht was asked by its chairman, Addis, in the next meeting what his future discount policy would be. But he showed not the slightest inclination to yield, only modifying his former statement to the effect that "he could no longer assume the responsibility for transfer by that particular means (i.e. out of borrowed money)".[189] That was close to repeating his provocative statement, and the General Council, who certainly did not always back Schacht[190], expressed disapproval of his hostility to the transfers. Schacht had to correct his statement in the meeting on 1 August, partly on the insistence of Gilbert[191], as he was forced to state that his earlier remarks "did not mean that, even if a final settlement of reparations were not reached, he intended to make any change in the fulfilment of his obligations under the Dawes Plan to facilitate transfers by every means in his power".[192] Schacht also cultivated his personal animosity to Gilbert. In July he opposed the Agent-General's membership of the organisational committee for the Bank for International Settlements (BIS), which was to carry out the transfers under the Young Plan. Schacht wanted to "expurgate the atmosphere of the Luisenstrasse" (where Gilbert's office was), as Bruins noted[193], and he held to his opposition, even when it became clear that Gilbert's candidature was supported by, Young and J.P. Morgan.[194]

In questions of finance policy Schacht's relation to the cabinet remained difficult, as he tried to use finance policy to compensate for the weakening of his

---

186 Reuter, Schacht, p. 90; Müller, Zentralbank, p. 87; Vogt, Entstehung, pp. 272f.
187 Bruins diary, 14 June 1929 (Schacht).
188 Parker Gilbert to Bruins, 24 May 1929, BP 93; See Notes 169 and 182.
189 Bruins to McGarrah, 3 July 1929, BP 118; Bruins to Parker Gilbert, 20 July 1929, BP 93.
190 James, Reichsbank, p. 24.
191 Parker Gilbert to Bruins, 30 July 1929, BP 93.
192 Bruins to McGarrah, 1 August 1929, BP 118 and Bruins to Parker Gilbert, 1 August 1929, BP 93.
193 Bruins diary, 27 June 1929 (Schacht), and 5 July 1929 (idem); James, Reichsbank, p. 82.
194 Bruins diary, 5 July 1929 (Schacht) and 19 July 1929 (idem).

position in reparation policy, which he felt as a serious loss of domestic prestige. Even during the Paris conference he had only unwillingly lent his support when it was a question of easing the cash problems faced by the Minister of Finance, Hilferding.[195] Then at the beginning of July he criticised the growing indebtedness of the public corporations particularly sharply in the General Council, expressing the opionion that foreign bankers should not supply them with credits any longer.[196] That was doubly regrettable in the cabinet's view: firstly, Schacht was making a solution to the tight cash position more difficult, and secondly, his criticism of public financial policy could easily affect German credit. Since floating a big reparation loan for the Reich, the proceeds of which were to enable France to repay part of her debts to the United States, was a basic element in the Young Plan, any damage to German credit would be bound to affect the viability of the new arrangement.[197] When rumours that Schacht was endeavouring to establish a finance policy "dictatorship" (Schäffer) were rife in government circles[198] the General Cpuncil could no longer be in doubt about Schacht's position here as well. The cabinet still had to feel it.

Even before the Reich Committee to petition for a referendum about the Young Plan had been formed on 9 July 1929, with Hugenberg (German National People's Party), Seldte (Veterans' League), Class (Pan-German League) and the still largely unknown Hitler (National Socialist German Workers Party)[199], Schacht had made it clear to Bruins, the General Council and the reparation agent that he rejected the transfer, Gilbert and the new arrangement altogether. The moral tone of the movement against the Plan, which was supported by all prominent opponents of the Weimar Republic and provided Hitler with the first opportunity to prove his oratoric skills on a national platform, was set by Class by describing Stresemann as "the essence of all the dangerous tendencies of our nation (whose) psychic degeneracy is clearly derived from his political decadence". After the formation of the Committee Schacht thought it best to refrain form public support for the Plan, as he had done on 28 June. When Secretary of State von Schubert asked Schacht on 10 July to deny a remark reportedly made by Albert Vögler, a director of the steel trust Vereinigte Stahlwerke and a member of the delegation in Paris – he was said to have commented that it had repeatedly been affirmed in the delegation that agreement to the Young Plan would be the same as acknowledging the lie over Germany's war guilt (its supposedly sole responsibility for the outbreak of war in August 1914) – Schacht answered laconically that he did not think much of such denials.[200] Schacht therefore made it plain to the government that he would do nothing to prevent the public forming the opinion that he did not feel morally bound by the Plan.

Nevertheless, Schacht went to the conference in The Hague in mid-August, where the diplomatic battle for the evacuation of the Rhineland was to be fought out.

---

195 Maurer, Reichsfinanzen, pp. 65ff.

196 Bruins to McGarrah, 3 July 1929, BP 118.

197 Link, Stabilisierungspolitik, pp. 405f.

198 Schäffer diary, ED 93/6, 4 June 1929, p. 199.

199 Braun, Weimar, p. 256; Hardach, Weltmarktorientierung, p. 105; H. Timm, Die deutsche Sozialpolitik und der Bruch der Grossen Koalition im März 1930, Düsseldorf 1953, p. 144.

200 ADAP B, XII, p. 171, Note 1. Quoted by Craig, Germany p. 527; ADAP B, XII, p. 171, Note 1.

With regard for the Reich Committee and the President of the republic, von Hindenburg, who was only prepared to give his authority to the Young Plan upon a speedy evacuation of the Rhineland[201], the German delegation under Stresemann had to come home with definite assurances on that issue. But Schacht, who had informed the British delegation that it should hold to its opposition to the Plan[202], concentrated as always mainly on the question of the annual payment. Shortly before the end of the conference, on 28 August, he proposed that even the slightest changes to the Young Plan be rejected and the negotiations broken off: "I am against any increase in the annual payment, and I wish this to be recorded".[203] Next day he stated that he wished to talk to Stresemann about his leaving the delegation, and only after that meeting did he agree to leave The Hague that evening, quietly, and not to cause any further difficulties.[204] Stresemann and the others had simply passed him over, and Schacht felt this as a humiliation he was never to forget.[205]

After the first conference in The Hague Schacht continued to contest the new Plan. In September he opposed the appointment of Pierre Quesnay, head of the Statistics Department in the Banque de France, to the important post of general manager at the BIS, since he saw him as a puppet of Moreau and Gilbert[206], and because he wanted at any price to prevent the BIS becoming a new reparation commission like the one Gilbert had headed.[207] Although only a short time later he supported the plan publicly for the last time[208], he was not prepared to offer constructive buttress for the formation of the BIS, and now, shortly after Stresemann's death, he was waiting for a chance to strengthen his position vis à vis the cabinet.

Again he decided to attack the government's reparation policy through finance policy. On 1 October he had anew spoken out in the General Council against an increase in Reich indebtedness.[209] When Hilferding began negotiating a loan with Dillon, Read & Co (New York) in mid-October – despite the Banking Act of 1924, according to which only the Reichsbank had power to secure foreign loans on behalf of the Reich – Schacht saw this as an attempt to bypass him. He also suspected that Hilferding wanted to put off the finance reform, which he thought was necessary and with the help of which the cash difficulties were to be structurally solved, until the second Hague Conference, the final conference of the revision process[210], and for that reason Schacht informed Gilbert, who was afraid for German credit on account of the reparation loan. Gilbert intervened, and Hilferding had to break off the negotiations, being left to look foolish.[211]

---

201 Meissner to Pünder, 7 August 1929, ADAP B, XII, p. 331.
202 Schäffer diary, ED 93/6, 12 August 1929, p. 285.
203 Loc. cit., 28 August 1929, p. 323.
204 Loc. cit., 29 August 1929, p. 327.
205 Loc. cit., ED 93/7, 27 December 1929, pp. 585f. See below.
206 Bruins diary, 24 September 1929 (Schacht), and 1 November 1929 (idem).
207 James, Reichsbank, p. 86.
208 Müller, Zentralbank, p. 88.
209 Bruins to McGarrah, 1 October 1929, BP 118.
210 Notes by Bruins on the meetings of the Reichsbank directorate, 1 November 1929, BP 140.
211 Maurer, Reichsfinanzen, pp. 95f; James, Reichsbank, pp. 112f.

Schacht's main concern was to make sure that Hilferding implemented the finance reform as quickly as possible, for without it the German delegation's position in the negotiations at the final conference in the Hague would be weak: "The more the members of the delegation need the 700 million (the difference between the last Dawes payment and the first under the Young Plan – H t C), the less resistance will they be able to offer", as Schacht explained in the intimate circle of the Reichsbank board of directors.[212]

In his view putting the public finances in order was the most important precondition for successfully resisting the new arrangement[213], and it was clearly Schacht's intention to perform this task of heroic resistance personally, for on the same day as he spoke to the Reichsbank directors, he wrote to the cabinet recommending himself as a member of the delegation to the final conference.[214] In short, his aim was an ex post improvement to the Young Plan, on the assumption that his position would be stronger because of Stresemann's death and the intended financial reform than at the first Hague conference.

In his decision to work for a change in the new arrangement at the final conference, and so to distance himself, at least indirectly, from the Young Plan, Schacht was influenced by events in foreign policy and at home. At the first Hague conference, for instance, the British finance minister Snowden had succeeded in achieving an increase in the British share of the German annuity, so that it did seem possible in the extremely difficult revision process to change settled questions subsequently. Schacht's desire to try to do so was further strengthened by the rise of the National Socialists. Although he maintained after the collapse of the Third Reich that it was only after the enormous success of the Nazi party in the Reichstag elections in September 1930 that he devoted any attention to the NSDAP[215], he was already expressing the fear that the Plan would not win a majority were elections to be held on 18 November 1929, after the first tiny gains by the Nazi party in Baden and Lübeck:[216] "The appeal of the Hitlerites was their uninhibited national feeling. Many of them were actually more anti-mammon than the Socialists. They attracted a lot of idealists. Schacht saw the gains by the NSDAP, like those of the Communists, as a manifestation of the fermentation in the German people", as Bruins wrote in his diary.[217] Apparently the Reichsbank President assumed that in the referendum in December (which was the work of the Reich Committee which petitioned for it) the Government would have to take a defeat. Following that, he calculated, he would be able to offer resistance at the final conference and enforce a better arrangement.

---

[212] See Note 210.

[213] Schacht never spoke of any other than the above reparation policy reasons for this decision. Naurally he was concerned with the sensational collapse in share prices on the New York stock exchange, but he saw the significance of this in that a growing demand for fixed-interest securities, German bonds as well, would result, with the familiar and undesirable effects on the foreign exchange reserves. See Note 210 and James, Reichsbank, p. 109; see also Wandel, Schäffer, p. 120.

[214] Schacht to Müller, 1 November 1929, ADAP B, XIII, pp. 189ff.; Vogt, Entstehung, p. 48.

[215] See above and Note 11.

[216] On 27 October the NSDAP won 7% of the votes in Baden, a stronghold of the Weimar coalition in 1928, and on 11 November it won 8% in Lübeck. See Hamilton, Hitler, p. 237.

[217] Bruins diary, 18 November 1929 (Schacht).

In the meantime the former government advisor and head of the delegation was no longer being included in the consultations on reparation policy. The question of the choice of delegates for the second and final conference in The Hague was also undecided. Stresemann's successor, the former Economics Minister Curtius, wanted to wait for the result of the referendum and only then decide whether Schacht was to go with the delegation to The Hague.[218] Schacht, who rightly felt isolated, strove all the more stubbornly for financial reform, which he needed for the opposition he was to offer. When the Foreign Minister chastised Schacht, on a chance encounter with him, for his derogatory remarks in Berlin society on the government's policy, Schacht called the Finance Minister Hilferding "a bankrupter...and more than that".[219] In the General Council he advised every banker to refrain from giving the Reich further credits, as that would be "a very risky business".[220] Again he personally called upon Hilferding to put forward a plan for reform before the Hague conference. But the Finance Minister did not respond.

As the time was getting short, Schacht finally took recourse to public opinion, and informed the cabinet on 4 December that he would "dissociate himself" from its finance policy.[221] In fact, although he had apparently felt "too much mental strain" during the day (Schäffer) to deal with routine matters[222], Schacht published a manifesto the following evening criticising the government's finance and reparation policy.[223] Since the government's financial position was indeed so precarious that it could not get through the end of the month without the assistance of the central bank[224], the cabinet did not dare to take any action against Schacht. On the contrary, in its bitter answer the cabinet was forced to announce the publication of a draft for financial reform, and within a week this *Lex Schacht* was approved by the Reichstag. So Schacht had achieved his first objective. Nevertheless, Hilferding continued his discussions with American bankers in the following weeks. As the President of the Reichsbank had intervened in finance policy, the Finance minister in turn intervened in Reichsbank policy. As in October, Parker Gilbert also intervened and Hilferding had to capitulate a second time within three weeks. This time he handed in his resignation. Naturally, this form of open war between the Reichsbank President and the cabinet dented foreign confidence in German credit still further. The influential New York house of J.P. Morgan had already decided to back out of Germany because, as Morgan put it to his partner Thomas W. Lamont, "From what I can see of the Germans they are second-rate people and I would rather have the business done for them by someone else". This distrust was the reason "second-rate bankers" like Dillon, Read & Co. managed to negotiate with Hilferding in the first place.[225]

---

[218] Schäffer diary, ED 93/7, 11 November 1929, p. 441.

[219] Note by Curtius, 30 November 1929, ADAP, B, XIII, p. 338. See Vogt, Entstehung, p. 49.

[220] Bruins to McGarrah, 3 December 1929, BP 118.

[221] Schäffer diary, ED 93/7, 5 December 1929, p. 493.

[222] Loc. cit., p. 495.

[223] For the text of the memorandum see Schacht, Ende der Reparationen, pp. 105ff. See also Vogt, Entstehung, p. 50; Lüke, Stabilisierung, pp. 248ff.; Wandel, Schäffer, p. 120; Th. Vogelsang (ed.), Hermann Pünder, Politik in der Staatskanzlei. Aufzeichnungen aus den Jahren 1929–1932, Stuttgart 1961, p. 28.

[224] Schäffer diary, ED 93/7, pp. 496, 510, 523, 537, 559.

[225] Morgan to Lamont, 30 August 1929, quoted by James, German Slump, p. 56; Maurer, Reichsfinanzen, pp. 102ff.; James, Reichsbank, pp. 112f.

In his memorandum Schacht had criticised, not the Young Plan but the government, arguing that the changes it had been responsible for since June had changed what had been originally an excellent plan into a ruinous instrument of enslavement. His onslaught improved the chances of the Reich Committee, and the plebiscite it had applied for was to take place on 22 December. Schacht was expecting the acceptance of the referendum to result in a postponement of the final conference.[226] Another aim in appealing to public opinion was probably also to secure himself an invitation to the second Hague conference. But the cabinet's efforts in getting the referendum turned down by the electorate succeeded, despite the anti-republican smear campaign launched by the Reich Committee. Schacht's prognosis had proved false, and to Bruins he indicated that he did not want to join the delegation to The Hague any longer.[227]

It was not until 27 December that the cabinet dealt with the question of whether Schacht should be sent to The Hague. He himself stated that at the conference the delegation should "do nothing beyond the Young Plan, since they would otherwise compromise the German experts, for if the governments were to agree to higher payments, the experts' standpoint that the Young payments are too high would no longer be tenable". But it would only be possible consistently to reject any change in the Plan if the delegation would be willing "to drop the Plan as well".[228] The cabinet ignored these peculiar arguments, as it still had to reckon with Schacht, because it still needed his help in its precarious financial situation. Moreover, the American high financiers, such as J.P. Morgan, who had cabled to congratulate Schacht on achieving the financial reform[229] and perhaps some industrialists and bankers, like Max Warburg, the most influential member of the Reichsbank General Council, saw Schacht as the guarantor of a sensible finance policy.[230] So Reich Chancellor Müller and Hilferding's successor, Finance Minister Moldenhauer (German People's Party), agreed that he should join the delegation, despite his views and remarks. But Schacht at first refused to go. This was his first opportunity to speak to the cabinet since June, he said. During the first Hague conference he had put forward his views, but they had been ignored. "I shall probably not be in a position to sign in The Hague. I would then have to depart suddenly and that would be worse than if I did not go in the first place".[231]

A day later it was agreed that Schacht would participate in the delegation anyway, but not as one of its leaders. Schacht was merely to go as a financial expert

---

226 On 12 December he said to Schäffer that "the second conference will not take place before around April", Schäffer diary, ED 93/7, 12 December 1929, p. 531. See Bruins diary, 17 December 1929 (Parker Gilbert) and Note 210.

227 Bruins diary, 23 December 1929 (Schacht); loc. cit., 27 December 1929 (Snouck Hurgronje).

228 Schäffer diary, ED 93/7, 27 December 1929, pp. 581ff.

229 Prittwitz to the Foreign Office, 4 February 1930, ADAP B, XIV, p. 176; James, Reichsbank, p. 116.

230 Neebe, Grossindustrie, pp. 52, 221, and Warburg to Bruins, 22 December 1929, BP 124; James, Reichsbank, pp. 114f.

231 Schäffer diary, ED 93/7, 27 December 1929, pp. 585f.; James, Reichsbank, p. 89.

on questions regarding the BIS, the new reparations bank.[232] As in December 1928 he revealed his tactics to the opposing side when he informed the representative of the American banking consortium which was to put up the money out of which Germany could pay reparations through the BIS, De Sanchez, that the Reichsbank could only decide in its taking part in the BIS after The Hague conference, since it would have to wait and see whether the conditions of the Young Plan worsened at the conference.[233] Clearly he intended to open up discussion of all the so-called deteriorations in the Plan since June in The Hague[234] and he let this be known to the cabinet by sending its members a copy of his letter to de Sanchez.[235] Although Schacht proposed again at the meeting of the delegation on 2 January that the Plan should if necessary be rejected, and despite the Chancellors distrust[236], he was not removed from the delegation since the government still needed his services for its financial problems.[237] Moreover, the cabinet was aware that German credit in the United States, the maintenance of which was one of the conditions for the success of the huge reparation loan, depended partly on Schacht.[238] For that reason too the Reich ministers rejected a French proposal to "combat Schacht energetically" (Briand).[239] The cabinet could only wait and see if he would remain loyal.

VII. Resignation

Immediately before the first meeting of the organisation committee for the BIS, which started in the Hague on January 13th, the chairman, the American banker Reynolds, made an offer to Schacht to withdraw his letter to De Sanchez, the contents of which had long been known to Gilbert[240] and the French delegates.[241] But Schacht refused with the words "This is the hour of my life". So when the meeting opened, Schacht's letter was read out to the representatives of the creditor nations, and in the ensuing discussion he not only stuck to his standpoint, saying he could not yet decide about the participation of the Reichsbank and he repeated the arguments stated in his December-manifesto on what he regarded as the deteriorations in the Young Plan since the Paris conference.[242] The sensation was total and the meeting had to be broken off.

---

232 Vogt, Entstehung, p. 356.

233 For the text see Schacht, Ende der Reparationen, pp. 111ff. See also Vogt, Entstehung, p. 55 and Curtius, Young-Plan, p. 81.

234 See Note 227.

235 Schäffer diary, ED 93/8, 2 January 1930; Vogt, Entstehung, pp. 53, 363. See Bruins diary, 12 January 1930 (Vocke).

236 Schäffer diary, ED 93/8, 2 January 1930, p. 6.

237 Loc. cit., 31 December 1929, p. 4.

238 Bruins diary, 14 January 1930 (Parker Gilbert).

239 Note by Schmidt, 5 January 1930, ADAP B, XIV, pp. 23f.

240 See Note 238.

241 See Note 239.

242 "Because we do not want to pay", as Schacht is reported as saying: Schäffer diary, ED 93/8, 13ff. January 1930, p. 22.

In a first discussion between the German delegates Schacht was sharply criticised by the four Reich ministers present. Moldenhauer, the Reich Finance minister urged him to resign.[243] The Foreign Minister, Curtius, hoped that Schacht would do so that very evening.[244] The reaction of the foreign delegates was, if possible, even greater outrage. The French Premier, Tardieu and the British Finance Minister, Snowden, indicated to German journalists that the cabinet would have to take appropiate measures against Schacht[245] and Gilbert was busy behind the scenes trying to whip up an American action against him.[246] The most radical suggestion seems to have come from Francqui, the Governor of the Banque de Belgique: "The only solution is a bullet!"[247]

Schacht endeavoured to calm the ministers by proposing, with Curtius' agreement, that other German banks could participate in setting up the BIS instead of the Reichsbank. The American financial magnate, J.P. Morgan, who was the decisive figure in the matter of the huge reparation loan, despite his misgivings about "second-rate Germans", insisted that Schacht and the Reichsbank must take part in the BIS and sent a dispatch to this effect to one of the Italian delgates, the industrialist Pirelli. Pirelli then informed the German delegation.[248] That eliminated the alternative, which in any case would hardly have been feasible for formal reasons, of the government forcing Schacht to resign against the vote of the General Council. This left the cabinet with only two possibilities: it could either force Schacht to participate in establishing the BIS, or wait and see if he did so voluntarily. To force him to participate would involve finding a way around the Banking Act of 1924, which laid down the independence of the Reichbank from domestic political currents and therefore stipulated that its President was not elected and dismissed by the cabinet but by the General Council. It was highly questionable whether the General Council and Morgan would agree to that. Secondly, as Müller stressed, trying to do something like this could create the impression of "sacrificing Schacht to obtain international financial control", and Schacht could make use of this later as "a foil".[249] On the other hand, Schacht seemed to be willing to support setting up the new international bank if the cabinet took the responsibility.[250] For these reasons the cabinet kept to its decision that the cooperation of the Reichsbank must be laid down in the new statutes for the BIS. Only if Schacht "were to raise the creditor powers against us" would Müller be less reluctant.[251]

243 Reuter, Schacht, p. 93.

244 Schäffer diary, ED 93/8, 22 January 1930, p. 26.

245 Loc. cit., 14 January 1930, p. 24; ADAP B, XIV, pp. 173f.

246 "No government worthy of the name could permit the head of its central bank to dictate foreign policy and override its international agreements, and the German Government will have to assert its sovereign rights if Schacht forces them", telegram from Parker Gilbert to McGarrah, Harrison, Young, Lamont, Jay and Fraser, 12 January 1930, quoted by James, Reichsbank, p. 117.

247 Bruins diary, 30 January 1930 (Schacht).

248 Loc. cit., 14 January 1930 (Parker Gilbert); Vogt, Entstehung, p. 365.

249 Schäffer diary, ED 93/8, 14 January 1930, pp. 25f.

250 Loc. cit. p. 23 and Bruins diary, 16 January 1930 (Schacht).

251 Schäffer diary, ED 93/8, 14 January 1930, p. 23; See Vossische Zeitung, No. 114, 8 March 1930.

By declaring himself willing to accept any viable solution "after all these not inconsiderable difficulties" (Pünder)[252] Schacht had made the limits of its scope for action plain to the cabinet. Schacht had not only damaged German prestige but also his personal standing. Men who had been his opponents in the past now were his enemies. Among these were Briand, Tardieu, Snowden, Francqui and Moreau,[253] and at home the SPD fraction.[254] Curtius, Moldenhauer, Müller and Schmidt, the Economics Minister.[255] The international financial world, which still decided on the election and dismissal of the Reichsbank President through the General Council, was divided in its view. Francqui, Moreau, Gilbert and Warburg[256], who wanted Schacht's resignation, were opposed by the American bankers Morgan, Traylor, Reynolds, the Chairman of the General Council Addis and Commissioner Bruins, who regarded Schacht as indispensable.[257] Schacht himself assumed that Reich President Hindenburg would stand by him.[258]

After Schacht's return from The Hague the only question that mattered was whether he would be constructive in cooperating over the establishment of the BIS or continue his campaign against the Young Plan.[259] To Reichsbank Commissioner Bruins he seemed very calm again by 16 January.[260] But the next day he made another oratorical derailment when he said to the American representative of the BIS banking consortium, De Sanchez, "...that he was about to be crucified by a gang of corrupt politicians. He dwelt at length upon his honesty, truthfulness and patriotism".[261] A week later he was agitating against Quesnay's candidature for the post of General Manager at the BIS, which had been a subject of controversy since September, 1929[262] and Schacht withdrew from the work in the bank, disappointed and depressed.[263] He flatly refused to nominate a German member of the organisational committee for the international bank, so it was still not clear whether the Reichsbank would in fact participate in the establishment of the BIS.[264]

This persistance in a tactical passive resistance made Schacht's Reichsbank colleagues extremely nervous, and they quickly organised a secret meeting between Schacht and his oldest friend in financial circles, Governor Norman of the Bank of England, in the Belgian sea resort Ostend in the hopes that he would succeed in talking Schacht round. The Reichsbank President was now actually promising to keep out of politics, and he communicated this piece of happy news in confidence, as it were, to the Secretary of State in the Finance Ministry.[265] Bruins then told Max Warburg[266], the Hamburg private banker, who enjoyed excellent relations with the cabinet[267] and had demanded that Schacht should explain himself to the General Council.[268] At the same time Reich Chancellor Müller let it be known that should new difficulties arise with Schacht he would confront the Reich-President with the choice

---

[252] Pünder to the German Foreign Office, ADAP B, XIV, p. 70; Hardach, Weltmarktorientierung, pp. 105 and 109; Craig, Germany, p. 530. In view of the fact that this crisis was mastered within a few hours, some accounts seem exaggerated. See for instance Bracher, Auflösung, pp. 263ff.; Timm, Sozialpolitik, p. 145; Curtius, Young-Plan, p. 82; Lüke, Stabilisierung, p. 252.

[253] Vogt, Entstehung, p. 367.

[254] C. Severing, Mein Lebensweg, Vol. II, Cologne 1950, p. 227.

[255] Maurer, Reichsfinanzen, p. 110.

[256] Bruins diary, 27 January 1930 (Warburg).

[257] Loc. cit., 16 January 1930 (Parker Gilbert), and 18 January 1930 (Addis).

[258] Pünder to the Foreign Office, 14 January 1930, ADAP B, XIV, p. 70.

between firing Schacht or seeing the Reich Chancellor resign and the coalition cabinet leave with him.[269]

Schacht attempted to ward off this pressure from the Chancellor by stressing repeatedly in informal discussions with members of the government and the Agent-General that any measures against him, whatever they might be, would only harm German credit abroad, particularly with J.P. Morgan. Parker Gilbert had already mentioned this to Thomas Lamont, Morgan's partner, and to Harrison, Strong's successor at the Federal Reserve Bank, making the challenging remark that "he, Schacht, is busy circulating stories about the many letters and cables he has had from America in support of his December Memorandum. At the same time he is trying to cultivate the fear that any effort of the German Government to discipline him will ruin German credit abroad".[270] What Gilbert wanted was Harrison and Lamont to arrange for a derogatory remark on Schacht by Morgan to clear the way for his resignation.[271] But Schacht had not the remotest intention of resigning. In his view the cabinet did not have a chance of getting the agreement with Poland, in which both states mutually renounced all the financial claims arising from the war and the peace treaty, through the Reichstag[272] and so there would not be a majority for the Young Plan either, as he told Bruins.[273]

The deterioration of Schacht's position engineered by Warburg and Gilbert gave an extraordinary tension to the meeting of the General Council on 31 January. Even before the meeting opened Schacht was so bold as to avoid a conversation with Addis, who had so far regarded him as indispensable. Thereupon Addis and Bruins, after checking with Gilbert, drew up a resolution in keeping with the Chancellor's tactics demanding that Schacht participate in the work of setting up the BIS without further ado. This proposal was rejected most emphatically by the Reichsbank directors, loyal to Schacht. After Addis had heatedly reproached the Reichsbank President Schacht did appear to be prepared to accept a resolution by the Council, but then categorically rejected it (calling it "a humiliation"), when he recognised

---

259 See Note 244.

260 Bruins diary, 16 January 1930 (Schacht).

261 De Sanchez to Lamont, 28 April 1934, quoted by James, Reichsbank, p. 88. See also James, German Slump, p. 59.

262 Bruins diary, 22 January 1930 (Schacht), and 30 January 1930 (Addis). See above.

263 Loc. cit., 24 January 1930 (Vocke); Schäffer diary, ED 93/8, 22 January 1930, p. 97.

264 Loc. cit., ED 93/8, 24 January 1930, p. 97a and Bruins diary, 27 January 1930 (Warburg).

265 Schäffer diary, ED 93/8, 25 January 1930, p. 30.

266 Bruins diary, 28 January 1930 (Vocke/Warburg).

267 Another partner in M.M. Warburg & Co. was Carl Melchior, Schacht's deputy at the Paris conference.

268 Bruins diary, 28 January 1930 (Warburg).

269 Severing, Lebensweg, II, p. 227; Vogt, Entstehung, p. 35.

270 See Note 246.

271 In a letter to Governor Strong of 29 January 1930 Parker Gilbert again said that Schacht was repeating that measures against him would ruin German credit abroad (reference from Professor Dr. K. Borchardt, Munich. Source Federal Reserve Bank of New York).

272 Krüger, Aussenpolitik, pp. 501ff. This treaty followed the Allied requirement at The Hague conferences that a new reparation settlement should be accompanied by a German-Polish détente.

273 Bruins diary, 30 January 1930 (Schacht), see Pentzlin, Schacht, p. 131.

Gilbert's typed version. But eventually Schacht did have to give a solemn promise that the participation of the Reichsbank in the BIS was "assured"[274], upon which the General Council stated that the confidence and cooperation of all concerned was essential if the new bank was to operate successfully.[275] So the Council had succeeded in taking a middle line between the furious Schacht and the equally raging Gilbert (who called Schacht "not only a damned fool, but also a damned liar")[276]

Although Schacht had also completely ruined his relations with the General Council as well now, he was still not prepared to resign. Again he told Curtius, the Foreign Minister, that Morgan stood by him unconditionally, a statement the German Foreign Office ordered to be checked with all speed.[277] In a discussion with the German ambassador in Washington Morgan made clear that he had in fact sent a cable to Schacht congratulating him on the finance reform he had achieved in December, but that further incidents must be avoided, in the interests of the authority of the government and Schacht's personal standing. Although he did not want to be singled out as Schacht's "compurgator", he explicitly confirmed that Schacht was "an essential factor in German credit".[278] Evidently Morgan believed that Schacht's resignation would have negative effects on the floating of the reparation loan (or something to that effect). Because Morgan wanted Schacht to stay on, Gilbert's attempt to bring him down failed utterly.

At the beginning of February Schacht had therefore strengthened his position and he could continue his tactics of passive resistance. He endeavoured particularly to prevent Quesnay's nomination as general manager of the BIS, as in fact did the Reich government. He favoured Bruins, and he held to his objection even after Gilbert and Norman had informed him that the American bankers would welcome Quesnay's appointment.[279]

Presumably with Gilbert's agreement Owen Young sent Schacht a telegram around 18 February, in Morgan's name as well, stating that they did approve of Quesnay's appointment but apologised for their strong support of the French candidate, explaining that they had preferred Quesnay because they believed that Schacht also agreed with this choice. Bruins reports that Schacht did not interpret this telegram as a last ironic warning but as meaning that Young and Morgan were also beginning to dissociate themselves from the Young Plan. When Schacht attacked the cabinet's foreign policy again in his reply of 20 February, listing nine differences between the original Young Plan and the final protocol of The Hague conference, he probably thought that the former delegates to the Paris conference would still be able to stop the Plan if they held together. Thus he concluded his despatch by assuring that he was and would remain an opponent of the new

---

274 Bruins diary, 31 January 1930 (General Council) and 1 February 1930 (idem).
275 Bruins to McGarrah, 1 February 1930, BP 118.
276 Bruins diary, 1 February 1930 (Parker Gilbert).
277 Curtius to Prittwitz, 1 February 1930, ADAP B, XIV, p. 176, Note 2.
278 Prittwitz to Curtius, 4 February 1930, ADAP B, XIV, p. 176.
279 Curtius to von Hoesch, 13 February 1930, ADAP B, XIV, p. 278 Note 1; von Hoesch to Curtius, 27 February 1930, loc. cit. p. 300; Bruins diary, 11–19 February 1930 (Schacht/Norman).

arrangement[280], that he intended to resign[281], and that he gave Young permission to make use of that information.[282] Schacht himself had now provoked the incident which Morgan wanted to avoid and Chancellor Müller had been waiting for.

Owen Young, no doubt after consulting Morgan, did not, however, set in motion the desired action by the experts. On the contrary he reported receipt of the telegram and the news of Schacht's intended resignation to the German embassy in Washington[283] and to Gilbert, who in turn informed Bruins, but without mentioning Schacht's resignation.[284] In the last week of February Young and Morgan telegraphed their answer to Schacht, making no attempt to prevent him from leaving office. After Schacht had received this reply, he certainly seemed very depressed on 1 March, and for the first time since 16 January he indicated to Bruins that he might indeed resign.[285] While the Reichsbank directors and Bruins again tried to direct Schacht back to his dayly work at the bank, the Washington embassy informed the cabinet in Berlin. Since Schacht was not planning to leave as long as the acceptance of the Plan in the Reichstag was still pending owing to the middle-of-the-road Centre Party's package, which made its agreement dependent on a second finance reform[286], he did not show the cabinet his dispatch stating his intended resignation, and formally the government therefore knew nothing about his intentions. Schacht continued to keep silent on this for two more weeks.

It was not until 3 March that J.P. Morgan personally intervened to clarify this tragi-comic situation. He held conversations in Berlin with Bruins, Parker Gilbert and Schacht[287], and presumably he spoke to members of the cabinet as well. On the same day the Reich Finance Minister Moldenhauer went to see Schacht and asked to be informed of the despatch containing the statement that he intended to resign. Since Morgan was now in Berlin Schacht could hesitate no longer. He admitted to the cabinet[288] that he had intrigued against the government's policy in the United States. In The Hague the Chancellor had indicated that he would probably have to take action should Schacht stir up the creditor nations against Germany.[289] So the situation in which Müller could face Hindenburg with the choice of dismissing either Schacht or the Reich Chancellor had finally arrived.

Schacht was fully aware of this. He did not wait for the cabinet to attack but informed them that he would ask the General Council to accept his resignation, however, he intended to inform the Reich President first.[290] This was not only for the formal reason that Hindenburg needed to approve his dismissal by the General

---

280 Bruins diary, 1 March 1930 (Schacht), see Vogt, Entstehung, p. 57 and Maurer, Reichsfinanzen, p. 220.

281 Bruins diary, 1 March 1930 (Schacht); Vossische Zeitung No. 114, 8 March 1930.

282 Bruins diary, 1 March 1930 (Schacht).

283 Vogt, Entstehung, pp. 57f.

284 Bruins diary, 3 March 1930 (Parker Gilbert).

285 See Note 282.

286 Bruins diary, 1 March 1930 (Dreyse); Vogelsang, Hermann Pünder, pp. 29ff.

287 Bruins diary, 3 March 1930 (Morgan).

288 Schäffer diary, ED 93/8, 4 March 1930, p. 78; Hardach, Weltmarktorientierung, p. 78; Vogt, Entstehung, p. 58.

289 See above.

290 Schäffer diary, ED 93/8, 4 March 1930, p. 80.

Council[291], it was for domestic policy reasons as well. To Bruins he explained his tactics as: should the coalition cabinet survive, it would succeed in getting a majority for the Plan. In that case, under the constitution the right-wing Nationalists and the Communists in parliament could put forward a parliamentary motion to postpone the Young Plan legislation. Presumably the majority which supported the cabinet would then formally declare the new laws a matter of urgency. If the Reich President Hindenburg in that event would refuse to sign and declare public the new laws, the only constitutional way out of the dead-lock would involve a second referendum.

Schacht considered a second plebiscite necessary: "The decision would be an extremely difficult one for the Reich President. His (Schacht's – Ht C) personal conviction was that because the Plan affected the essential interests of the German people, a referendum should be held. Should the Plan be rejected in the referendum, the evacuation of the Rhineland would of course be delayed, some financial hurdles would need to be taken and there would be an outcry in the foreign press, but all in all he expected a better outcome for Germany. The idea that a new arrangement would have to be made had already taken such strong hold that new negotiations would probably have to take place, and in the end the results would probably be better", as Schacht told Bruins. To increase the pressure on Hindenburg to hold a second plebiscite Schacht had decided not to send a representative to the organisational committee for the BIS, and for that reason he had also telegraphed to Young, as the faithful Bruins concluded.[292]

Now that he had alienated everybody but the politicians of the (extreme) right, Schacht set his last hopes in Hindenburg. In a discussion on 3 March, however, the President of the Reich did not seem very impressed by Schacht's prophecies of doom. Whether he would ask Schacht "only to keep silent, or to stay in office as well" (Pünder) was something he still had to decide.[293] Thereupon Schacht agreed to inform Hindenburg before taking his final decision.[294] Next day he stopped talking about resigning, and told Bruins that he was still being supported by J.P. Morgan, although this was probably incorrect.[295]

But there was not much time left to Schacht to persuade Hindenburg to hold the referendum he wanted. On 6 March, when the second reading of the Young legislation started in parliament, Schacht again went to see the Reich President and asked him to permit him to give a speech in the Reichstag.[296] He probably intended to polemicise against the cabinet or publicly announce his resignation. But Hindenburg refused Schacht's request, on the grounds that he could only decide after the Plan had been accepted in the Reichstag whether he would be able to lend it his authority.[297]

That left Schacht, who had finally alienated the President as well, no other way out. On the same evening he handed in his resignation to Reichsbank vice-president

[291] See Schacht to Hindenburg, 3 March 1930 (copy), Schäffer papers, ED 93/29, p. 50.

[292] Bruins diary, 4 March 1930 (Schacht); See E. Eyck, Geschichte der Weimarer Republik, Zurich 1954, p. 303.

[293] See Note 290.

[294] Schacht, 76 Jahre, p. 327.

[295] Bruins diary, 4 March 1930 (Schacht) and 5 March 1930 (Vocke).

[296] Loc. cit., 12 March 1930 (Dreyse).

[297] Vogt, Entstehung, p. 58; Maurer, p. 112; See Schacht 76 Jahre, pp. 327f.

Dreyse, after two attempts by the directors of the central bank to stop him had failed[298], and the next morning he announced it at a meeting of the Central Committee of the Reichsbank shareholders in Hamburg. The move surprised Bruins, who had gone to Holland[299], and probably Hindenburg as well, and it certainly surprised the general public. The prominent journalist and intellectual Georg Bernhard wrote in the liberal Vossische Zeitung: "Why he is actually laying down his office now, no-one knows".[300] But no-one was prepared to support him any longer, neither the General Council, nor Young, nor Morgan, nor Hindenburg.

On 8 March 1930 his resignation was either welcomed in the press or merely accepted as a fact. The step failed to arouse any unease on Wall Street.[301] Schacht himself seemed quite cheerful about "the historic day yesterday". His wife had asked him in the morning whether he was happy. "No man is ever completely happy, but I do feel extraordinarily relieved now that I have cast off this moral burden".[302] Although he emphatically denied in a newspaper interview[303] that he intended to go into politics, Bruins wondered whether he would become a second Ludendorff[304], the dictatorial World War I general who had morally encouraged Hitler to perpetrate his ludicrous Beer Hall Putsch back in 1923.

VIII. Conclusion

A survey of the reparation policy pursued by Reichsbank President Hjalmar Schacht shows that the formulaic debunking of Schacht as an opportunist dilettante with a presumptuous personality can be called in question. It seems a misepresentation of the importance of his policy and an underestimation of its success. Following the Thoiry-catastrophe, Stresemann advocated a reparation policy of passive revisionism. He wanted 'to direct the reparation issue away from the former political discussion and more into economic and financial channels', but he did not say how that was to be done except by waiting for a spontaneous swing round in American public opinion. As the godfather of the Rentenmark, the manager of a stable Reichsmark, the architect of the financial, economic and political cooperation with the United States, and last but not least as a central bank president who used discount policy to his political advantage, Schacht succeeded in convincing Strong and Parker Gilbert of the need for a prompt revision of the Dawes Plan. As the head of the German delegation he went to the Paris conference to negotiate a new and cheaper arrangement. When it became evident that the American policy-makers were unwilling to solve the problem of German reparations in connection with the pending question of inter-allied debts, Schacht's reparation policy and the cabinet's had failed. Even after November 1929, when he decided to move closer to the Reich Committee and thus to Hitler, because the national-socialists were incessantly

---

298 Bruins diary, 8 March 1930 (Dreyse).
299 Loc. cit., 7 March 1930.
300 Quoted by Peterson, Schacht, p. 98.
301 Vossische Zeitung, 8 March 1930, No. 114.
302 Bruins diary, 8 March 1930 (Schacht).
303 See Note 301.
304 See Note 302.

fighting the Young Plan, and intervened in finance policy in order to acquire a new significance in reparation policy, Schacht was still supported by the American banking world, as German credit seemed to depend on him, until he tried to stir up Young and Morgan against the New Plan. When Morgan and Reich President Hindenburg no longer backed him and it was clear that the Reichstag would accept the Young Plan, he brought himself down before the cabinet could do so. Both his undeniable successes and his later defeats were based on an Atlantic concept of reparation policy. This in turn was rooted in Schacht's conviction that the problem of reparation payments could not be regarded as a European let alone as a German-French affair, but that it was a question that could only be dealt with with American cooperation. If it all, the tragedy of Schacht's reparation policy lies in the one-sidedness of his Atlantic orientation, which was characteristic of his Weimar career and, at least according to some of his contemporaries, of his character.

To dismiss Schacht as a dangerous amateur who put expedience before principle is also to suggest that his reparation policy was inexpiably incompatible with Stresemann's foreign policy of reconciliation and compromise. Possibly qualifications such as these become the domestic policy endeavours of the 'Schacht Redivivus' (H. James)[305] in 1931–1932, when the former Reichsbank president publicly joined the national-socialist troupe. Schacht's gradual shift from the left-liberal DDP to the NSDAP, however, started as early as May 1926. He became interested in nazism in November 1929, quite some time before Hitler seemed to have any chance of coming to power at all. For years his overall concept in reparation politics matched the economic-Atlantic constituent of Stresemann's political fundamentals and for that reason in a field of tension between cooperation and confrontation, after 1925 a close association developed between him and Stresemann. With his monopoly position as a man who was trusted by Wall Street, Schacht was better suited than any other representative of the Weimar Republic to negotiate on foreign policy affairs involving packages of financial compensations and territorial revisions. For that reason the Foreign Minister made use of Schacht's prestige and pushing power when it seemed useful to do so. With Stresemann's agreement Schacht sounded out Belgian financiers on Eupen-Malmédy in 1925, discussed Polish affairs with Governor Norman in 1926 and promoted the publication of the Gilbert memorandum on finance policy in 1927. The informal joint responsibility for reparation policy between the cabinet and Schacht, that had been established in October 1928, culminated in his appointment as leader of the delegation in Paris in January 1929. Schacht's doubts about the possibility of reaching a advantageous new financial settlement had already dawned on him by then, a feeling of uncertainty that Stresemann shared with him. Because he was not prepared to take public responsibility for the failure of the policy he had helped to formulate, as formally he was not obliged to do, he resentfully dissociated himself from the policy of reconciliation of the moribund Stresemann. The last year of his first term as Reichsbank President formed both the afterpiece to his reparation policy and the first act of his domestic political efforts á la Ludendorff. For an appraisal of his entive career as a Weimar reparation politician, however, it is essential not to pay attention to this tragicomic epilogue alone.

---

[305] James, Reichsbank, p. 335ff.; Turner, Faschismus, p. 26. See Neebe, Grossindustries p. 59, 122f.

Cartels as a Form of Concentration in Industry: The Example of the International Dyestuffs Cartel from 1927 to 1939

Harm G. Schröter

Concentration in the economy is one of those fundamental themes which need to be taken up periodically, and are. A similar process is evident in the writing of economic history.[1] Helmut Arndt and Günter Ollenburg defined concentration as "a concentration of economic forces".[2] This definition was adopted by historians[3] and it also forms the basis of this article. That cartelisation is closely related to concentration is stressed by all sides, but even the views on the nature of the relation diverge. Wolfram Fischer saw the degree of cartelisation between the wars as furthering concentration.[4] Hans-Heinrich Barnikel also saw "cartels in all their variety and with all their surrogate forms" in one of their variants as a form of concentration.[5] Hans Otto Lenel pointed out that cartels generally increase concentration.[6] But from the Marxist view Helga Nussbaum reaches a conclusion that is in some ways the opposite: the merger of existing companies is prevented, while the companies in the cartel show above-average growth.[7] These statements are to be examined in this article, using the dyestuffs cartel as an example. However, the main focus will be somewhat different: Lenel and Nussbaum see cartelisation and concentration as two different things, while describing one set of causes and effects. Their considerations are based on concentration of ownership, while in this article the cartel is examined

[1] In 1978 Hans Pohl and Wilhelm Treue published a collected volume, Die Konzentration in der deutschen Wirtschaft seit dem 19. Jahrhundert, Supplement 11 to the Zeitschrift für Unternehmensgeschichte, and in 1985 another collected volume, edited by H. Pohl, appeared, Kartelle und Kartellgesetzgebung in Praxis und Rechtsprechung vom 19. Jahrhundert bis zur Gegenwart. In 1986 a separate section at the 9th International Congress of Economic Historians was devoted to this subject.

[2] H. Arndt/G. Ollenburg, Begriff und Arten der Konzentration, p. 7, in: H. Arndt (ed.), Die Konzentration in der Wirtschaft, Berlin 1971², pp. 3–40.

[3] With some deviations and greater precision ("the concentration of economic power"): W. Fischer, Bergbau, Industrie und Handwerk, p. 807, in: H. Aubin/W. Zorn, Handbuch der deutschen Wirtschafts- und Sozialgeschichte, Vol. 2, Stuttgart 1976.

[4] Loc. cit., p. 810. The extensive tables on the strikingly high degree of cartelisation in the German economy underline what Fischer has to say on the world slump and the Nazi period (p. 811). They also show that further research is needed, since they are based simply on the number of cartels. The "concentration of economic power" (see above), measured by turnover, however, shows differences of at least 1:1000 between major cartels such as e.g. of the heavy industry and the local brickworks agreements. A survey, and if possible a weighted one, would be very desirable.

[5] Barnikel, H.–H., Die Konzentrationspolitik nach 1945, in: Pohl/Treue, loc. cit., pp. 54–73, p. 54.

[6] Lenel, H.O., Ursachen der Konzentration unter besonderer Berücksichtigung der deutschen Verhältnisse, Tübingen 1968², pp. 231, 234.

[7] Nussbaum, H., International Cartels and Multinational Enterprises, p. 138, in: A. Teichova/M. Lévy-Leboyer/H. Nussbaum (ed.), Multinational Enterprise in Historical Perspective, Cambridge/Paris 1986, pp. 131–144.

as a concentration of market power, as in the above definitions. From the perspective of the buyer the concentration of market power could certainly seem the most important and relativise the differences that persisted, no matter what they were.

To assess concentration we need to quantify it. "A combination of various quantitative features, adapted to the branch of industry concerned over time, would appear to be the best criterion for the development of company and plant sizes".[8] The problems arise in the selection and from the frequent lack of such features. The Reich Statistical Office published surveys on share capital according to capital size class and industry.[9] Hans Pohl has pointed out the importance of the number employed by a firm as the only long-term flow of figures available (from 1875).[10] Methodological studies for the time after the World War II take the company's turnover as the central measurement – in the case of Germany, because of the possible statistical accumulative effect through trade within vertically structured enterprises, the figure taken is net production value.[11] But that material is not always easy to acquire, even for modern studies, and it is all the more significant that the figures for our case study could be compiled from various company archives, at least in the form of key figures. In addition, the available material is also enough to meet a second central requirement: "The approach to research on concentration can therefore only be (sectoral) branch analysis".[12] The further requirement, that the branch approach can be replaced by the more specific production method[13], is largely superfluous for our study, because generally the dyestuffs in the entire industry were cartelised. The cases where a products cartel was more comprehensive than the industry agreement are examined separately at the end of this article. It has been pointed out that qualitative elements in concentration can be examined only inadequately, if at all, with quantitative methods, a factor that applies particularly to cartels.[14] For these reasons, and because qualitative aspects play an important role in our example, special attention is devoted to this.

The degree of concentration in the German economy, which was generally relatively high, both regarding agreements above the level of individual firms and company concentration, has often been stressed, and we do not need to discuss this further here. It applies very particularly to the German chemical industry. Even before World War I groupings of companies had formed, and when IG-Farbenindustrie AG was established in 1925 it represented more than one third of all the capital invested in the chemical sector.[15] The establishment of the firm was an event of worldwide significance: "There was no operation of chemical industry which it

---

[8] Pohl, H., Die Konzentration in der deutschen Wirtschaft vom ausgehenden 19. Jahrhundert bis 1945, in: Pohl/Treue, loc. cit., pp. 4–44, p. 5.

[9] Stat. Jb. des Dt. Reiches 1938, p. 433, for example.

[10] Loc. cit., p. 6.

[11] Marfels, Chr. Erfassung und Darstellung industrieller Konzentration. Statistische Grundlagen und Möglichkeiten, Baden-Baden 1977, p. 23f.

[12] Pohl, loc. cit., p. 6.

[13] Marfels, loc. cit., p. 29.

[14] "For all concentration that is not, or at least not solely, based on private property, a qualitative analysis is necessary instead of the quantitative measurement, or at least in addition to it", Arndt/Ollenburg, loc. cit., p. 15; see also Pohl, loc. cit., p. 7.

[15] Of a total of RM 3.3 billion, RM 1.15 billion in 1931: Die chemische Industrie, Vol. 1923, p. 861.

would not undertake, and no industrial combine in the world which it could not face or outface".[16] With the great expansion of IG Farben in the thirties its share in the German chemical industry grew so much that it came close to acquiring a monopoly.[17] For a number of products, indeed for whole groups of products, this role was uncontested, and it was also the way IG Farben saw itself. Although there was an Association for the Preservation of the Interests of the German Chemical Industry (Verein zur Wahrung der Interessen der Chemischen Industrie Deutschlands), and IG Farben was a member, the company acted internally and externally as representing the entire German chemical sector.

Perhaps we should point out that for the purposes of this article the term "dyestuffs" does not include paint, but pigments used mainly for textiles, printing, paper and similar purposes. IG Farben's sales, broken down by users, also give a rough idea of the world dyestuffs market in this meaning of the word:

Table 1. Sales by IG Farben in Germany in 1941 in % of value[a)]

To textile producers			63.11
of which:	1. from vegetable fibres (cotton, linen, etc.)	25,67	
	2. from animal fibres (wool, etc.)	21,02	
To producers of paints			7.29
To paper producers			6.36
To leather goods producers			3.17
To producers of printer's ink			2.92
To others			to 100.00

[a)] Kugler, p. 1f.

It is interesting that the producers listed under "others" are so broken down that no single group has more than 2%, and sales to dealers amount to less than 4%. The cartelised dyestuffs were almost exclusively for the processing industry.

The production of dyestuffs in Germany was entirely concentrated in IG Farben, the only exception being the investment by the Swiss firm J.R. Geigy AG in Grenzach near Basle. Measured by total German production, the production in Grenzach was qualitatively of high standard but the quantity was low, for the Grenzach production capacity was less than 2% of the entire German output. Other producers of chemical products who might possibly have worked their way towards dyestuffs production from their product range or the technical facilities available to them were prevented from taking such steps at an early stage by the appropriate agreements.[18]

[16] Reader, W.J., Imperial Chemical Industries. A History, Vol. I, The Forerunners 1870–1926, London/New York/Toronto 1}70, p. 412.

[17] Pohl, loc. cit., p. 38.

[18] On 15./18.12.1933 IG Farben and Silesia, Verein Chemischer Fabriken Ida- und Maxhütte, Saarau, near Schweidnitz in Silesia, concluded a contract that was to run until 31.12.1938 and be

Table 2. Production of tar dyes in 1926

Country	Production in 1000 t	Production in 1000 t	Production in 1000 t	Production in 1000 t	Production in Capacity in 100 t/a	Capacity utilisation in %	Shares: Share in production in % (quantities) in %	Shares: Share in production in % (quantities) in %	Shares: Share in production in % (values)	Shares: Prod. value/ prod. quantity (calculated from	Shares: Production in RM mill.
	(a)	(b)	(c)	(d)	(a)	(a)	(a)	(b)	(a)	(a)	(a)
Germany	63	68.0	74.8	75	160	39.4	41.2	41.6	49.9	1:1.21	344
USA	36	39.9	39.9	43	54	66.7	23.6	24.4	22.3	1:0.92	154
France	11	17.1	17.1	14	14	78.6	7.2	10.4	6.2	1:0.86	43
GB	14.8	13.5	13.7	18	24	61.7	9.7	8.3	10.7	1:1.10	74
Switzerland	9	9.0	8.7	10	13	69.2	5.9	5.5	9.1	1:1.54	63
Italy	–	7.0	7.0	6	–	–	–	4.3	–	–	–
Japan	–	7.5	–	8	–	–	–	4.6	–	–	–
Others	19	1.5	–	10	23	82.6	12.4	0.9	1.8	1:0.15	12
Total	152.8	163.5	–	184	288	53.1	100.0	100.0	100.0		690

a) From Kugler, p. 29. The figures for 1924 and 1928 in Tammen only partly agree with those in this table; but he himself says some are doubtful (Tammen, H., Die IG Farbenindustrie AG, 1925–1935, Berlin 1978, p. 35).
b) From "Weltproduktion an Teerfarben", compiled by the IG Farben Central Economics Department (for 1925–28), Hö 1094.
c) Reich Statistical Yearbook for 1932, p. 48.
d) 1927: Svennilson, I., Growth and Stagnation in the European Economy, Geneva 1954, p. 290.

Before World War I the dominance of the German tar dyes industry was uncontested worldwide, and it accounted for roughly 90% of all exports throughout the world. Beside the Germans, only Switzerland had a dyestuffs export industry, and this was important mainly for its quality. This extreme concentration was broken during and after World War I, but the ban on the exports of dyes, issued by Germany in September 1914, to be extended only a few days later to pre-products and raw materials, did not put the desired economic constraints on the entente. On the contrary, the industrialised countries built up their own national industries, and in many cases the sequestered German direct investment provided an important basic stock. The Swiss dyestuffs industry enjoyed an almost fairytale boom.[19] All were aware that when the war was concluded the export business would be very much more difficult. And on all sides an answer was seen in the gathering of national forces. In 1918 the three large Swiss producers, CIBA, Geigy and Sandoz, joined to form a Swiss interest association (see below). IG Farben followed in 1925, a year later the British I.C.I. (see below). Nevertheless, the Germans succeeded in remaining by far the most important producers, as the following table shows. In 1926, before international cartelisation became a major factor, the production of dyestuffs was as shown in Table 2.

The table is informative in several regards, but only two aspects need to be singled out here. Firstly, the deviations between the sources, some of which (France!) are considerable. In some cases the Statistical Yearbook uses a different basis for collecting the figures – i.a. the dyestuffs group of rapidogenes were not included as tar dyes – and so the figures differ. In the table below the extent of the deviation is of fundamental importance. The Central Economics Department of IG Farben shows the figures for Germany (!) and Switzerland as estimates, but the most important deviation is in the case of France. Kugler's figures are based on the figures from the Preparatory Committee for the International Economic Conference of the League of Nations and the Cartel of Three (see below). It is probable that Kugler's account is closest to the truth, but it remains to be said that these aggregate figures as well are rather indicators of size than absolute figures. But in all these accounts the Soviet Union is missing. Secondly, there are major shifts in the relation between production value and production quantity. While Switzerland produced particularly high-grade products, the "others" restricted themselves to cheap mass goods. The discrepancy for the French C.M.C. is also interesting, as is the narrow gap between

tacitly prolonged for a year at a time, if not terminated. Silesia, producer of auxiliary materials and raw materials for dye works, refrained from producing dyes, subjected its output quantity to quotas imposed by IG Farben, and also limited its sales territorially. The agreement went into great detail. IG guaranteed in return to take a fixed amount of the output. The production quota agreement was annulled in the summer of 1943 on the basis of the state Order on Quotas of 29.1.1943, but the agreement to refrain from producing dyes was maintained by the exchange of letters (1.6. and 19.7.43) between the firms. (Activities of IG Farbenindustrie AG in the Dyestuffs Industry, Economics Division Decartelization Branch Control Office, 5.6.1946, Archives of Hoechst AG, Frankfurt/M. (HÖ) no number, quoted from Kugler. This account was given by Dr. Hans Kugler, who was i.a. procurist at IG Farben in Frankfurt from 1928 to 1945, and from 1930 headed the main office for dyestuffs agreements there.

19 For instance, the turnover of Sandoz rose from SFr. 6 million in 1914 to SFr. 52 million in 1920 (Sandoz historical archive, C 102).

Germany and Great Britain. Although in my view some doubts must be entertained on this last point, this figure was of importance in the cartel negotiations between IG Farben and I.C.I. (see below).

Some factors remain to be pointed out, since they determined the structure of dyestuffs production and sales. Almost the only purchasers were the textile, leather and paper industries, and for these customers the price of the dyes was of minor importance, since it hardly affected their cost structure. "As a result the consumption of dyes cannot have been affected by raising or lowering prices, it depended entirely on the business trend in the consumer industries".[20] Wage and raw materials costs for dyestuffs production were low, but investment was high.

The annual turnover of a plant when fully utilised corresponded to the sum of investment.[21] So utilisation was, with price formation, the decisive factor in profitability[22], and large plants were very much cheaper to run than small plants.[23]

Unlike Germany, the United States had several major dyestuffs producers, and in 1938the sales breakdown was as follows:

Table 3. US dyestuffs producers by sales (value) in 1938 in percent[a)]

E.I. Du Pont de Nemours & Co.	26
National Aniline & Chemical Co. (Nacco)	24
General Aniline & Film Corp.	20
Dow Chemical Co. }	
Cincinnati Chemical Works Inc. }	25
Calco Chemical Co. Inc. }	
About 90 others	5
	100

[a)] Kugler, p. 11.

Du Pont was by far the most important company in this list, very much more so than these percentages show.

Although Du Pont only began producing dyes in 1917, the firm grew to be of great importance, structurally as well, through its own development and skilful acquisitions of other firms (including Newport Co. in 1931). It had the broadest production range of all the US dyestuffs producers. However, this was not its main area of activity, for dyestuffs was only one of many divisions in Du Pont.[24] In size,

[20] Ter-Meer, F., Die IG Farben-Industrie-Aktiengesellschaft. Ihre Entstehung, Entwicklung und Bedeutung, Düsseldorf 1953, p. 74.

[21] Kugler, p. 29.

[22] Of course the degree of depreciation was important too, and here the old-established German and Swiss producers had an advantage. The same factor also played a major part in the nitrogen sector (Schröter, H.G., Privatwirtschaftliche Marktregulierung und staatliche Interessenpolitik: Das internationale Stickstoffkartell 1929–1939).

[23] Because of the large number of dyes that had to be produced (Kugler, p. 29).

[24] Dutton, W.S., Du Pont, One Hundred and Forty Years, New York 1942.

the company could only be compared with I.C.I. and IG Farben, and its importance is evident in that IG Farben saw in Du Pont worldwide its only competitor of equal strength. Nacco was created in 1917 by the merger of five companies, but it made mainly mass-produced goods. Du Pont and Nacco were also the major US exporters. They were particularly active on the Far Eastern markets. General Aniline & Film Corp.[25] was a fullyowned subsidiary of IG Farben.[26] Its shares were held indirectly through the Internationale Gesellschaft für Chemische Unternehmungen AG in Basle.[27] Dow began to produce dyestuffs in the mid-twenties. It is striking that its sales went through the sales organisation of the Swiss IG in the United States. Cincinnati was a subsidiary of the Swiss IG from 1920. Its function was similar to that of General Aniline, to produce the dyes that could no longer be exported to the United States, owing to government measures (customs duties, etc.).

The Swiss dyestuffs industry was even more strongly exportoriented than the German, and about 90% of its output went abroad. The three major producers, Gesellschaft für Chemische Industrie AG, Basle (CIBA), J.A. Geigy AG, Basle and Chemische Fabrik vorm. Sandoz AG, Basle, had formed an interest association in 1918. Unlike the German IG Farben the Swiss IG, also known as Baseler IG, had not come about through a merger. The companies remained legally independent, and the Swiss production plants, and those directly linked with them, also remained independent. This created a rather complicated picture. Like many Swiss companies, CIBA and Geigy had invested abroad, and they only showed part of this investment as legally independent subsidiaries. The other investment was a plant owned by the parent company and located abroad. Administratively and for accounting purposes it was incorporated directly in the accounts of the Basle company, without drawing up independent statement. That applied to Geigy's works in Grenzach in Germany, near Basle, and to the small factory in France near Rouen, and to the CIBA works in St. Fons on the Rhône. Legally independent subsidiaries, such as the British Clayton company in Manchester, owned by CIBA, were made the joint property of Baseler IG. The shares were not held by a body of the IG but directly, to the appropriate amount of the IG share, by the three parent companies. The same construction was used for new foreign investment, like the Cincinnati Chemical Works.[28] In Switzerland, apart from Baseler IG, Durand & Huguenin AG, Basle, and Chemische Fabrik Rohner AG in Pratteln, were also producing dyestuffs. Both were greatly influenced by IG Farben, which held 50.25% of the capital of Durand & Huguenin and in 1928 acquired 100% of Rohner.[29] The shares in both companies were held by the holding company of IG Farben, I.G. Chemie, Basle. The Swiss companies had the following sales:

---

[25] Up to 1939 General Aniline Corp., and before that General Aniline Works (GAW).

[26] On the build-up of investment in the US by IG Farben see Schröter, V., Participation in Market Control through Foreign Investment: IG Farbenindustrie in the United States, 1920–1938, in: A. Teichova, Multinational Enterprise, pp. 171–184.

[27] This was a pure holding company, and is often called IG Basel. It had no connections with Baseler IG or Schweizerische IG.

[28] Whereas in other mergers which also left the parent companies legally independent (like that of Vereinigte Stahlwerke in 1926), the management was merged, it remained separate in Baseler IG. As a result Baseler IG was dissolved in 1952 after heated arguments.

[29] Kugler, p. 103f.

Table 4. Sales by Swiss dyestuffs producers in 1938 in % of Total[a)]

CIBA	45
Sandoz and Geigy	41
Durand & Huguenin	12
Rohner	2
	100

[a)] Kugler, p. 12.

Sandoz and Geigy are shown together in the table. Sales by CIBA, Geigy and Sandoz were divided internally in the Swiss IG in a ratio of 52:24:24.[30] It may be assumed that in 1938 as well the sales by Sandoz and Geigy were about the same, so that each would have had a share of about 20% in total Swiss production. The high share shown for Durand & Huguenin is due to the fact that this company bought high quality vat dyes from IG Farben and processed these to top quality printing dyes (indigosoles).[31] On account of the high prices for the basic products and the relatively low degree of process range the company's sales are relatively overvalued in the statistics.

The most important chemical company in Great Britain was Imperial Chemical Industries Ltd. in London (I.C.I.). It had been established in 1926, not least to compete with IG Farben. I.C.I. was similar to Du Pont in many regards, including size and structure. In both firms the dyes sector was important, but not the main area of activity. Both had the largest range of dyes in their own country, but not a full range, as IG Farben had. Table 5 shows the role played by I.C.I. among British producers:

Table 5. British dyestuffs producers by sales in 1938 in %[a)]

I.C.I. (incl. subsidiaries)[b)]	58.0
Clayton Aniline Co., Ltd., Clayton	24.0
L.B. Holliday & Co., Ltd., Huddersfield	13.5
12 others	4.5
	100.0

[a)] Kugler, p. 13.
[b)] According to a list kept by the cartel ("Subsidiaries of D.I.G. and our cartel partners") of 4.9.1937, and drawn up by the Central Accounting Department in Frankfurt for the Cartel Control Commission, I.C.I. held (at least 51% – H.G.S.)
- British Dyestuffs Corporation Ltd., Manchester
- British Alizarine Co., Ltd., Manchester
- Scottish Dyes Ltd., Grangemouth
- British Synthetics Ltd., Manchester
- Emco Dyestuffs Ltd., Hull
- Oliver Wilkins & Co. Ltd., Derby
- Leech, Neil & Co., Spondon

(Bayer Works archive, BAW 13/21). On Trafford Chemical Co. Ltd. see below.

[30] Bürgin, A., Geschichte des Geigy-Unternehmens von 1758 bis 1939, Basle 1958, p. 246.
[31] Kugler, p. 12.

In France, the last major country producing dyestuffs, the picture was more differentiated.[32]

Table 6. French dyestuffs producers by sales in 1938 in %[a])

Compagnie Nationale des Matières Colorantes et Manufactures de Produits Chimiques du Nord Réunies, Etablissements Kuhlmann, Paris	59%
S.A. des Matières Colorantes et Produits Chimiques de Saint-Denis, Paris	26%
Comp. Française de Produits Chimiqes et Matières Colorantes de Saint-Clair-du-Rhône, Paris	12%
Etablissements Steiner, Vernon Durand & Huguenin, Huningue Soc. des Produits Chimiques et Matières Colorantes de Mulhouse, Paris S.A. pour l'Industrie Chimique, Mulhouse/Dornach Mabboux et Camell, Lyon Soc. des Matières Colorantes de Croix-Wasquehal (Burel), Roubaix/Rième Ertvelde	3%
	100%

[a]) Kugler, p. 17.

But the concentration was very much more far-reaching, in two respects, than the list suggests. Firstly, all the producers were in the Centrale des Matières Colorantes, Paris (C.M.C.), an interest association.[33] Ets. Kuhlmann held large shares of a number of the companies in the list.[34] It held the majority in the following firms: St. Clair du Rhône (capital Ffr. 24 million), Mulhouse (share capital Ffr. 12 million), Mabboux et Camell (share capital Ffr. 2.2 million), Croix-Wasquehal, Durand & Huguenin[35], and the Polish Winnica firm, as well as a minority in St. Denis. The cartel agreement in 1929 was signed by J. Frossard for Ets. Kuhlmann and St. Clair, and by Thesmar for St. Denis and Mulhouse and de Kap Herr for Ets. Steiner and Durand & Huguenin. This is evidence of further ties. Certainly Ets. Kuhlmann had accumulated far more than 70% of all sales.

[32] The other countries are discussed in the section on the international dyestuffs cartel.

[33] The C.M.C. had a capital of Ffr. 250 000 and it also acted as a cartel partner.

[34] Volkswirtschaftlicher Bericht (of IG Farben – H.G.S.) 4070, Konzerndarstellung Ets. Kuhlmann, 27.7.1940 (BWA 91.1).

[35] Only D & H Huningue. According to the report mentioned in Note 38, Ets. Kuhlmann and D & H merged in 1935, and since then the works had been closed. But the IG Farben Central Accounting Department included D & H in the Swiss IG in 1937 (see Note 34). That is not altogether clear.

After Germany and Switzerland, France was the country with the greatest concentration in the dyestuffs sector. But in Great Britain and the United States as well, a few major producers dominated the market. So there were two structural factors which basically favoured cartelisation: high expenditure on research and development in the major dyestuffs sectors[36], and a limited number of powerful producers. But there were other factors which had the opposite effect, such as the large number of patents, and their impact was underlined by the need for many years experience in dyestuffs production.[37]

IG Farben and the Swiss IG in particular were interested in international cartels. Both groups had had good experience with this before World War I[38], and both depended on exports to survive, since far more than two thirds of output went abroad. "So it was always the main task for the management of the IG to ensure that foreign sales of dyestuffs were promoted with all possible means".[39] The following table will illustrate this:

Table 7. World exports of dyestuffs in 1913 and 1926[a)]

Country	1913 1000 t	1913 mill. gold m.	1913 % (values)	1926 1000 t	1926 mill. gold m.	1926 % (values)
Germany	109	218	88.6	36.60	195.6	64.8
Switzerland	9	23	9.3	7.80	49.6	16.4
GB	3	4	1.6	3.80	12.5	4.1
France	1	1	0.4	2.50	10.0	3.3
USA	–	–	–	11.70	25.1	8.3
Czechoslovakia	–	–	–	0.90	3.0	1.0
Netherlands	–	–	–	0.80	2.6	0.9
Italy	–	–	–	0.30	1.9	0.6
Belgium	–	–	–	0.30	1.1	0.4
Poland	–	–	–	0.08	0.5	0.2
Total	122	246	100.0	64.78	301.9	100.0

a) Compiled and calculated from Kugler, p. 30

Only Germany had had to concede percentages to all the others after the war, and even if it still dominated the export market, with a share of almost two thirds, the pressure from the new producers was very real and potentially very strong. The solution was seen in extensive cartelisation of the export market.

---

36 Natural dyestuffs and the simple traditional dyes, such as logwood extract, were not cartelised.

37 In many cases, even if they had an outside patent, companies were not able to produce the patented dyes to the same quality. This required factory experience, so that technical assistance was needed as well as the patent. Very few companies could manage without this (most easily IG Farben).

38 For Geigy, see Geigy-Hagenbach, K., Kurzer Überblick über die Entwicklung der Firma Joh. Rud. Geigy, Basle 1919, p. 28 (Geigy AG historical archive in the CIBA-Geigy archive, no number).

39 ter-Meer, p. 73.

IG Farben's first major success in the pursuit of its international cartel strategy[40] was the contract with the C.M.C. in 1927. But this entailed a number of preparatory steps, such as building up basic trust, or at least, the conviction that the same interests were being pursued. There was a particular need for this, for most of the French dyestuffs production used dispropriated German plant. But it could then be assumed that there would be a need for technical assistance on the French side, and such a contract was in fact signed in 1921.[41] So the German chemical industry had very quickly come to terms with the new situation after the war. Very considerable political pressure had also been exercised by Paris, and it may be regarded as a feature of German-French relations in the chemical sector that the governments were involved far more than was the case with other countries. The contract with the C.M.C., however, was very advantageous to the German side[42], and its premature termination by C.M.C. owing to the struggle over the Ruhr was greatly regretted.[43] The French had to hand over 50% of their profit, renounce exports outside their territories and pay a single indemnity of Ffr. 16.7 million. The contract was to have run to 1965![44]

Nevertheless, contrary positions did not develop, and feelers were soon put out for new negotiations. At the same time Stresemann, the German Foreign Minister, was striving for a political agreement with France, and the iron and steel and electrical industries were negotiating as well.[45] On November 15, 1927 the C.M.C. and IG Farben concluded a most unusual and pioneering agreement. It was new firstly in its simplicity, and secondly in its scope. The chemical industry had great experience in cartels with individual dyestuffs or their equivalents, but the offsetting had always been a weak point in these agreements. In most cases the agreement was based on real sales or production figures, which then had to be converted to fictive figures, such as 40% colour pigment or 100% of a certain chemical compound, without regard for other factors. 750 chrome black dyestuffs, for instance, were converted in this way to 5 offsettable types.[46] Sometimes it was also possible to evade agreements by producing new or different compounds. Even if far less use was made of this possibility than would have been technically conceivable, for this would have affected the standing of the company generally as a partner in agreements – these two complexes do show what the problems in the individual dyestuffs cartels were: although they involved considerable bureaucratic expenditure they were difficult to

---

40 See Schröter, V., Die deutsche Industrie auf dem Weltmarkt 1929 bis 1933. Aussenwirtschaftliche Strategien unter dem Druck der Weltwirtschaftskrise, Frankfurt/M./Bern 1984, esp. the chapter on international cartels as an instrument of market regulation under crisis conditions, pp. 290–383.

41 See also the memorandum by IG Farben for V. Maltzan, councillor in the Trade Policy Division of the German Foreign Office, in 1940 (PA AA, HaPol, HA Sammlung V.L.R. Dumont).

42 Contract of 31.1.1921 in BWA 19 Farbstoffe 15.

43 The "dual injustice", see Memorandum of 1940, Note 41.

44 Holdermann, K., Im Banne der Chemie – Carl Bosch, Düsseldorf 1953, pp. 191 ff.; Kugler, p. 28 and Ter-Meer, p. 59.

45 Pohl, K.-H., Weimars Wirtschaft und die Aussenpolitik der Weimarer Republik, Düsseldorf 1979.

46 Similarly, 450 auramine dyestuffs were converted to 3, 360 rhodamine dyestuffs to 6 and 230 types of Victoria blue to 8 offsettable types (Kugler, p. 31).

control. The German-French agreement solved this dilemma at a stroke, by grouping all dyestuffs, without exception, together in a single overall reckoning. That was also to apply to products invented in the distant future, and it marked the step from the cartel on products to the industry cartel. The relation between the IG Farben/C.M.C. production values had been fixed at 88.5:11.5[47], and internally IG Farben called this the "Two Party Cartel".[48]

Despite its importance, the Two Party Cartel was seen as a provisional arrangement. The aim was an even more extensive agreement, to cover almost the entire chemical production of the two countries. The text of the contract states on this: "From the discussions that have taken place between leading personalities in the French and German chemical industry full agreement and conviction has emerged that fully integrated cooperation, firmly anchored financially, is appropriate in the three areas of dyestuffs, nitrogen and coal processing, to achieve rational manufacturing processes and sales, a limitation of costs and cheaper output".[49]

The Two Party Cartel was seen as a provisional arrangement in another regard as well. Right from the beginning its expansion to include other members was desired. Various discussions were held by IG Farben with I.C.I. and the Swiss IG, and the latter in turn had built up extensive cartel relations with the biggest member of C.M.C., Kuhlmann. However, the provisional nature of Two Party Cartel was not underlined in that it was considered preliminary, could be changed and so not so important. On the contrary, it was clear to all concerned that the agreement was pionneering precisely because of its uniqë scope.[50] In fact, this contract not only de facto fixed the German-French ratios for the following agreements as well, it also contained a large number of instructions on procedure and evaluation.

Various major agreements had been concluded between the German and Swiss chemical industries even before World War I[51], and both sides could look back on many years of experience. After 1918 further agreements were signed in the dyestuffs field, of which the most important were the Chrome Black Convention of 17 June 1924 and the Agreement on Vat Dyes of June/July 1927.[52] Both covered modern dyestuffs of major economic importance.

A further agreement, known as the "Russian agreement", was not of the same economic importance, but it should be mentioned here since it is of historical interest. As a result of the dispropriation without compensation Switzerland had lost

---

47 The text of the contract is in Hö 305.

48 But in the Swiss IG the German-Swiss agreement of 1929 was called the "Twosome Cartel", see below.

49 Hö 305.

50 Similar provisional agreements, generally to test the partner in practice, were used as a preliminary to more comprehensive cartel agreements in several cases. The German and French partners in the potash industry, who dominated the world market, "tested" each other particularly intensively. In 1924 they concluded a one-year agreement for the United States and Sweden, and in 1925 a one-year agreement for the world market.
The real contract was not signed until 1926 (Schröter, H.G., Die internationale Kaliwirtschaft 1918 bis 1939, Kassel 1985, pp. 35–41).

51 Bürgin, p. 253.

52 BWA 19.1.

considerable assets in Soviet Russia.[53] It did not join in the military sanctions but it did in the economic ones; it also refused to acknowledge the USSR, and as late as 1934 was still trying actively to prevent its acceptance into the League of Nations. The chemical industry, especially J.R. Geigy AG, had also lost investments.[54] To be able to supply without losing face, the Swiss IG concluded what was known as the Russian Agreement with IG Farben, under which the firms in Basle acquired a fixed quota of the sales by IG Farben in the USSR. Sales went exclusively through Germany. The agreement ran formally from 1 January 1927 until 1 July 1929;[55] The Three Party Cartel had already come into force on 1 January 1929.

There were agreements between the Swiss IG and Ets. Kuhlmann on the production and sales of vat dyestuffs (of 11 June 1926 and 3 February 1927 respectively).[56] In both the shares were 50% each, but they only applied to the French territories (including the colonies, etc.). Possible French exports were limited by quantity, and in addition dependent on the approval of the Swiss IG. Finally, on 15 October 1928 a cartel agreement was concluded by the same partners to fix the status quo for the entire dyestuffs field.[57] It was expressly described as "provisional" in regard to a French-German-Swiss agreement, and it had only a brief period to run.[58]

At the time of the Swiss-French agreement negotiations had been proceeding for a long time between the Basle IG and IG Farben. The discussions had actually progressed so far that IG Farben had achieved its first goal, namely to prevent the agreement that was threatening between the Swiss firms and the British I.C.I.[59] For that combination would have made nonsense of IG Farben's aim to combine all continental dyestuffs production. Nevertheless, IG Farben made stringent demands in the negotiations which appear to have caused "many a headache" in Basle:

"1) A conditio sine qua non for us is the implementation of internal centralisation, incorporating a uniform and indissoluble Swiss group, to be the only partner in discussions for us and the French; in connection with this full centralisation of production and sales in the Basle head ofice and uniform sales organs outside.

2) Acceptance of the principle of capital integration laid down in the preamble to the French contract".[60]

But all the plans to concentrate Swiss dyestuffs production beyond the interest association in a large enterprise had always met with rejection in Basle. So the first objective for the Swiss in negotiating was to get round this condition.[61] The argument

---

53 Rauber, U., Schweizer Industrie in Russland, Zurich 1985.

54 Dyestuffs factories in Lithuania and Moskow. The biggest turnover was achieved in 1915 at 1.3 million roubles (CIBA-Geigy historical archive, FA Geigy FL2 (His), KAR 1, KAR 1a).

55 Appendix 1 to the contract of 27 April 1929, p. 12 (WA Sandoz Kartellbeziehungen No. 1); letter of 27 November 1929, p. 6, loc. cit.

56 Characteristically, nearly all the dyestuffs incorporated by the French side were based on licences from IG Farben, while the Swiss had their own products, loc. cit.

57 The reference period was from 1 January 1924 to 30 June 1928, loc. cit.

58 It was valid from 1 October 1928 to 31 December 1929, loc. cit.

59 "The rapid negotiations certainly achieved a major objective, namely blowing apart the negotiations between the Swiss and the British" (letter from Prof. Meyer of 19 October 1928 to Dr. Krekeler, both of IG Farben, HO 312, p. 1).

60 Minutes of 23 January 1928, p. 2.

61 Bürgin, p. 253f.

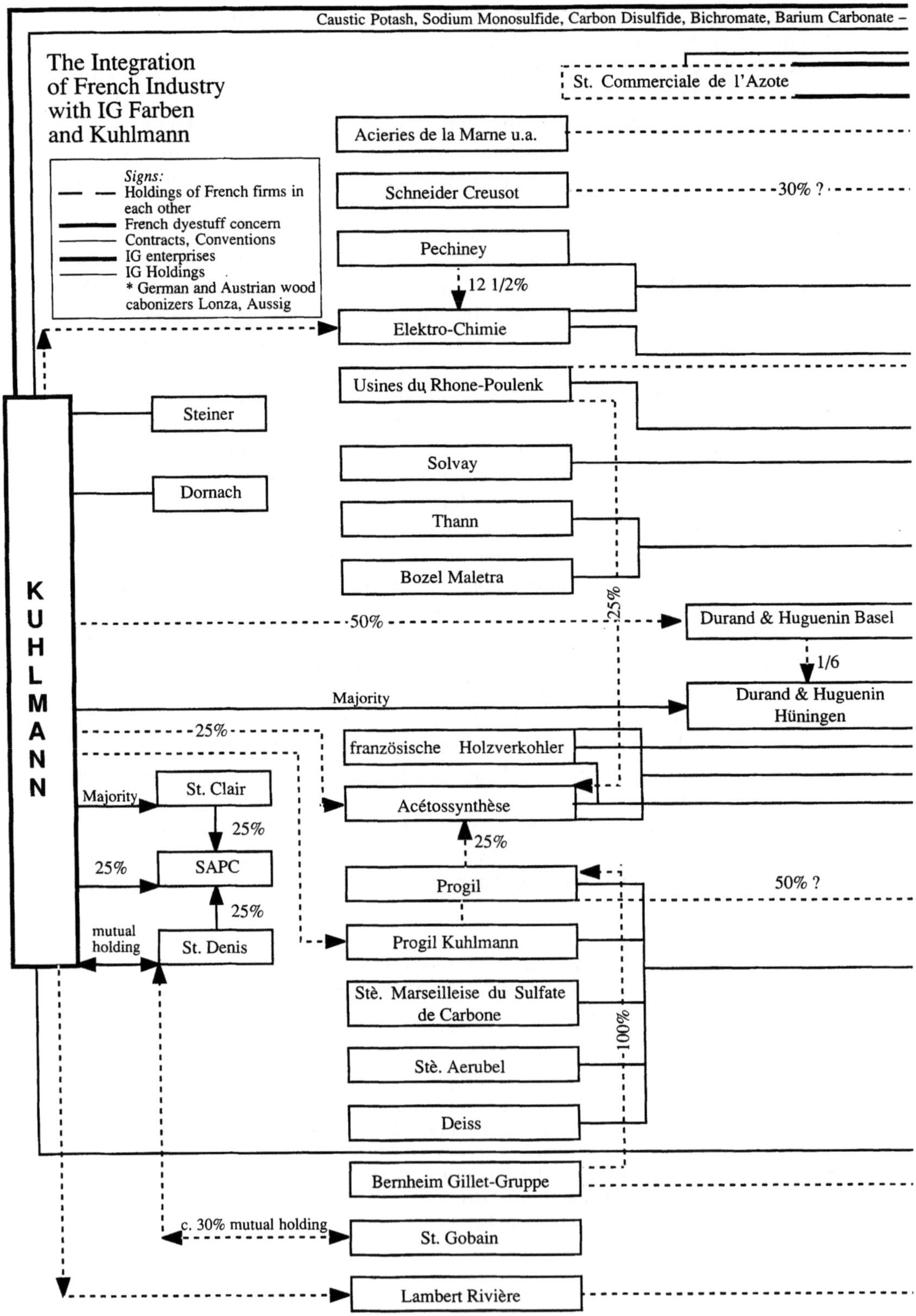
Caustic Potash, Sodium Monosulfide, Carbon Disulfide, Bichromate, Barium Carbonate –
The Integration of French Industry with IG Farben and Kuhlmann
Signs:
Holdings of French firms in each other
French dyestuff concern
Contracts, Conventions
IG enterprises
IG Holdings
* German and Austrian wood cabonizers Lonza, Aussig
St. Commerciale de l'Azote
Acieries de la Marne u.a.
Schneider Creusot
30% ?
Pechiney
12 1/2%
Elektro-Chimie
Usines du Rhone-Poulenk
Steiner
Dornach
Solvay
Thann
Bozel Maletra
KUHLMANN
50%
25%
Durand & Huguenin Basel
1/6
Majority
Durand & Huguenin Hüningen
25%
französische Holzverkohler
Majority
St. Clair
Acétossynthèse
25%
25%
25%
SAPC
Progil
50% ?
25%
mutual holding
St. Denis
Progil Kuhlmann
Stè. Marseilleise du Sulfate de Carbone
100%
Stè. Aerubel
Deiss
Bernheim Gillet-Gruppe
c. 30% mutual holding
St. Gobain
Lambert Rivière

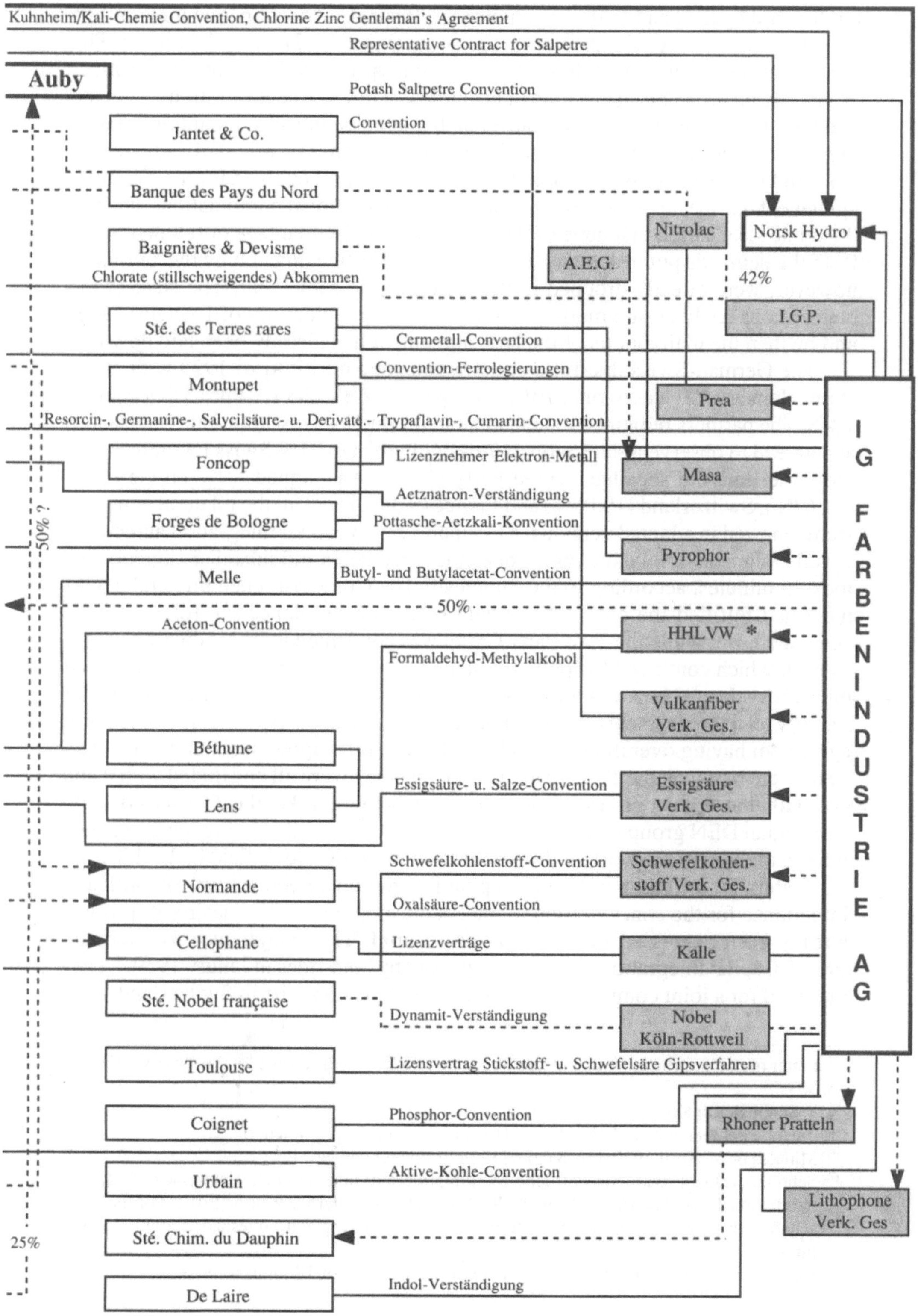
Kuhnheim/Kali-Chemie Convention, Chlorine Zinc Gentleman's Agreement
Representative Contract for Salpetre
Auby
Potash Saltpetre Convention
Jantet & Co.
Convention
Banque des Pays du Nord
Nitrolac
Norsk Hydro
Baignières & Devisme
A.E.G.
Chlorate (stillschweigendes) Abkommen
42%
I.G.P.
Sté. des Terres rares
Cermetall-Convention
Montupet
Convention-Ferrolegierungen
Prea
Resorcin-, Germanine-, Salycilsäure- u. Derivate.- Trypaflavin-, Cumarin-Convention
Foncop
Lizenznehmer Elektron-Metall
Masa
Aetznatron-Verständigung
Forges de Bologne
Pottasche-Aetzkali-Konvention
50% ?
Pyrophor
Melle
Butyl- und Butylacetat-Convention
50%
Aceton-Convention
HHLVW *
Formaldehyd-Methylalkohol
Vulkanfiber Verk. Ges.
Béthune
Lens
Essigsäure- u. Salze-Convention
Essigsäure Verk. Ges.
Schwefelkohlenstoff-Convention
Schwefelkohlenstoff Verk. Ges.
Normande
Oxalsäure-Convention
Cellophane
Lizenzverträge
Kalle
Sté. Nobel française
Dynamit-Verständigung
Nobel Köln-Rottweil
Toulouse
Lizensvertrag Stickstoff- u. Schwefelsäre Gipsverfahren
I G FARBENINDUSTRIE AG
Coignet
Phosphor-Convention
Rhoner Pratteln
Urbain
Aktive-Kohle-Convention
Lithophone Verk. Ges
25%
Sté. Chim. du Dauphin
De Laire
Indol-Verständigung

put forward by the head of the negotiations in Basle, C. Koechlin, that three sellers would be more successful than one, was not accepted by Dr. von Schnitzler. The concentration in Germany of 8 or 11 into one enterprise had been entirely positive: "Certainly there can be no question of business lost through centralisation".[62] On the contrary, he saw the mutual German-French guarantee of sales, including sales of French products through the German sales organisation, as particularly advantageous: "In fact, we are of the opinion that the form of cartel evolved for the dyestuffs agreement has the advantage over all the other international combinations, such as the crude steel cartel, that none of the partners can suffer damage or fall behind".[63] Both the demands put in January 1928 as a conditio sine qua non by the Germans, however, were already dropped in the spring of the same year. The state of the negotiations could be summarised in the Heidelberg Guidelines of 1 August 1928, and by then the main points of the later agreement had already been laid down.

The German-Swiss dyestuffs cartel was signed on 27 April 1929 with effect from 1 January.[64] It was to run for the same period as Baseler IG, until 31 December 1968. The partners remained independent in production, research, sales and so on, and agreed to observe a sales ratio of 79% IG Farben to 21% Swiss IG (values). At the same time the socalled "Three Party Cartel" was signed between Germany (71.67%), Switzerland (19.00%) and France (9.33%), and all the bilateral contracts were renewed in adapted versions; a German-French capital integration agreement was also signed. Simply the signing of all the agreements and subsidiary agreements took 35 minutes, according to the minutes![65] The German-French bilateral agreement had fulfilled the expectations held of it, and its pioneering role had been confirmed. But while the Two Party Cartel was confirmed in its production quotas as well, which continued to apply, the shares in the Three Party Cartel were based on sales' values. The German-French link was therefore a dual one. For greater security all the agreements applied independent of each other, with the Three Party agreement having overall legal validity. The dyestuffs agreements in the next few years were based on the Three Party Cartel, and they were all concluded with it and not with the whole group of partners (see below). Like the German-British-Norwegian DEN group in the nitrogen field, the German-Swiss-French agreement formed the core of the worldwide cartelisation in the dyestuffs field in the thirties.[66]

Naturally, the German-French capital integration agreement was of particular importance for the concentration in the chemical industry. The desire for this had already been expressed in the Two Party Cartel. The "Guidelines for German-French Capital Integration" had been approved by both sides in Janury 1929.[67] They provided for a joint company to be founded with its domicile in Switzerland, to be

[62] Letter from Koechlin to V. Schnitzler, 30 January 1928, and the answer of 2 February 1928, HÖ 303.

[63] v. Schnitzler to Koechlin, loc. cit., p. 2.

[64] The other agreements in BWA 13/18; HA Sandoz; see also Tammen, p. 32f.

[65] Minutes of 27 April 1929, HA Sandoz, Kartellbeziehungen No. 1.

[66] Schröter, H.G.: Privatwirtschaftliche Marktregulierung und staatliche Interessenpolitik: Das internationale Stickstoffkartell 1929–1939, in: H.G. Schröter/C. Wurm (Eds.): Politik, Wirtschaft und internationale Beziehungenin der Zwischenkriegszeit, Wiesbaden 1990 (forthcoming).

[67] HÖ 305 for both the Guidelines and a letter to Dr. Schmitz of 18 January 1929.

guaranteed by a fixed agreement. Its capital was to be "big enough to ensure that the heads of the individual companies could never, not even in the distant future, take it upon themselves to jeopardise large parts of the substance of their companies by behaviour contrary to the agreement, or by endeavouring to cancel the agreement altogether".[68]

The capital was to be provided in a ratio of 4:1 IG Farben to C.M.C., and it was intended that the German side should incorporate the shares in its Swiss holding company IG Chemie Basle. The link was intended to ensure both a profit pool and an exchange of technical experience.[69] Large sections of the guidelines also referred to a possible participation by the Swiss IG, although it was stated that "on the Swiss side the final conditions for capital integration are not yet given, mainly for internal reasons as well".[70] A relation of 60 : 25 : 15 was envisaged should Switzerland be included. In view of the above cartel relation of 71.67 : 19.00 : 9.33 this constituted a concession on the part of IG Farben. The Guidelines extended for ten pages, but they were shortened to only one brief page of text for the final contract, and altered in some points.[71] The capital was increased to a total of Sfr. 105 million, but the C.M.C. share was lower, at Sfr. 11.7 million, or 11.1%, than the French share in the Two Party Cartel (11.5%). Although the Swiss company that was to be founded was to be formed "immédiatement après la signature",[72] it was never formed. According to Kugler that was due to a French request.[73] But internal negotiation papers in IG Farben show that doubts were entertained in the usefulness of the profit pool and the exchange of experience with C.M.C.[74]

So although financial integration of the German and French chemical industries never took place, there were so many common interests and points of contact through the cartel agreements in dyestuffs and nitrogen compounds that a diagram of the two major companies seems appropriate (cf. the following diagram). It will also show the internal structure of the French dyestuffs group. The abbreviation "SAPC" is "Mulhouse" (see above). The incorporation of other French chemical companies in the IG Farben contracts is also very impressive, all the more as this picture dates from

---

68 Loc. cit., p. 2f.

69 Loc. cit., p. 4.

70 Loc. cit., p. 2. "Although Switzerland, as stated above, is not yet seen as ripe for capital integration, the moment when it is mature for this may perhaps come very much more quickly than some of the gentlemen in Basle imagine. Some of them already see integration as a fact in the immediate future. In that case nothing further need be done than to include Switzerland with the amount originally envisaged for it, and which is also identical with the amount to be deposited under the cartel agreement now to be concluded. If only for that reason, and because figures were calculated for the key of three which take adequate account of the original aims of security and the preservation of interests for both sides, the amounts for the German-French capital integration should remain at Sfr. 24 million shares of the Swiss institute of IG, which would initially be an estimated 72 million Sfrs., and accordingly a French incorporation to the countervalue of about 18 million Sfrs". See Bürgin, p. 254.

71 A copy of the contract is in BWA 13/19.

72 Loc. cit., see Schröter, V., Weltmarkt, p. 298.

73 Kugler, p. 45.

74 File note of 1 February 1928 on a discussion on 23 January 1928, p. 4 (HÖ 302). From the material available it is not possible fully to clarify that question.

1930, when IG Farben had not yet finished building up its network of agreements and was still busily engaged in doing so.

After the formation of the Three Party Cartel the British firm I.C.I. remained the only major dyestuffs company in Europe outside the agreements. In 1930 I.C.I. accounted for 43% of the British output of dyestuffs;[75] and IG Farben estimated the breakdown as follows:[76] (see page 120).

Table 7a. Shares in British dyestuffs production in 1925

I.C.I.	44%
Clayton	21%
Brotherton	10%
Brit. Alizarine	9%
Holiday	7%
Diverse others	9%
	100%

The differences to Table 5 are still significant if I.C.I.'s acquisition of British Alizarine is taken into account: the biggest company was developing with a remarkable dynamic.

As early as 1927 a cooperation agreement between I.C.I. and IG Farben was being discussed. Duisberg and Woolcock, among others, were in favour.[77] In a letter to Bosch of 24 November of that year, Ludwig Mond of I.C.I. suggested interest compensation in all major areas.[78] But in the dyestuffs sector as well, indeed particularly, the German IG did not want to accept the British as equal partners. Moreover, in their eyes the British producers were too fragmented. I.C.I. had also put very far-reaching demands, such as that the Empire to be regarded as a home market, and the sale to it of the Swiss investment, Clayton, so that an agreement was inconceivable. Indeed, a heated controversy developed over prices and patents. Nevertheless, the two sides saw a joint agreement as the only possible ultimate end. I.C.I. achieved big successes with its patents, but it did not succeed in taking its dyestuffs production out of the red against the price pressure from the Three Party Cartel. Once the business positions were established and clarified, there was nothing to stand in the way of an agreement. Moreover, I.C.I. and IG Farben had had cartel links since 1929 in the nitrogen DEN group. Against that background Dr. von Schnitzler informed Koechlin in a confidential letter of 4 July 1930 that his company was ready to negotiate: "In keeping with the facts of the situation and the general friendly relations between I.C.I. and our firm (!) the discussion was extended to the

75 Haber, L.F., The Chemical Industry 1900–1930, London 1971, p. 87.

76 Letter to Krekeler of 21 February 1929 (HÖ 310).

77 Note of 5 July 1927, BA NL Silverberg 236. Woolcock was the Director of the Association of British Chemical Manufacturers, while Duisberg was Chairman of the Supervisory Board of IG Farben.

78 HÖ 310; see Reader, Imperial Chemical Industries. A History, Vol. 2, The First Quarter-Century 1926–1952, London/New York/Toronto 1975, pp. 40ff.

general world dyestuffs situation...We could confirm that there is now a very large degree of agreement on principle between the views of I.C.I. and those of the members of the cartel on the conduct of the world dyestuffs business, and that all sides would welcome it if a formulation was speedily found for a general agreement that would ensure, on the basis of the present division of business, the independence and technical progress of all concerned".[79] After further negotiations the contract (for the "Four Party Cartel") was signed between I.C.I. and the Three Party Cartel on 26 February 1932, with effect from 1 January that year. Its period of validity was adjusted to that of the Three Party Cartel – until 1968. The ratios were 8.467% of the sales' values for I.C.I. and 91.533% for the Three Party Cartel. This gave the following ratios within the Four Party agreement:[80]

IG Farben	65.602%
Swiss IG	17.391%
C.M.C.	8.540%
I.C.I.	8.467%
	100.000%

With that agreement all the major producers in Europe were concentrated in a cartel, and a number of smaller producers also joined the agreement.

Most of the outsiders, and the most important of them, were in Great Britain. For that reason the British firms, especially since they can be regarded as representative, will be used to show the attitude taken by the cartel to outsiders.

The following figures will give an overview of the British dyestuffs companies. The table (unlike Table 5) is drawn up according to share capital. Apart from Brotherton, which mainly produced chemicals, the other companies were mainly or exclusively dyestuffs producers:

Table 8. British Dyestuffs Producers in 1940[a]

Company	Share capital in £ 1000s
I.C.I. Dyestuffs group (I.C.I. concern 74203)	5019
Brotherton & Co. Ltd., Leeds	2000
Clayton Aniline Co. Ltd., Clayton	600
British Alizarine Co. Ltd.[b]	600
Major & Co., Hull	450
L.B. Holliday & Co., Huddersfield	250
J.W. Leitch & Co., Ltd., Bradford	200

[a]) Manuscript for an economic report of 21 November 1940 (BWA B4, Eur. GB, 1a).
[b]) Subsidiary of I.C.I.

[79] HÖ 310, p. 1f.
[80] The most exact figures, those given here, are in Kugler, pp. 33 and 56.

Other firms of note, not listed in the table were:

1. J.C. Oxley's & Chemicals Ltd, Dewsbury
2. J. Robinson & Co. Ltd, Huddersfield
3. British Celanese Ltd.
4. Colne Vale Dye & Chemical Co.
5. Cornbrooke Chemical Co.
6. Williams Bros. Hounslow[81]

To IG Farben, Holliday was particularly important: "The turnover of the individual producers is insignificant in comparison with Holliday, but as a whole they from a considerable group among the outsiders".[82]

Even in the preliminary negotiations I.C.I. had several times been requested to create order in this variety, and was urged to buy up some of the smaller firms. It did in fact acquire Alizarine in 1931, so making the negotiations that had been proceeding since 1929 between this company and the Three Party Cartel superfluous.[83] The company also endeavoured to reach an agreement with Brotherton, and the internal preparations for this in IG Farben were commenced in June 1928.[84] A good year later the "larger Dyestuffs Committee" was able to receive an appropriate report on the negotiations; this was on the main hydrosulphite group of dyestuffs.[85]

On 1 January 1930 the appropriate agreement for hydrosulphites, rongalite and decroline came into force.[86] The shares in sales were frozen at the current level and the sales markets split up between the members.[87] The cartel was to be kept secret, and the obligations undertaken were to be fulfilled, even in the other side's exclusive zone, so as "to avoid undesired attention from customers".[88] When the agreement came to an end, on 31 December 1931, it was renewed "for another two years initially, on a basis favourable to the IG".[89] Of particular interest in this is that IG Farben tacitly negotiated for the Three Party Cartel as well. Although the partners did not take part in the discussions, and the contract was only concluded between Brotherton and IG Farben, Baseler IG had to take some of the load (C.M.C. had generally agreed not to export to Great Britain, among other places): "The Basle group (the Swiss IG) will be informed of the necessary details in writing, so that an agreement between the Basle group and Brotherton, to run concurrently, can lay down the undertaking by the Swiss firms not to export hydrosulphite products to England. For the rest, in accordance with an earlier agreement the Swiss group will

---

[81] Lecture by Dr. Loehr (1937), p. 14, HÖ 2508.
[82] Loc. cit.
[83] Letter to J.R. Geigy AG of 22 August 1929, HÖ 303.
[84] Minutes of the Kaufmännische Kommission of 6 June 1928, p. 8, BWA 13/8.
[85] Compiled on 10 September 1929, see below, HÖ 109.
[86] Copy in BWA 19 Verträge, Hydrosulfit 1.
[87] The IG agreed not to supply the British Isles and Brotherton not to sell in Europe. Moreover, Brotherton was only to sell to British India, Japan, China, Mexico, South America and Australia, markets where the firm was already established, loc. cit., para. 4.
[88] Notes of meeting of the enlarged committee on 18 March 1930, HÖ 109.
[89] Loc. cit., 22 January 1932, HÖ 110.

take a share of the burden, in itself not of any weight, of the new agreement in the relation of the basic ratios".[90]

It was also possible to reach agreements with other British firms which bound them to the cartel. Robinson was obliged not to expand its range for seven years, only to supply certain markets and not to undercut the cartel prices.[91] Oxley's Dyes was bound in a similar way.[92] Since Major & Co. is never mentioned in the minutes, it may be assumed from the material available that it offered no competition. Possibly the firm did not export, but it is also conceivable that it was tied by an agreement with I.C.I. The IG Farben Annual Report for 1932 mentions only Holliday and Leitch as British competitors.[93] While Leitch is very rarely mentioned, suggesting that it was not a competitor of note, the problems with Holliday were a frequent point of discussion at the meetings of the IG Farben Dyestuffs Committee. Both the frequency with which the topic was raised and the choice of words suggests that the little Holliday company was a considerable source of irritation, indeed of rage, to IG Farben.

Holliday in fact accounted for an over-proportional share of British exports of dyes with about 25% (I.C.I. had 75%).[94] IG Farben was particularly affected by Holliday's offensive in Scandinavia.[95] When the Scandinavian countries followed the devaluation of the pound sterling in 1931 the IG Farben products, like other German exports, were left around 30% higher in price, and the concern registered with bitterness that Holliday did not use the occasion to raise its prices but utilised the price advantage from devaluation and embarked on a strong offensive to expand its market share. IG Farben always countered attempts of this kind with determination. "There is agreement that on no account must business be let fall to Holliday, and if necessary the price advantages offered by Holliday must be matched with a *'special discount'*".[96]

IG Farben had evolved particular tactics for price battles to avoid the problem of other cartels: if a cartel was forced into a price battle by an outsider, it was always extremely difficult after the battle had been fought out to convince customers that a return to the old higher prices was necessary. The International Raw Steel Export Community, for instance, or the World Potash Syndicate needed several years of strong demand to get back to the price level of before their battles. IG Farben avoided this dilemma by fixing lower price thresholds for its dyestuffs. If a price battle forced it below that threshold, a new name was invented and the same goods put on the market under the new name and at the lower price, while the old price was maintained for the old name. When the battle was over the new product that had been

---

90 Minutes of the IG Farben Dyestuffs Committee meeting on 6 January 1937, p. 7, HÖ 110.

91 Quoted by Etzold, H., Der Konkurrenzkampf zwischen der deutschen und der englischen Teerfarbenindustrie während der Weltwirtschaftskrise, thesis, Halle 1966, p. 260.

92 Loc. cit.

93 P. 17, sent by Dr. v. Schnitzler on 26 January 1933, HÖ 110.

94 Talk by Dr. Loehr, p. 10, HÖ 2508.

95 On Anglo-German rivalry in Scandinavia, in the chemical sector particularly, see Schröter, H.G., Aussenpolitik und Wirtschaftsinteresse. Skandinavien im aussenwirtschaftlichen Kalkül Deutschlands und Grossbritanniens 1918–39, Frankfurt/M./Bern 1983, pp. 244–321, and for a more general account, Nilson, B., Handelspolitik unter skärpt konkurrens, Lund 1983.

96 Italics in the text. Minutes of the meeting of the "enlarged Dyestuffs Committee" on 9 October 1931, p. 3, HÖ 110.

used in the struggle was withdrawn, and in this way it was relatively easier to regain the old level.[97] But it must be stressed in this context that the success of such tactics depended on certain structural conditions.[98] Generally, every partner in a cartel "should defend its position in the individual countries and dyestuffs groups, regardless of the price situation".[99]

Beside price battles the Four Party Cartel had a number of other ways of exerting pressure. The British firms were, for instance, greatly dependent on supplies of pre-products from I.C.I., and this was used, with other means, to put pressure on Holliday. IG Farben expected a speedy result: "There are prospects that we will, after all, be able to put an end to the competition from Holliday in the course of this year".[100] But it was not so easy to get at Holliday, and as late as the summer of 1938 a joint letter went to I.C.I. from the top representatives of the French, Swiss and German partners demanding that it should put an end to the matter and buy Holliday out. An additional £150 000 were provided for this purpose from the continental partners[101], and Holliday was to be offered £650 000. Although the importance of the company was played down[102], the matter is significant because it was a singular occurrence, not repeated in this form or with these contents. Finally, however, the urgency of the matter was expressly stated in the letter: "We hope that by the foregoing proposals and suggestions we are offering a constructive contribution towards the solution of the Holliday problem which occupies our minds more or less since the formation of the Four Party Cartel".[103]

In fact, Holliday had developed into a problem which the Four Party Cartel had to take seriously[104], and IG Farben's optimism was misplaced.[105] Four years later the Four Party Cartel's share of the British market had fallen from 88% to 83%.[106] I.C.I. and IG Farben had to share the loss, for the Swiss were able to expand their share of the business, as were the outsiders. Among these, of which there were about twelve, Holliday had the lion's share of the sales value, at around 40%. It was also Holliday

---

97 Etzold, p. 177; Reader, p. 194; Schröter, V., Weltmarkt, p. 305; Schröter, H.G., Aussenpolitik, p. 274.

98 Various factors were involved here: dyestuffs customers generally had little in-depth knowledge of the products, and most of them depended on technical assistance and instructions from the manufacturer. The price of the dyes also made little difference in the cost of their goods to customers (the textile industry, and so on), so that price fluctuations for dyestuffs did not affect their end prices very greatly. A steel company, for instance, would be very much more dependent on the price of steel.

99 Minutes of the meeting of the Dyestuffs Committee, quoted from Schröter, V., Weltmarkt, p. 305.

100 Annual Report by Dr. v. Schnitzler, 26 January 1933, p. 17f., HÖ 110.

101 Joint letter from Dr. v. Schnitzler, C. Koechlin and J. Frossard to Mr. Walker of I.C.I., of 9 June 1938, BWA 13/20.2.

102 "... the Holliday question is one which in the first line concerns the Cartel partners in the Great Britain market, since we are of the opinion that the elimination of Holliday at this stage will not bring about a change worth mentioning in the competitive situation in foreign markets", loc. cit.

103 Loc. cit. The letter ends by assuring Walker that I.C.I. is the party that must take action in Great Britain, and that the Three Party Cartel, and its members, will refrain from any unilateral steps.

104 See Schröter, V., Weltmarkt, pp. 308–310.

105 "Holliday can really only be seen as an independent (sic!) competitor in basic dyestuffs. Its activities in the other production areas are rather sporadic and, moreover, built on pre-products from I.C.I.", (Dr. v. Schnitzler's Annual Report of 26 January 1933, p. 17, HÖ 110).

106 See also the following figures in the lecture by Dr. Loehr, 1937, pp. 13ff., HÖ 2508.

that systematically put pressure on the cartel. It was able to do this by exploiting the British system of import licences, which was intended to protect the domestic industry from the all-powerful German competition. As soon as a dyestuff could be produced in adequate quantities in Great Britain, the company could apply for the state import licences to be withdrawn. I.C.I. had made much use of this possibility in the struggle against the Three Party Cartel, but it agreed to refrain from using it when entering into the arrangement with the Four Party Cartel. After it had signed, I.C.I., as in other cases, held with extreme care to the spirit and letter of the agreement, but Holliday made all the more use of the mechanism. While the Swiss were easily able to stand up to Holliday through their British holding in Clayton, I.C.I. was not, for technical reasons, in a position to embark on a production that would compete with Holliday in its special fields. As a result, IG Farben and I.C.I. suffered the most damage, IG Farben from the blocking of German exports, and I.C.I. from the loss of sales that were bound to the cartel ratio.[107]

For a time IG Farben was able to counter the activities of Holliday by utilising its broad product range, and replacing the goods that could be imported with another product of a similar colour effect[108], but this could only be a temporary solution. In 1935 and 1936 Holliday's applications for protection became ever more numerous and comprehensive: "What Holliday is doing now is tantamount to a wide breach in the reserve positions of our range".[109] But once the full extent of the problem was recognised action was swift. The Trafford Chemical Company was founded in the spring of 1938 jointly by I.C.I. and IG Farben. It was a further and visible sign of the good relations which persisted between the leading British and German chemical firms right up to the Second World War[110], in contrast to the political tension.[111] Trafford was also a sign that the Cartel, and especially IG Farben, would not tolerate any fundamental market shifts to its disadvantage. But the case of Holliday also shows that, despite extreme concentration, small firms could persist and grow in the dyestuffs field as well, if they pursued a strategy of exploiting market niches.[112]

Table 9. Italian dyestuffs producers by sales in 1938 (values) in %[a)]

Aziende Colori Nazionali Affini, Milan (ACNA)	51.6
Soc. Chimica Lombarda A.E. Bianchi & Co., Rho	15.6
Industria Chimica Dot. Saronnio, Melegnano	13.1
Industria Piemontese Colori Anilina (IPCA), Ciriè	5.1
Others, incl. Soc. Begamasca per l'Industrial Chimica, Seriate	15.1
	100.0

a) Kugler, p. 15.

107 The ratios for the British market for I.C.I. to the Three Party Cartel had been fixed at 53.80 : 46.20.

108 For instance, indanthrene brown BR was supplied for indanthrene brown R and G, and naphtogene blue RR was replaced with diazo indigo blue BR and so on, loc. cit., p. 17.

109 Loc. cit.

110 For more details see Schröter, H.G., Aussenpolitik, pp. 313–318.

111 Wendt, B.-J., Economic Appeasement. Handel und Finanz in der britischen Deutschlandpolitik 1933–1939, Düsseldorf 1971.

112 Another case was the Italian firm "Melegnano", which had specialised in supplying a local market with wool dyes.

After this outline of the build-up of the cartel and the market relations for the main European countries, let us now turn to the other European and non-European countries where dyes were produced, with some major individual markets as examples. In 1938 Italy was producing 2.9% of the world dyestuffs, and within Italy the breakdown was as follows (See table 9).

At the beqinning of the 1920s the Hoechst subsidiary Cassella had bought up the shares of Bianchi. When ACNA had to declare itself bankrupt in 1930/31, despite a government subsidy, it was taken over by the Italian chemical concern Montecatini. In that context (1931) IG Farben was able to agree a very advantageous exchange of shares between Bianchi and ACNA, and bind ACNA into the Cartel.[113] The Bergamasca company was a subsidiary of the Swiss IG.

Poland produced 1.3% of world output of dyes in 1938. Its main producers were:

Table 10. Polish dyestuffs producers by sales values in 1938 in %[a])

Pemrysl Chemiczny Boruta Sp. Akc., Zgierz	40
Zaklady Chemiczne W. Winnicy Sp. Akc., Winnica	30
Pabjanicer AG for Chemische Industrie, Pabjanice	21
Chemizna Fabryka Wola Krzystoporska, Wola Krystoporska	6
Others	3
	100

[a]) Kugler, p. 16.

Winnica had been founded in 1929 by IG Farben and Kuhlmann, Paris, jointly, but although each held 50%, only Kuhlmann appeared as representative of the firm. Even in negotiations, and on some occasions on the internal IG Farben list, Winnica appears as part of the Kuhlmann concern. It may be surmised that political motives played a part in this, but there is no evidence in the sources. Pabjanicer AG was part of the Swiss IG; it had been founded in 1899 by CIBA.[114] So the Three Party Cartel accounted for half Polish output, which does not, of course, include imports. In 1932 the socalled "Polish group" – Boruta and Wola – concluded a provisional agreement with the Three Party Cartel, which was followed by a firm contract in 1934 that was to run for eight years.[115] Based on a ratio of 29.5 to 70.5 between the Polish group and the Three Party Cartel, the Polish group was allowed an annual increase of 0.5% in its ratio. One year later IG Farben was able to conclude a contract with the small Polish dyestuffs producer Chemische Fabrik Bruno Schülde in Lodz[116], bringing virtually all the Polish manufacturers under the Three Party Cartel.

113 After the exchange the IG had 49.0% of ACNA, and 51.01% of Bianchi, while Montecatini held the rest in both cases. On ACNA see Schröter, V., Weltmarkt, pp. 428–430.

114 Report by the Management Board of CIBA to the Board of Directors, 17 August 1899 (CIBA-Geigy historical archive, FA CIBA, KG 2.15.04).

115 The contract is in the Sandoz historical archives, Kartellbeziehungen, no number.

116 Schülde undertook not to sell dyestuffs from its own production for more than Zl 400 000 (about RM 188 000) a year. Any loss in turnover would be made good by IG Farben through direct payments (25%) (Kugler, p. 124).

In Czechoslovakia, "Aussig"[117] was the only dyestuffs producer, and in 1938 its sales value was 0.5% of world sales. The firm was the largest chemical company in the successor states, producing mainly heavy chemicals. With its size, its broad product range and the government protection it enjoyed, and with its close links to Solvay as well as direct investment in Poland, Austria, Hungary, Yugoslavia, and Romania it was regarded as a serious future competitor.[118] From 1924 to 1928 the Three Party Cartel supplied 95% of the dyestuffs used in Czechoslovakia, of which IG Farben accounted for 77%.[119] But the cartel's share was falling, and in 1934 it concluded an agreement with Aussig that was limited to five years.[120] Aussig's total turnover in dyestuffs was to be increased successively by 100% from the 1933 level (about RM 3 million). At the same time agreements were reached on Aussig's exports.[121] The contract was seen in a very positive light inside IG Farben[122], mainly because the last potentially serious competitor in Central and South-East Europe was thus bound to the cartel.[123]

The Netherlands accounted for 0.8% of world sales in 1938. 80% of this came from N.V. van Chemische Producten Vondelingenplaat, Schiedam, and 20% from Niederländische Farben- und Chemikalienfabrik, Delft.[124] Schiedam was one of the few producers that remained independent of the cartel – until the Netherlands was occupied by German troops. All the attempts to persuade Schiedam to join the cartel failed. The company bought the pre-products and raw materials it needed from the United States or Great Britain, where there were companies that only made pre-products and were not closely related to the cartel. IG Farben held 95.9% of Delft, and this company, like some of the following, came close to being no chemical producer of its own, since its main activity was now only preparing the dyyestuffs for the end-consumer, that is, mixing, reducing, bottling, and so on.

The following five countries accounted for 0.8% of world sales in 1938:

Spain:	Fabricacion Nacional de Colorantes y Explosivos, Barcelona (F.N.C.E.); Chimica Industrial Espanola SA Quiesa
Romania:	Colorom Chemische Fabrik R.A.O., Zeiden, Codlea
Bulgaria:	Coloriska S.A., Sofia
Greece:	SA Oeconomides & Co., Piraus
Brazil:	Cia de Productos Industriales M. Hamers S.A., Rio de Janeiro

117 Verein für chemische und metallurgische Produktion in Aussig, from 1939 in Prague, also known as the Aussiger or Prager Verein.

118 See Teichova, A. Internationale Kartelle und die chemische Industrie der Vormünchner Tschechoslowakei, in: Tradition 1972, pp. 143–175.

119 Vorträge Dr. Loehr, p. 8, HÖ 2508.

120 Sandoz historical archive, Kartellbeziehungen, no number.

121 Immediately after it came into force this agreement was used to exert pressure in the negotiations with the Polish companies, since they bought their pre-products mainly from the Three Party Cartel itself or from Aussig.

122 Vortrag Dr. Loehr, p. 15, HÖ 2508.

123 See Schröter, V., The IG Farbenindustrie AG in Central and South-East Europe, 1926–38, in: Teichova/Cottrell, International Business and Central Europe, 1918–1939, Leicester/New York 1983, pp. 139–172.

124 Kugler, p. 16.

IG Farben had a decisive influence on all of them through participations and/or agreements.

So the only major competitors on the world market were companies in the United States and Japan, since the Soviet Union did not export dyestuffs.[125] The Japanese dyestuffs industry was only in its beginning, and in 1938 3.2% of the world sales came from Japan, from the following firms:

Table 11. Japanese dyestuffs producers by sales values in 1938 in %[a)]

Nippon Senryo Saizo Kabushiki Kaisha, Osaka (N.S.K.)	60
Mitsui Bussan Kaisha Ltd., Tokyo Mitsui Kozan Kabushiki Kaisha, Tokyo/Miike }	20
Mitsubishi Dye Co., Tokyo	10
Others	10
	100

[a)] Kugler, p. 15; the figures for Japan are based on estimates, in my view (H.G.S.), not calculations, as in the other tables.

After some controversy over patents IG Farben and N.S.K. concluded cartel agreements in 1934 and 1935 on major dyestuffs groups. The companies of the China Six Party Agreements (the Four Party Cartel and Du Pont and Nacco, see below) signed a contract with Mitsui in 1935 dividing up indigo turnover. The agreement established relations between the European cartel system and Japan, regulating the important market segments for the product range and sales markets.[126] But this did not enable them to exert any influence on the further development of the industry in Japan. Unlike the new type of industry cartels in Europe, the agreements with Japan were traditional product agreements. In the United States conditions were similar, and here too the influence of the cartel was very much less than in Europe. IG Farben (General Aniline) and the Swiss IG (Cincinnati) were producing in the United States, but the biggest manufacturers there were Du Pont and Nacco (see above). Moreover, the legislation in the United States kept its firms out of the cartel agreements which otherwise applied worldwide.

However, this would not have prevented the US companies from concluding agreements on exports, as they did in other cases. In fact, IG Farben and Du Pont were negotiating very intensively during the first few months of 1929 on such an agreement.[127] But it did not prove possible to include this major producer in the cartel, and only gradually could agreements be reached on certain product and market groups. Dr. von Schnitzler commented on that point in his annual report for

[125] Interestingly, the Soviet Union did not approach the cartel, either, to request compensation payments for refraining from exporting, although it was quite successful with this in other fields, see Schröter, H.G., Kaliwirtschaft, pp. 53–57.

[126] Japan, China and the areas under Japanese influence, such as Korea, Manchuria, Formosa and so on, and Hong Kong as well.

[127] Letter of 16 April 1929, HÖ 303.

1932 as follows:[128] "Our major competitors are still the two American firms, Nacco and Du Pont. Now that internal American relations to these two concerns have been put on a friendly basis and the American dyestuffs business is largely conducted on the basis of Gentlemen's Agreements, a number of openings for exports have arisen, and during the last two years we have succeeded in concluding special agreements, particularly on the Chinese market, a good 80% of which is now governed by quota agreements with the Americans. The Americans are working freely on the other makkets, but with a large number of agreements of a loose nature to maintain the price level in the interests of all concerned. America's percentual share of world dyestuffs exports is remaining constant at about 8%, and no major changes are expected in the immediate future".

One of these "agreements of a loose nature" was the China Six Party Agreement mentioned above, and we can briefly outline it here as an example.[129] Under the leadership of IG Farben the Four Party Cartel and Du Pont and Nacco agreed in 1920 to observe price and quota arrangements for the main dyestuffs on the Chinese market, including Hong Kong. But as with the prolongation in 1934 a contract was not signed. Later, Dow Chemical, ACNA and Mitsui were directly or indirectly included through IG Farben.[130] The Four Party Cartel concluded similar agreements with Nacco in the mid-thirties for the Indian and Indonesian markets, and with Nacco and Du Pont for the Argentinian and Belgian markets, as IG Farben did with Du Pont. The US firms only supplied a few selected countries, so that these agreements regulated the main export markets. But since they all only covered specific products on specific markets – even if the most important of both – and quotas were not agreed in every case, although prices were, it is not possible to make an exact quantification of the US share of the regulation of the world dyestuffs market from the available material. Like the Japanese companies, the European type of comprehensive industry cartel could not be transferred to the United States, and the agreements remained specific product cartels.

The world dyestuffs market was not only regulated by written and informal quotas and price agreements, there were also flanking agreements on production renunciation, patents and technical assistance. Only a few companies could be induced to refrain from producing in return for compensation payments. The reason why the dyestuffs producers behaved differently on this point from the nitrogen producers, for instance, may be that dyestuffs offered far greater opportunities for profits than other sectors of the chemical industry. The few compensation agreements that are known were negotiated with IG Farben, but the other members of the cartel had to provide some of the funds. Characteristically, in all three cases other factors had to be taken into account in addition to dyestuffs sales: in the case of B. Schülde (see above) IG Farben practically had a monopoly of supplies of the pre-products needed. In the contract with von Heyden (takeover of Aussig in 1938)

---

128 Confidential memorandum to certain members of the Central Committee of IG Farben and to Professor Bosch, Professor Duisberg and Dr. v. Weinberg of 26 January 1933, p. 18, HÖ 110.

129 A full, if brief account is in Schröter, V., Weltmarkt, p. 310f.

130 In retrospect Kugler said: "The above agreements achieved a substantially complete regulation of competition in the China market, particularly in indigo, the most important single manufacturing type". (p. 35).

political motives played a part, while Norsk Hydro's later membership of the nitrogen cartel had to be taken into account.[131]

IG Farben also included clauses on exports in agreements on patents and technical assistance to facilitate the export market. As examples we can take the contract with N.S.K., which limited the company to exports to China, and that with Canadian Industries Ltd., which was only allowed to sell its entire production to one New York firm. However, these flanking agreements to the cartel were of only secondary importance in regulating the market.

It is interesting to see how IG Farben was at the centre of the network of agreements to regulate the dyestuffs market. A number of agreements were only negotiated and signed by it. The other cartel partners were then given a share according to their quotas.

The cartel agreements, especially those of the Three and Four Party cartels, had strict confidentiality clauses. Nevetheless, they did not, at least in their essentials, remain a secret from those who knew the industries for long. The exact extent of the agreements, however, was known only to a few, and on several occasions this proved a valuable source of information on movements by cartel outsiders. Mr. Jeffcott, head of the US Calco dyestuffs group, for instance, attempted to organise a technical exchange of experience outside the cartel, by visiting "all the firms and concerns in Europe that are free of cartels or which he thought were such – mainly ACNA, Rohner and Aussig. Rohner has fully informed us of what Mr. Jeffcott wanted...", as Dr. von Schnitzler in IG Farben commented.[132]

We are fortunate that material exists on the exact extent and relative importance of the cartels: in a long letter from IG Farben to the Reich Government on the peace plans in 1940 the share of the German economy in world dyestuffs production in 1938 is put at 27% (quantity) and 40% (value), with 55% of world exports.[133] In 1933 this was still around 60%.[134] These figures correspond with the following. (See table 12).

According to the list, 68.2% of the world sales in 1938 were to the account of the dyestuff cartels. Since some of the US and Japanese sales were also cartelised, the regulated share of the market, and so the degree of concentration, was certainly over 70%, and including the Gentlemen's Agreements, over 80%. Both are very cautious estimates.[135]

Most companies sold most of their output in their own countries and politically dependent territories, the big exceptions being Switzerland (exporting about 90%) and Germany (about 60%). For most of the smaller companies outside the cartels this

131 Schröter, H.G., Aussenpolitik, p. 290f.

132 Confidential report of 26 January 1933, p. 18, HÖ 110.

133 Strictly confidential report from IG Farben, signed by V. Schnitzler/Krüger, to a senior official in the Reich Ministry of Economics, Dr. Schlotterer, on 3 August 1940, reprinted in Eichholtz, D., Die IG Farben – Friedensplanung, in: Jahrbuch für Wirtschaftsgeschichte 1966, Part III, pp. 280ff.

134 Internal memorandum from the Dyestuffs Division Management of IG Farben to Dr. Struss, p. 1, 12 March 1934, HÖ 1094.

135 Tammens gives 61% (P. 33), but that may be quantities. Since his figure is given without reference figures – there are big differences between values and quantities – and without a year or source, it is not very helpful.

Table 12. Dyestuffs sales in 1938[a])

	in 1000 Gold marks	in %
IG Farben incl. Subsidiaries	319.241	46.0
Swiss IG incl. subsidiaries	73.934	10.6
C.M.C. incl. subsidiaries	29.438	4.2
Total for Three Party Cartel	422.613	60.8
I.C.I. incl. subsidiaries	31.832	4.6
Total for Four Party Cartel	454.445	65.4
Italian production	11.033	1.6
Polish production	4.341	0.6
Czech production	3.705	0.5
Total for Four Party Cartel with associated companies	473.524	68.2
US production without IG Farben subsidiariesb)	119.700	17.2
Soviet production	60.600	8.7
Japanese production	22.000	3.2
Holliday and British outsiders	6.500	0.9
Schiedam	4.30	0.6
Others	8.000	1.2
Total	694.754	100.0

[a]) Calculated and compiled from Kugler, p. 17.
[b]) This does not show whether the Cincinnati subsidiary of the Swiss IG is included in the figures for the parent company or not.

Table 13. Export shares on the Asian market in %[a])

Country of origin	1933	1937	1938
Germany	58.27	63.66	57.3
Switzerland and France	13.17	8.96	12.83
Total for Three Party Cartel	71.44	72.62	70.14
Great Britainb)	7.43	11.64	12.47
Approximate figure for Four Party Cartel	78.78	84.62	82.61
Czechoslovakia. Italy and Netherlands	1.32	0.75	0.80
Share under contract	80.19	85.01	83.41
USAc)	15.59	9.09	6.13
Japan	4.22	5.90	10.46
	100.00	100.00	100.00

[a]) Calculated and compiled from Kugler, p. 19.
[b]) Outsiders account for a small share of the GB figures
[c]) IG Farben's subsidiary was bound under contract not to export. It may be taken that there was a similar contract between the Swiss IG and Cincinnati.

tendency was even stronger. Consequently, the cartels had much bigger shares in world exports than in production. Since the main markets in Europe and the United States were largely protected by state and inner-industry measures, the main free export markets were in Asia and Latin America. The volume of dyestuffs sales to Asia was about RM 123 million in 1937, and RM 104 million in the crisis year 1938.[136] The individual export countries accounted for the following shares. (See table 13).

Since most of the US exports to Asia and a substantial part of the Japanese exports were also cartelised, the regulation of the Asian market must be assumed to have been much higher than shown here. For the Latin American market the corresponding figures were:

Table 14. Export shares on the Latin American market in %[a])

Country of origin	1933	1937	1938
Germany	71.1	63.8	59.9
Switzerland and France	17.8	22,0	25.2
Total of Three Party Cartel	88.9	85.8	85.1
Great Britain[b])	0.6	2.7	2.5
Approximate figure for Four Party Cartel	89.5	88.5	87.6
USA[c])	8.8	10.0	10.6
Others	1.7	1.5	1.8
	100.0	100.0	100.0

a) Kugler p. 20
b) See table 13
c) See table 13

The total volume of sales in Latin America in 1937 was RM 27 million, and in 1938 RM 25.9 million.[137] For Latin America the US producers were not tied into the cartel system to the same extent as for Asia, but here too the regulated part of the market must be assumed to have been higher than the figures in the table show. Europe was still the most important dyestuffs market, and here the position of the cartel was absolutely uncontested. It must be said to have been almost as strong on the world export market, since the Four Party Cartel accounted for about 90% in 1938 alone.[138] The 90% must include exports by companies that were tied directly or indirectly into the Three or Four Party Cartel. Very few of these contracts were dissolved or not prolonged before the outbreak of World War II.[139] The main build-

136 Calculated in current prices by Kugler, p. 19.
137 Calculated from Kugler, p. 19f.
138 Kugler, p. 34 (p. 33 on Tammen's figure of 88%), see Note 135.
139 They have deliberately been excluded here, but we can take the following as an example: the agreement of 1931 with Mitsui Bussan on sulphur black on the Chinese market was not prolonged

up of the dyestuffs cartels was concluded in 1932. The world slump may have accelerated this process, although it certainly did not cause it or even spark it off. The basic company strategies were decided in the early to mid-twenties.[140] A few major individual contracts were signed after 1933, and this phase only ended with the outbreak of the war. Until then there was no real decline in cartelisation and so no reduction in concentration.

Prices were not raised through cartelisation. The declared aim was to maintain the existing price level. That goal was fully realised, and even the outsiders held to the price network in the cartel system. The price level was such that 15 to 25% of the appropriate turnover in goods was paid in cash for renunciation of production and a virtual transfer of quotas. A large part of earnings, which were very substantial, were used to finance the very expensive research and development, for other products as well, in some cases[141], and the dyestuffs cartels are a good illustration of Helga Nussbaum's statement that there was a close connection between cartelisation and research.[142] Dr. ter-Meer[143] stressed that the dyestuffs cartels "protected the small producer", and that this proved its worth "particularly in times of sales crises".[144] That is indeed so, and it also underlines the general view put forward by Hans Otto Lenel on small companies and cartels.[145]

The concentration in the dyestuffs sector was already considerable in the twenties, and it rose considerably again as a result of cartelisation in the thirties. In Europe there was no company of any significance outside the Cartel. Worldwide, too, the main producers were largely bound in with the Three Party Cartel, the core of the European contract system of agreements. The Four Party Cartel controlled about 70% of world production and 90% of world exports. The inclusion of further elements, such as patents, supplies of pre-products and so on, enabled the Three Party Cartel particularly, and IG Farben and the Swiss IG as the major constituent parties, both of determine the supply to individual markets and affect the development chances of smaller firms. Until they de facto came to an end on the outbreak of World War II[146], the cartels were extremely successful, measured by their aims: regulation of quantities and prices on markets and access to these. The concentration only increased slightly during the second half of the thirties. But that it could reach so high a degree at all through cartelisation was not only a result of the specific

---

in 1933 at the request of the Japanese. As a result, sulphur black was released in 1937 in the China Six Party Agreement as well.

140 For a summary see Schröter, V., Weltmarkt, pp. 341–346.

141 Bürgin, pp. 253 and 256f.

142 Nussbaum, International Cartels, p. 139.

143 Dr. ter-Meer was a member of the Management Board of IG Farben.

144 ter-Meer, loc. cit., p. 73.

145 Lenel, Ursachen, p. 229. His statement (p. 230) that small companies were basically inferior to large companies in the cartel, since competition was shifted from production and sales to organisation and legal disputes does not, however, apply to the dyestuffs cartels. But an account of how the disputes were fought out would be beyond the scope of this article.

146 Some contracts remained formally in force and others, especially in the German occupied territories, continued to be effective right through the war.

features of the dyestuffs sector. Cartelisation generally in the chemical industry was very advanced, and other major agreements were in some cases a condition for participation in the dyestuffs cartel (e.g. in the case of I.C.I.), which conversely also had an effect on the development of these other agreements. The whole system of chemical cartels is one of the reasons for the firmness of the individual agreements, as well as for the remarkably high degree of concentration.

A Review of the New Literature on Business History*

Beate Brüninghaus**

Foreword

Yet again in 1987 there was a great interest in business history in the Federal Republic of Germany and this is not only evident in the large number and the high quality of the publications. The enterprises themselves have become aware that their history is part of the business culture and should be used to develop a corporate identity. A large number of commemorative publications from enterprises is also an indicator of a good economic situation. Considering the substantial time and financial effort involved, an enterprise's decision to produce such a commemorative paper is because of financial reasons certainly more easily made during an economic boom than during a period when the business has to concentrate all its efforts on overcoming a fall in sales. In addition to this an enterprise would probably prefer to write a "success story" than a history of a crisis. The continuous good economic conditions in the Federal Republic of Germany evidently provide a reason for the busy publication activity of enterprises for their jubilees, but also for publishers to publish business historical works written by scientists. With approximately 275 business history publications which appeared in 1987 there were published less than in the two preceding years, but there still was a continuation of the trend already apparent in the preceding years of an increasing number of business historical publications being written without an order from an enterprise. About 164 business historical papers resulted from a contract with an enterprise or association, 111 – more than ever before – were independent of such sponsorship. This clearly shows that business history enjoys increasing interest as part of a scientific discipline and has finally been able to assert itself. Once again a selection has had to be made of the publications on business history which appeared in 1987. The most important criterion for the choice was, as before, the value of their contribution to research work.

* Publications which appeared in 1987 in the Federal Republic of Germany, except from works on banking history which are mentioned in the article by Monika Pohle. For the rest reference is made to the bibliography which appears periodically in the "Zeitschrift für Unternehmensgeschichte" and which tries to consider all works on business history and biography.

** I have received much help in compiling the bibliography and obtaining the books. I am particularly grateful to Mrs. Erika Hermanns of the Institut der deutschen Wirtschaft in Cologne, Mr. Gerhard Alschner in Munich, Mr. Günther Berthmann of the Gesamtverband der Versicherungswirtschaft in Cologne as well as Mrs. Martina Mundorf of my staff. Finally I would like to thank my teacher Prof. Dr. Hans Pohl, University of Bonn, for his critical advice.

1. General Studies on Individual Industries

Knowledge of the sources in enterprises, Chambers of Commerce and associations is essential for business historical research. In this respect the revised edition of the Führer über deutsche Wirtschaftsarchive (Guide to German Economic Archives), which first appeared in 1978 and received an addendum in 1982, fills a gap.[1] This archives' guide contains more than 370 archives in enterprises, Chambers of Commerce and associations with a total of 1170 sources. The editors who published the reference book on behalf of the German Society for Business History are mainly experienced business archivists.

The Handbuch der europäischen Wirtschafts- und Sozialgeschichte (Handbook on European Economic and Social History) by the economic historian Wolfram Fischer from Berlin has finally been completed. Volume 6 which appeared in 1987 covers the period from the First World War to the present day.[2] As in the previous volumes it has been organized systematically and not according to political or military events. The economic part is of particular use to business historians who are concerned with publications on individual sectors within Europe, especially since it was written using an excellent basis of sources. The book is made easier to use by a register also for the hurried reader.

Students and colleagues published a three volume commemorative work on occasion of the 65th birthday of the economic historian Wolfgang von Stromer from Nuremberg.[3] It contains 46 contributions including two in French and one in Italian and covers the period from the 12th to the 19th century. The thematical emphasis is placed – as a result of von Stromer's particular research interests – on the trade and money movements in the late Middle Ages. Of relevance to business history are, strictly speaking, the contributions from Winfried Reichert on the traders in upper Italy and the mining entrepreneurs in the East of central Europe during the 14th century. Ekkehard Westermann examines the business links between the families of the Praun, Froler and Mulich from Nuremberg, Erfurt and Lübeck in the second half of the 15th century and Othmar Pickl the foreign traders and mining works of the Ze(i)ringers from Steiermark who became famous as large mining entrepreneurs in Nuremberg. The essay by István N. Kiss on the role of the farming traders in import and export within the Hungarian Kingdom from the 16th to the 18th century, that by Anton Spiesz on industry, business and trade in eastern Europe during the 18th century and Uwe Bestmann's analysis of Schumpeter's concept of an innovative entrepreneur using as example the innovative processes of the late Middle Ages are also of interest.

---

[1] Klara van Eyll/Beate Brüninghaus/Sibylle Grube-Bannasch et al. (Eds.), Deutsche Wirtschafts-Archive. Nachweis historischer Quellen in Unternehmen, Kammern und Verbänden der Bundesrepublik Deutschland, Vol. 1, 2nd entirely revised ed., Stuttgart (Steiner) 1987, 471 p.

[2] Wolfram Fischer (Ed.), Wirtschafts- und Sozialgeschichte vom Ersten Weltkrieg bis zur Gegenwart (= Handbuch der europäischen Wirtschafts- und Sozialgeschichte, Vol. 6), Stuttgart (Klett-Cotta) 1987, 1136 p.

[3] Uwe Bestmann/Franz Irsigler/Jürgen Schneider (Eds.), Hochfinanz, Wirtschaftsräume, Innovationen: Festschrift für Wolfgang von Stromer, Trier (Auenthal) 1987, Vol. 1: 570 p., Vol 2: 390 p., Vol. 3: 310 p.

In celebration of the 65th birthday of the economic historian Wolfgang Zorn from Munich, his colleagues and co-editors of the "Vierteljahrschrift für Sozial- und Wirtschaftsgeschichte" (Quarterly Journal for Social and Economic History) edited a commemorative work with 22 contributions.[4] Karl Erich Born's contribution on the Department of Economic- and Social History of the University of Tübingen, where several publications concerning business history, in particular the history of associations and banks, have been published, deals with business history in its narrower sense, an area Zorn has done important research work on. Wolfram Fischer writes on the relationship between business history and economic history and about the difficulties of accommodating micro- and macroeconomical aspects. Hans Pohl, Wolfgang Zorn's successor as professor in Bonn, shows in his survey of a quarter of a century of economic and social historical research at the Historisches Seminar der Universität Bonn (Historical Seminar at the University of Bonn) that there business history has increasingly become a main research topic in the last few years. Hans Jaeger's contribution on tendencies and perspectives of Augsburg's economic development, Wolfgang Zorn's birthplace, during the 19th and 20th century also provides several examples of business history. Jürgen Kocka compares German-American railway administrators during the Industrial Revolution and Wolfgang Köllmann describes the industrialist Friedrich Harkort from Westphalia. Joachim Riebartsch compares the equity capital and the state of enterprise in trading companies in Augsburg during the 15th and 16th century.[5] During this phase the Augsburg foreign traders were gripped by a new economic spirit which led to the introduction of several organizational innovations and foreign financing into the trading business. This thesis from Munich examines twelve trading companies from Augsburg, the development of which was always heavily influenced by the owner families. The emphasis of the investigation lies on the company contracts, the proprietor's capital and the accumulation of assets as shown in the tax volumes which are completely available for the 15th and 16th century.

The Hohenheim conference of the "Gesellschaft für Sozial- und Wirtschaftsgeschichte" (Society for Social and Economic History) in 1985 provided the proceedings edited by Hans Pohl on the influence of customs and other trading barriers on economy and society from the Middle Ages to the present day.[6] The detailed introduction by Hans Pohl and the 16 papers from mainly young German economic historians cover the topic chronologically and occasionally over-lap. There are two papers for the Middle Ages and two for the Early Modern Times. There are eight papers dedicated to the period from 1806 to 1914 and four papers covering the period

---

[4] Hermann Kellenbenz/Hans Pohl (Eds.), Historia socialis et oeconomica. Festschrift für Wolfgang Zorn zum 65. Geburtstag (= Vierteljahrschrift für Sozial- und Wirtschaftsgeschichte, Supp. 84), Stuttgart (Steiner) 1987, 369 p.

[5] Joachim Riebartsch, Augsburger Handelsgesellschaften des 15. und 16. Jahrhunderts. Eine vergleichende Darstellung ihres Eigenkapitals und ihrer Verfassung, Bergisch-Gladbach, Cologne (Eul) 1987, 441 p.

[6] Hans Pohl (Ed.), Die Auswirkungen von Zöllen und anderen Handelshemmnissen auf Wirtschaft und Gesellschaft vom Mittelalter bis zur Gegenwart. Referate der 11. Arbeitstagung der Gesellschaft für Sozial- und Wirtschaftsgeschichte vom 9. bis 13. April 1985 in Hohenheim (= Vierteljahrschrift für Sozial- und Wirtschaftsgeschichte, Supp. 80), Stuttgart (Steiner) 1987, 397 p.

from the end of the First World War to the present day. Gert Kollmer provides an approach, interesting for business history, where he follows the results and crises of the Tariff-Union using three micro-economic investigations from the southwest of Germany. The other contributions concentrate on the basic conditions for the development of enterprises and not on the specific effects on the enterprises.

A further conference provides the book on Policy and Effectiveness of the "Deutscher Industrie- und Handelstages (DIHT)" (German Industry- and Trade Association) and the Chambers of Commerce from 1861 to 1949, edited by Hans Pohl.[7] This symposium taking place in 1986 in Ludwigshafen should commemorate the 125th anniversary of the "DIHT". There were papers on the sources of the history of the "DIHT" by Klara van Eyll, Friedrich Peter Kahlenberg and Wilfried Reininghaus as well as contributions to the attitude of the "DIHT" to the economic and social policies from 1861 to 1914 by Harald Winkel, Friedrich-Wilhelm Henning, Hans Pohl and Karl Erich Born. The Chambers of Commerce during the re-building phase from 1945 to 1949 were covered by Dieter Schäfer, Diethelm Prowe, Franz Greiß and Jürgen Weise.

The Federal Republic of Germany also has, in addition to private and state enterprises, municipal enterprises owned by towns and communities. This tradition dates back about 2000 years and for the period from the Middle Ages to the present day it was covered by a conference of the German Society for Business History in Cologne in 1985.[8] Friedrich-Wilhelm Henning's paper reviews the municipal enterprises in the pre- and early industrial age and the following contributions deal with the period from the mid-19th century to the present day. Willi A. Boelcke describes the legal forms and the organizational structure of the municipal enterprises while Wilhelm Treue describes their co-operation with political committees. Dieter Burgholz is concerned with the economic development of markets, trade fairs and slaughter-houses, Gerold Ambrosius with gas-, water- and electricity works, Jakob Kandler with transport enterprises and Josef Wysocki with savings banks and pawn shops. The podium discussion on the future of municipal enterprises comes to the conclusion that also in the future they will exercise an indispensable function in the entrepreneurial landscape of the Federal Republic of Germany.

Karl M. Brousek reports in his handbook-like work, which reduces the extensive details to the point, on the Bohemian big industries from 1848 to 1918.[9] This work, which resulted from a project led by the historian Karl Bosl from Munich and sponsored by the "Deutsche Forschungsgemeinschaft" (German Research Association), is based on the analysis of Czechoslovakian literature, on reports of the

---

[7] Hans Pohl (Ed.), Zur Politik und Wirksamkeit des Deutschen Industrie- und Handelstages und der Industrie- und Handelskammern 1861 bis 1949. Referate und Diskussionsbeiträge eines Symposiums aus Anlaß des 125jährigen Bestehens des Deutschen Industrie- und Handelstages am 1. Oktober 1986 in Ludwigshafen am Rhein (= Zeitschrift für Unternehmensgeschichte, Supp. 53), Stuttgart (Steiner) 1987, 158 p.

[8] Hans Pohl (Ed.), Kommunale Unternehmen. Geschichte und Gegenwart. Referate und Diskussionsbeiträge des 9. Wissenschaftlichen Symposiums der Gesellschaft für Unternehmensgeschichte e.V. am 17./18. Januar 1985 in Köln (= Zeitschrift für Unternehmensgeschichte, Supp. 42), Stuttgart (Steiner) 1987, 254 p.

[9] Karl M. Brousek, Die Großindustrie Böhmens: 1848–1918 (= Veröffentlichungen des Collegium Carolinum, 50), Munich (Oldenbourg) 1987, 223 p.

Chambers of Trade and Commerce as well as on reports of trade-supervisors. The original plan to include middle-sized business in this study, too, could not be carried out due to the state of the sources. A register of companies and people increases the usability.

In German publications on business history little attention is paid to tax legislation as well as to financial history probably because of the complexity of the material. With his work on corporate income tax in the period from 1918 to 1929[10] Thomas Brinkmann therefore enters an area which is important for entrepreneurial decisions and which has hardly been dealt with up to now. Corporate income tax was first legally introduced as a tax together with the Erzberger finance and tax reform in 1920 after vehement disputes. The author investigates the conditions and the motives for the emergence of this tax, its first unsuccessful trial period during and due to inflation and finally the re-organization of the bill and the real test between 1925 and 1929. Unfortunately the effect of the tax on enterprises is not touched in this study, too, since it emphasizes the legal and fiscal aspects.

The labour movement in the Weimar Republic is comparatively well researched. Heinrich Potthoff analyses the free union top level, the "Allgemeiner Deutscher Gewerkschaftsbund" (ADGB) (General Association of German Unions) in the years 1918 to 1933.[11] The investigation includes the organizational structure, labour market, wages and social policies of the association and the relationship of the ADGB to its political environment. The central theme of this work, which is mainly based on the union files of the Institut für soziale Demokratie (Institute for Social Democracy) in Berlin, is the proceeding of the free unions seen in context with the social relationships and the political structures during the first German republic. A register eases searching in the extensive presentation.

The proceedings of the conference on the Weimar Republic as a welfare state[12], edited by the economic- and social historian Werner Abelshauser from Bochum, and resulting from a project supported by the "Deutsche Forschungsgemeinschaft", are also concerned with the unions in the Weimar Republic. The title of this book is inasmuch slightly misleading as some of the papers do not refer to the welfare state at all. Of relevance to entrepreneurial history in its narrower sense are the papers by Michael Ruck on public building policies and by Michael Drupp on non-profit-making building associations. Johannes Bähr reports on the arbitration system, Dieter Schiffmann on the state as employer and mediator and Reinhard Neebe adds comments on the relationship between capital and labour during the international economic crisis.

Wolfgang Spohn describes the legal and institutional regulation of labour relations in the NS-State and in this context compares the business community to the

---

[10] Thomas Brinkmann, Die Körperschaftssteuer in der Zeit von 1918 bis 1929. Ein Beitrag zur Geschichte der Unternehmensbesteuerung (= Wirtschafts- und Rechtsgeschichte, 6), Cologne (Müller Botermann) 1987, 240 p.

[11] Heinrich Potthoff, Freie Gewerkschaften 1918–1933. Der Allgemeine Deutsche Gewerkschaftsbund in der Weimarer Republik (= Beiträge zur Geschichte des Parlamentarismus und der politischen Parteien, 82), Düsseldorf (Droste) 1987, 435 p.

[12] Werner Abelshauser (Ed.), Die Weimarer Republik als Wohlfahrtsstaat. Zum Verhältnis von Wirtschafts- und Sozialpolitik in der Industriegesellschaft (= Vierteljahrschrift für Sozial- und Wirtschaftsgeschichte, Supp. 81), Stuttgart (Steiner) 1987, 337 p.

community of the people.[13] The author, who supports a marxist view, is mainly concerned with the legal and political situation and less with the concrete operational facts. As basic sources he i.a. uses files from the Federal Archives (Bundesarchiv) in Koblenz, the Institut für Zeitgeschichte (Institute for Contemporary History) in Munich, the Welt-Wirtschafts-Archiv (World Economic Archives) in Hamburg and the Institut für Weltwirtschaft (Institute for World Economy) in Kiel.

The economic historian Fritz Blaich from Regensburg, who died in 1988, presented with his book on the economy in the Third Reich[14] the first volume of a series in which well-known authors introduce into the problems and the state of research and submit the most important sources. This didactical series is therefore aimed at both teachers and generally interested people. Blaich goes into the research topic in a short but precise introduction and after the part on the sources, which in some cases also includes rarely published documents, he reports on the research theses. Thereby he supports the thesis of the pre-eminence of politics, stressing however, that there was a far-reaching identity of interests between politics and economy.

As a result of the archives' opening, the post-war period has in the meantime developed into a central theme of historical research in the Federal Republic of Germany. In his thesis on economy and labour in East Germany 1945–1949[15] written under Dietmar Petzina in Bochum, Wolfgang Zank looks into reconstruction in the Soviet occupied territory. It is pleasing that the author, at the same time historian and economic scientist, does take a look not only limited to one branch of knowledge, in this field of research up to now mainly covered by social scientists. The basis of his paper is provided by sources from the archives of the Federal Republic of Germany – he had no access to the archives of the GDR – and literature.

In Bochum Dietmar Petzina has also supervised the thesis of Werner Plumpe on economic administration and entrepreneurial associations in the British zone.[16] This theme, which until now had rarely been dealt with, is covered by the author using sources from the Public Record Office in London, the Federal Archives in Koblenz and the Central Public Record Office (Hauptstaatsarchiv) in Düsseldorf. Since he had no access to sources of the associations he had to forgo an analysis of the internal structure. Above all Plumpe studies the reality of rationing and control of economy, the planning and the distribution. He shows that very soon after the end of the war the entrepreneurial associations and the Chambers of Commerce gained such a strong influence on the administration of the economy and the rationing practice that they were able to exert a veto position in case private economic interests were not sufficiently taken into account.

---

[13] Wolfgang Spohn, Betriebsgemeinschaft und Volksgemeinschaft. Die rechtliche und institutionelle Regelung der Arbeitsbeziehungen im NS-Staat, Berlin (Quorum) 1987, 507p.

[14] Fritz Blaich, Wirtschaft im "Dritten Reich" (= Historisches Seminar, 1), Düsseldorf (Schwann) 1987, 159 p.

[15] Wolfgang Zank, Wirtschaft und Arbeit in Ostdeutschland 1945–1949. Probleme des Wiederaufbaus in der Sowjetischen Besatzungszone Deutschlands (= Studien zur Zeitgeschichte, 31), Munich (Oldenbourg) 1987, 214 p.

[16] Werner Plumpe, Vom Plan zum Markt: Wirtschaftsverwaltung und Unternehmerverbände in der britischen Zone (= Düsseldorfer Schriften zur neueren Landesgeschichte und zur Geschichte Nordrhein-Westfalens, 22), Düsseldorf (Schwann) 1987, 364 p.

The law of co-determination in the coal, iron and steel industry ratified in 1951 is considered to be the most important socio-political innovation in the history of the Federal Republic of Germany. It was the legalization of an agreement reached in 1946/47 which guaranteed the employees' representation in the management boards of those factories of the iron and steel industry in the British zone which were about to be decentralized. Gloria Müller's work on co-determination in the post-war era[17] investigates the conditions, the political constellations and the reasons which led to the introduction of co-determination in the iron and steel industry at the end of 1946 and why a similar agreement was impeded outside this branch. The sources for this publication, which has been made easier to use through a register of persons, come from numerous business-, trade-union- and State archives and from interviews.

More recent investigations have found that impulses for supporting employment increasingly come from small and middle-sized companies, whereas in the last years big enterprises increasingly reduce their labour force. This development was investigated by the German Society for Business History on a conference, the papers and discussions of which have been published now.[18] The economic and social historian Karl Heinrich Kaufhold from Göttingen describes the contribution of middle-sized industries to the solving of employment problems from industrialization to the mid-20th century and the economist Horst Albach from Bonn examines the same question for the Federal Republic of Germany. Although both papers look at the question mainly from a macro-economic perspective, and, owing to the lack of suitable research works, have to concentrate on the basic theses of the development, they nevertheless provide an important contribution to the history of middle-sized businesses.

There are only few studies on the shareholders of joint-stock companies. In his work on the development of the shareholder structure of German joint-stock companies quoted at the stock exchange[19], Bernhard Iber looks at the period from 1963 to 1983 both theoretically and empirically. The basis for his hypotheses on the relationship between the shareholder structure and its influence, is the development in the 300 largest enterprises. He comes to the conclusion that the proportion of enterprises with a qualified majority of shareholders has considerably increased whilst the number of enterprises mainly in the hands of family members has greatly decreased.

The economic and social historian Willi A. Boelcke from Stuttgart has written an economic history of Baden-Württemberg from the Roman Ages until the present

---

[17] Gloria Müller, Mitbestimmung in der Nachkriegszeit. Britische Besatzungsmacht, Unternehmer, Gewerkschaften (= Düsseldorfer Schriften zur neueren Landesgeschichte und zur Geschichte Nordrhein-Westfalens, 21), Düsseldorf (Schwann) 1987, 314 p.

[18] Hans Pohl (Ed.), Mittelstand und Arbeitsmarkt. Löst der Mittelstand die Beschäftigungsprobleme der deutschen Wirtschaft? Referate und Diskussionsbeiträge der 11. Öffentlichen Vortragsveranstaltung der Gesellschaft für Unternehmensgeschichte e.V. am 10.6.1986 in München (= Zeitschrift für Unternehmensgeschichte, Supp. 49), Stuttgart (Steiner) 1987, 109 p.

[19] Bernhard Iber, Entwicklung der Aktionärsstruktur börsennotierter deutscher Aktiengesellschaften. Eine theoretische und empirische Analyse für den Zeitraum 1963–1983 (= Kieler Schriften zur Finanzwirtschaft, 1), Kiel (Wissenschaftsverlag Vauk) 1987, 288 p.

day.[20] In doing this he tries to combine both macro- and micro-economic points of view so that he often even refers to the enterprises themselves. This makes the study also of use for the business history. Unfortunately there are no footnotes which is a pity in view of the numerous new details e.g. from the area of business history. However the volume has been completed in an exemplary manner with a register of subjects, companies and people.

There are thirteen contributions in the omnibus volume resulting from a lecture series of the Berlin Chamber of Commerce entitled "Berlin und seine Wirtschaft" (Berlin and its Economy)[21]. The essay by Rudolf von Thadden on the integration problems of the Huguenots in Prussia and Berlin, the essay by Karl Heinrich Kaufhold on the Prussian mercantilism and Berlin entrepreneurs and the essay by Wolfram Fischer on the Prussian residency Berlin on its way to an industrial town all touch questions of business history. In addition Tilmann Buddensieg describes Berlin as a location of great industrial architecture, Thomas Nipperdey looks into the organization of sciences and their relations to the economy, and Werner Knopp deals with private art sponsorship. Jürgen Kocka writes on the relationship between entrepreneurs and the state during the First World War, and Wolfgang Schieder on state and economy during the Third Reich. A subject- and name register improve the use of the contributions which have been well matched.

On the occasion of the 100th anniversary of the Industrie-Club, founded in Hanover by the Factory Owners' Association in 1887[22], Dieter Tasch, a journalist has dealt with the economy in Hanover. Although this presentation does not claim to be scientific it is based on two years of careful research, i.a. in the municipal archives (Stadtarchiv) of Hanover and on the interpretation of literature. The text has been sensibly enhanced by good and well-commented photographs.

2. Studies on Individual Sectors

2.1 Mining

In his thesis written under Wolfgang Weber in Bochum, Peter Piasecki studies invention, innovation and diffusion in the German saline industry in the years 1550 to 1650.[23] Taken altogether 161 innovations were collected and classified, and with the exception of new establishments they were all connected with the terms energy and use of energy. This historical investigation into diffusion shows that after a phase of stagnation lasting until about 1570, there was an innovative push in the last third

[20] Willi A. Boelcke, Wirtschaftsgeschichte Baden-Württembergs von den Römern bis heute, Stuttgart (Theiss) 1987, 725 p.

[21] Industrie- und Handelskammer zu Berlin (Ed.), Berlin und seine Wirtschaft. Ein Weg aus der Geschichte in die Zukunft – Lehren und Erkenntnisse, Berlin (de Gruyter) 1987, 253 p.

[22] Dieter Tasch, Ein Jahrhundert hannoverscher Wirtschaft. Vom Fabrikanten-Verein zum Industrie-Club 1887–1987, ed. by Industrie-Club Hannover e.V., Hanover (publ. by the ed.) 1987, 197 p.

[23] Peter Piasecki, Das deutsche Salinenwesen (1550–1650). Invention, Innovation, Diffusion (= Wissenschaftliche Schriften, Series 9: Geschichtswissenschaftliche Beiträge, 104), Idstein (Schulz-Kirchner) 1987, 387 p.

of the sixteenth century which in particular extended to graduation methods. Several municipal and State archives as well as archives from General Mining Offices were analysed for this study.

The salt mining in Lüneburg has often been object of scientific research. Ulrich Hennings, born in Lüneburg, in his Freiburg legal-historical thesis[24], which is based on sources from several archives, describes the development of the Lüneburg salt monopolies granted in the 10th century for the production and the sale of salt. The economic decline of the salt mining in Lüneburg began in the 17th century and increased in the 18th century due to the repeated violations of the monopoly by salt imports. After 1830 the freedom of trade meant the final downfall of the Lüneburg monopolies and competition from home and abroad.

On occasion of the founding of the first mining office in the Ruhr coal-mining industry 250 years ago, the Märkish Mining Office in Bochum, Karl-Heinz Bader and Karl Röttger have published a study of the Märkish pit-coal mining industry which is limited to the present Bochum city area.[25] The publication provides a detailed chronicle of mining, in which all mines and collieries with more than 100 employees are listed and documents reprinted. A glossary on mining and geology helps to understand the specialist mining language. In addition to this the volume is completed by a register of people and subjects which also includes companies.

Coal mining in Ibbenbüren, south of Osnabrück, can be traced back to 1492. Hubert Rickelmann and Hans Röhrs have described the pit-coal mining in Ibbenbüren from the beginning till today.[26] This book, which was first published in 1983 and has now been revised, provides statistics for the annual output of the colliery now belonging to the Preussag, since 1758. Much space has been dedicated to the mining working- and social world. The detailed description is completed by photos, maps and a dictionary of the miners' language.

The thesis by Cäcilia Schmitz from Hamburg is concerned with the role of mining enterprises during the spread of towns in the industrialization era, using Gelsenkirchen as an example.[27] This work, which is based on mining companies' files in the Mining Archives of the German Mining Museum, has chosen Gelsenkirchen as a particularly typical town for the mid-Ruhr area. It is shown that the relationship between mining enterprises and the town was not without tension, a fact becoming evident especially when building company-dwellings.

Ernst Klein, the economic historian from Saarbrücken, has written a scientific history completed by tables of the pit-coal colliery Sulzbach-Altenwald in the period

---

24 Ulrich Hennings, Die Lüneburger Salzmonopole. Entwicklung und Niedergang (= Historische Forschungen, 21), Rheinfelden (Schäuble) 1987, 161 p.

25 Karl-Heinz Bader/Karl Röttger, 250 Jahre märkischer Steinkohlenbergbau. Ein Beitrag zur Geschichte des Bergbaus, der Bergverwaltung und der Stadt Bochum, Bochum (Studienverlag Brockmeyer) 1987, 232 p.

26 Hubert Rickelmann/Hans Röhrs, Der Ibbenbürener Steinkohlenbergbau. Von den Anfängen bis zur Gegenwart, 2nd revised ed., Paderborn (Schöningh) 1987, 350 p.

27 Cäcilia Schmitz, Bergbau und Verstädterung im Ruhrgebiet: die Rolle der Bergwerksunternehmen in der Industrialisierung am Beispiel Gelsenkirchen (= Der Anschnitt, 5) (= Veröffentlichungen aus dem Deutschen Bergbau-Museum Bochum, 39), Bochum (Deutsches Bergbaumuseum) 1987, 104 p.

from 1841 to 1932.[28] Unlike other collieries in the Saar territory this one was, from the beginning, state-owned and it was run directly by civil servants, although all important questions were decided by higher ranks. In his publication, which is based on material from the State Archives in Saarbrücken, Klein notes technical and economical aspects, social points are hardly mentioned.

Klaus Klemp's art historical master-work is concerned with the architecture of the administrative office of the colliery Dr. Geier.[29] This magnificent building, constructed in 1916, is one of the most impressive technical monuments of the mining industry which is also well illustrated by the numerous photos in the book. The manganese ore colliery in the Hunsrück and the Binger forest has stopped mining in 1971. The introduction to this work contains a historical summary of ore mining in the Hunsrück and in the Binger forest.

2.2 Energy

The bibliography on the history of energy production in Germany, edited by the economic and social historian Hugo Ott from Freiburg, provides a survey of the literature which since the 18th century[30] has appeared on the topic of energy production and -application. It arose as part of a project on historical statistics sponsored by the "Deutsche Forschungsgemeinschaft" dealing with the energy statistics for Freiburg. It contains 10,664 titles from the 18th century till 1985. A key-word register, a register of people and companies and a geographical register help finding the publications which also include numerous commemorative publications.

Thomas Herzig's very detailed thesis on the history of the electricity supply in the Saarland with special consideration of the Vereinigte Saar-Elektrizitäts-AG, was also written in Freiburg under Hugo Ott.[31] Electrical energy was first used in the industrial area of the Saar around 1880 as a result of an initiative of the private sector and the Prussian mining directorate. Herzig, as temporary employee of the company, had access to the company's archives from which he used a lot of material. In addition to this he has also visited numerous public archives and he has produced a very good business historical report.

For the 75th foundation anniversary of the Kaiser-Wilhelm-Institut for Coal Research, Manfred Rasch, historian at this institute, which meanwhile has been

[28] Ernst Klein, Geschichte der saarländischen Steinkohlengrube Sulzbach-Altenwald (1841–1932) (= Veröffentlichungen der Kommission für Saarländische Landesgeschichte und Volksforschung, 16), Saarbrücken (Minerva) 1987, 152 p.

[29] Klaus Klemp, Grube Dr. Geier. Monument des deutschen Erzbergbaus, Biebertal (im Biebertal) 1987, 167 p.

[30] Hugo Ott (Ed.), Bibliographie zur Geschichte der Energiewirtschaft in Deutschland. Eine Übersicht der seit dem 18. Jahrhundert zur Energieerzeugung und –verwendung erschienenen Literatur (= Historische Energiestatistik von Deutschland, 3), St. Katharinen (Scripta Mercaturae) 1987, 60 p.

[31] Thomas Herzig, Geschichte der Elektrizitätsversorgung des Saarlandes unter besonderer Berücksichtigung der Vereinigten Saar-Elektrizitäts-AG. Ein Beitrag zur Wirtschaftsgeschichte des Saarlandes (= Veröffentlichungen der Kommission für saarländische Landesgeschichte und Volksforschung, 17), Saarbrücken (Minerva) 1987, 414 p.

renamed into Max-Planck-Institut for Coal Research in Mülheim on the Ruhr, has written a publication on the background and foundation of this institute, illustrated with several photos and documents.[32] In this publication he shows the massive influence of the mining industry on the foundation of this institute. His study is based on extensive papers of the former Chief Mayor of Mülheim, Dr. Lembke, who had obviously watched the foundation of the Coal Research Institute with particular interest.

With the commemorative publication on the occasion of the 50th birthday of the Union Kraftstoff in Wesseling, Hans-Josef Joest, historian and journalist for an economic newspaper, has produced a well-written publication with many facts on the petrochemical industry in the area between Cologne and Bonn.[33] The hydrogenation plant, coming into existence in 1937 because of state pressure, was meant to secure the German mineral oil production on the basis of national mineral resources. According to the model of Leuna, where the IG Farben combine produced petrol from lignite since 1927, further hydrogenation plants were planned although this process was too expensive.

2.3 Metals

Johann Paul in his thesis, written in 1984 under Otto Dann in Cologne and revised there, studies the tense relationship between Alfred Krupp and the employees of his business during the critical years 1872–1879.[34] Using material from the Historical Archives of the Fried. Krupp GmbH in Essen and other archives, Paul from an indeological perspective describes the historical process of the development of the classes in detail, and he comes to the conclusion that at that time unification of the class structure was already advanced. However it was not until 1879 that the labour movement in Essen could send one of its representatives to the Reichstag, a fact Alfred Krupp had until then successfully been able to prevent. Paul turns towards the thesis that the "Kruppianer" were integrated and non-political on account of the extensive company welfare, but his argumentation does not convince.

The economic and social historian Jürgen Brockstedt from Berlin has published a paper on the history of the Husum iron factory in the period from 1852 to 1954.[35] Central points of this publication are the memoirs of the entrepreneur P.W. Matz which are printed and commented on. Between 1896 and 1914 the enterprise experienced its economic culminate; it was dissolved in 1954. Based on archives'

---

32 Manfred Rasch, Vorgeschichte und Gründung des Kaiser-Wilhelm-Instituts für Kohlenforschung in Mülheim a.d. Ruhr (= Zeitschrift des Geschichtsvereins Mülheim a.d. Ruhr, 60), Hagen (v.d. Linnepe) 1987, 214 p.

33 Hans-Josef Joest, Kraftakte. Ein halbes Jahrhundert Union Kraftstoff in Wesseling, Düsseldorf/Vienna/New York (Econ) 1987, 109 p.

34 Johann Paul, Alfred Krupp und die Arbeiterbewegung (= Düsseldorfer Schriften zur Neueren Landesgeschichte und zur Geschichte Nordrhein-Westfalens, 19), Düsseldorf (Patmos-Schwann) 1987, 300 p.

35 Jürgen Brockstedt, Husumer Eisenwerk. Mittelständisches Unternehmertum in einer Agrarregion 1852–1954 (= Schriften des Kreisarchivs Nordfriesland Schloß vor Husum, 9), Husum (Husum) 1987, 72 p.

material Brockstedt describes the history of a middle-sized industrial enterprise in a region strongly influenced by agriculture. The publication has been sensibly supplemented by tables on the number of employees and on the amount and value of production.

On the occasion of the 100th anniversary of the wire weaving mill and machine factory Haver & Boecker in Oelde in Westphalia, Toni Pierenkemper and Richard Tilly, economic historians from Münster, have presented a history of this enterprise.[36] They have tried to picture this family enterprise in comparison with the development of the whole industry of wire weaving mills. The history is based on material from the company itself, interviews, newspaper reports and literature and it has been supplemented by photos and tables.

The graduate engineer Hans Pischel has written a techno-historical study on the history of massive- and sheet metal reforming from antiquity to the present time.[37] It describes in detail the different presses for metal reforming. Interesting for business history is the description of the development of mechanical engineering shown at the example of the machine factory Siempelkamp which was founded in Krefeld in 1883 and originally produced presses for the silk industry. In view of the diversity of the facts presented the subject register is helpful.

Wolfgang-Ulrich Prigge has published a system-theoretical study on the employers' associations in the metal industry in Great Britain and the Federal Republic of Germany which is the revised version of a sociological habilitation paper.[38] Prigge is investigating virgin territory inasmuch as there are hardly any recent research works on the employers' associations or on the industrial labour relations allowing a comparison between different countries. Although the emphasis of this work lies on the present situation the historical development is also described. Sources for the work are scientific literature publications and discussions.

2.4 Mechanical Engineering

To mark the 5oth anniversary of the Zahnradfabrik Friedrichshafen in Gmünd, Gerd Noetzel, professor at the College of Education in Schwäbisch Gmünd, has presented a commemorative paper, based entirely on sources.[39] Each source is reproduced in detailwhile the interpretation and its classification into literature comes off badly. This work which on the whole is more of local historical value, is also of over-regional interest because it shows what efforts the national socialistic settlement policies undertook to convince industrial enterprises of the value of a new location.

---

[36] Toni Pierenkemper/Richard Tilly, Die Geschichte der Drahtweberei. Dargestellt am Beispiel der Firma Haver & Boecker, Oelde aus Anlaß des einhundertjährigen Bestehens 1887–1987 (= Zeitschrift für Unternehmensgeschichte, Supp. 51), Stuttgart (Steiner) 1987, 142 p.

[37] Hans Pischel, Geschichte des Massiv- und Blechumformens, Kleve (Boss) 1987, 243 p.

[38] Wolfgang-Ulrich Prigge, Metallindustrielle Arbeitgeberverbände in Großbritannien und in der Bundesrepublik Deutschland – eine systemtheoretische Studie (= Forschungstexte Wirtschafts- und Sozialwissenschaften, 18), Opladen (Leske + Budrich) 1987, 319 p.

[39] Gerd Noetzel, Vom Notstandsgebiet Schwäbisch Gmünd und den hiesigen Anfängen der Zahnradfabrik Friedrichshafen AG. Eine Darstellung aus zeitgenössischen Gmünder Quellen (= Gmünder Hochschulreihe, 2), Schwäbisch-Gmünd 1987, 266 p.

August Borsig was the founder of what was once the most important industrial business in Prussia. In addition to locomotives the Berlin enterprise also produced steam engines and later vacuum cleaners. In commemoration of the company's 150th anniversary Helmut Lindner and Jörg Schmalfuß, employees of the newly founded Museum for Transport and Technology in Berlin, have written a history of the enterprise, supplemented by numerous excellent illustrations. It concentrates on the technological history and the period after the turn of the century.[40] In Borsig's former factory building, now owned by the Museum for Transport and Technology which also took over parts of the Borsig archives, there now is a permanent exhibition on Borsig.

Ulla Galm has presented a well-written biography on August Borsig[41] who is considered to be one of the most impressive personalities of the Berlin economic life at the beginning of the Industrial Revolution. The basis for this work is the Borsig archives, which in addition to the Museum for Transport and Technology can also be found at the Deutsche Babcock in Berlin. This chronologically arranged publication is completed by a name register.

Babara Kasper, Lothar Schuster and Christof Watkinson are concerned with a dark capital of business history which usually is only briefly covered in most official commemorative publications. In their book on German and foreign workers in the armament production at Rheinmetall-Borsig between 1943 and 1945[42] they have interviewed 11 former Borsig workers including a Russian, two Dutchmen and a Polish woman. Based on these not very representative statements, which are supplemented by only rather meagre archives' material, the authors attempt to give a picture of the labour situation in the armament production of Rheinmetall-Borsig during the final stage of the Second World War.

2.5 Shipbuilding

Günter Stavorinus's thesis, written under Heinrich Volkmann at the Free University of Berlin, on the royal/imperial Danzig shipyard during the period from 1844 to 1918[43], is based on several decades of business experience in the shipping industry and on a study of political economy. The work is based on the file Kaiserliche Werft Danzig, which now is to be found in the Geheimes Staatsarchiv Preußischer Kulturbesitz Berlin (Secret State Archives of Prussian Cultural Possession), and on files from the Federal Archives/Military Archives Freiburg. The foundation of a fleet was not only a wish of the state but trade and industry also strived for it. Danzig

---

40 Helmut Lindner/Jörg Schmalfuß, 150 Jahre Borsig (= Berliner Beiträge zur Technikgeschichte und Industriekultur: Schriftenreihe des Museums für Verkehr und Technik Berlin, 7), Berlin (Nicolaische Verlagsbuchhandlung) 1987, 204 p.

41 Ulla Galm, August Borsig (= Preußische Köpfe. Industrie, 18), Berlin (Stapp) 1987, 143 p.

42 Barbara Kasper/Lothar Schuster/Christof Watkinson (Eds.), Arbeiten für den Krieg: Deutsche und Ausländer in der Rüstungsproduktion bei Rheinmetall-Borsig 1943–1945, Hamburg (VSA) 1987, 115 p.

43 Günter Stavorinus, Die königliche/kaiserliche Werft Danzig. Ein Beitrag zur Geschichte der Marine und der Schiffbauindustrie in Westpreußen 1844–1918, Berlin, Univ., thesis, 1987, 400 p.

was originally intended to be a provisional location but finally this proved to be wrong. Central points of the publication are on the one hand macro-economical aspects such as the influence of the arming of the navy on the regional and national economy while on the other hand micro-economical facts such as the shipyard personnel and the wages are described in detail.

Within a project to the history of ship-building revised at the University of Bremen, Hartmut Roder, a Bremen historian, has written a two volume work on the Bremer Vulkan AG.[44] The first part describes the enterprise's development from 1893 to 1914, the second part the period from 1914 to 1933. The short text which is based on material from the company archives, is supplemented by photos. The publication concentrates on production, whereas the social history is only briefly touched.

The two volume publication from Peter Kuckuk, historian and chief of the project on the Bremer Werft A.G. Weser resulted from the same project and it also makes a temporary cut with the beginning of the First World War.[45] The co-workers of this project try to link the historiography from "above", from the view of the managing level, with that from "below", from the employees' point of view, because they want to classify both kinds of historiography into the economical, technical, socio-historical and political events and structures. Neither of the publications resulting from this project has, however, met this high claim, probably because of the sources, since the company archives used by both Roder and Kuckuk appear to contain only little material on the labour force.

2.6 Production of Road Vehicles and Aircraft

In 1987 there once again were numerous new books on the history of the motor car. The journalist Horst Mönnich presents the second volume of his history of the Munich motor car company BMW, covering the period from 1945 to 1972.[46] This book which is based on research in the company archives and on interviews with contemporaries remains easily readable although it contains lots of details. For decisive stages of the company history also different interpretations are given as, for example, that of the chairman of the works council on the take-over of the majority of shares by Quandt. The book has subject and name register for easy reference.

When the old Bremen motor car company Borgward went bankrupt in 1961, it was the largest bankruptcy in the Federal Republic of Germany. In their very readable publication the authors Wilhelm Eberwein and Jochen Tholen, economists and social scientists at the University of Bremen, inquire into the trade-unions' view

---

[44] Hartmut Roder, Der Bremer Vulkan. Part 1: Von der Johann-Lange-Werft zum Bremer Vulkan 1893–1914, Part 2: Schiffbau und Werftarbeit in Vegesack 1914–33, both parts Bremen (Steintor) 1987, 48 p.

[45] Peter Kuckuk, Die A.G. "Weser". Part 1: Bis 1914. Von der Maschinenfabrik Waltjen & Leonhardt zur Großwerft, Part 2: 1914–1933. Vom Weltkrieg zur Weltwirtschaftskrise, both parts Bremen (Steintor) 1987, 48 p.

[46] Horst Mönnich, BMW – Eine Jahrhundertgeschichte, Vol. 2: Der Turm: 1945–1972, Düsseldorf (Econ) 1987, 259 p.

of the end of Borgward and of the crisis with the miscarried attempt at an agreement preceding the bankruptcy.[47] In addition to structural weaknesses they testify to those responsible economic-political and entrepreneurial dilettantism. As sources there were used materials from the Public Record Office Bremen, the Radio Archives in Bremen and an inquiry of all the residents of the Borgward settlement in Bremen-Arbergen.

One year after the company's 100th anniversary nine authors with different educational background have presented a history of the Daimler-Benz AG from their point of view.[48] The volume, edited by the Stiftung für Sozialgeschichte des 20. Jahrhunderts (Foundation for 20th Century Social History) in Hamburg contains essays which are of extremely different quality and often even contradict each other. The contribution provoking most opposition, both from the methodical and objective aspect, is by the director of the Hamburger Stiftung, the physician Karl Heinz Roth. His paper, which argues from the marxist view, presents the armament combine as agent of the Deutsche Bank, having made a vital contribution to the existence of the Nazi dictatorship and from this time participating in the policy of the Third Reich. Other contributions such as the one on forced labour have a much more solid basis and provide interesting details – some of which are verified by partly new sources from national and foreign archives – of the discussion on forced labour, which has been revived in the Federal Republic of Germany since the beginning of 1986.

In an additional volume from the Stiftung für Sozialgeschichte des 20. Jahrhunderts in Hamburg, the most important documents on the history of the Daimler-Benz combine in the years 1928 to 1948 have been printed and are briefly commented in the appendix.[49] Even if the sources exhibited do by no means support all the theses of the first volume, here some only hardly accessible sources, e.g. from archives of the German Democratic Republic, on the relationship of the Deutsche Bank to Daimler Benz are published for the first time. For easy reference the extensive volume has several registers.

The motor journalist Hanns-Peter Rosellen has published a two volume history on the Cologne motor-concern Ford.[50] The attempt to use an illustrative language is,

---

[47] Wilhelm Eberwein/Jochen Tholen, Borgwards Fall. Borgward, Goliath, Lloyd: Arbeit im Wirtschaftswunder, Bremen (Steintor) 1987, 256 p.

[48] Hamburger Stiftung für Sozialgeschichte des 20. Jahrhunderts (Ed.), Das Daimler-Benz-Buch. Ein Rüstungskonzern im "Tausendjährigen Reich" (= Schriften der Hamburger Stiftung für Sozialgeschichte des 20. Jahrhunderts, 3) (= Delphin Politik), 2nd ed., Nördlingen (Greno) 1987, 829 p.
cf. to this and to quotation 49:
Volker Hentschel, Daimler-Benz im Dritten Reich. Zu Inhalt und Methode zweier Bücher zum gleichen Thema, in: Vierteljahrschrift für Sozial- und Wirtschaftsgeschichte, Vol. 75, 1/1988, p. 74–100.

[49] Hamburger Stiftung für Sozialgeschichte des 20. Jahrhunderts (Ed.), Die Daimler-Benz AG 1928–1948. Schlüsseldokumente zur Konzerngeschichte, compiled by K.H. Roth and M. Schmidt (= Schriften der Hamburger Stiftung für Sozialgeschichte des 20. Jahrhunderts, 5), Nördlingen (Greno) 1987, 478 p.

[50] Hanns-Peter Rosellen, Ford-Schritte. Der Wiederaufstieg der Ford-Werke Köln von 1945 bis 1970, 2 Vols., Frankfurt (Zyklam) 1987/88, 416 p.

however, occasionally embarrassing. There are also numerous orthographical mistakes in this volume, possibly due to the book being printed in Yugoslavia. Rosellen's statements on the general policy of the American-German concern and his comments on the development of the motor-car industry are nevertheless worth reading.

To mark the 125th anniversary of the Adam Opel AG in Rüsselsheim[51], Hans-Jürgen Schneider has written a commemorative book. Opel which nowadays manufactures nothing but cars, has produced the first car only in 1899, before that sewing machines and until 1937 bicycles. Central point of the work is the presentation of the technical development which is illustrated by good photos. In 1929 General Motors took over the management of Opel. The strikes in 1930 and 1936 are mentioned as well as the closure of the car production in 1940, which was due to the war, and its replacement by the production of armament goods. After the entry of the USA into war in December 1941, the Opel factory was controlled by the National Socialists. At the end of the war the Rüsselsheim factory was destroyed to more than 50%. After 1945 the upturn at Opel mainly depends on the Blitz lorry and the motorcars Olympia and Kapitän. In 1953, the first post-war model, the Opel Ascona, is produced.

Dorothea Haaland's geographical thesis, written at the University of Mannheim, is concerned with the Schütte-Lanz airship produced in Mannheim in the years from 1909 to 1925.[52] It looks at the production processes of technical innovations from the ideas of an innovator, at the industrial effects, the prosperity and finally the end of the airship's innovation which experienced a continual technical decline after the First World War. This study is based on Johann Schütte's estates at the Landesmuseum für Technik und Arbeit (State Museum for Technology and Work) in Mannheim.

2.7 Data Processing and Optics

Seen from the side of economics Tilmann Driessen has concerned himself with the early history of data processing technology from 1880 to 1970.[53] With this work he has entered virgin territory because up to war business history has scarcely dealt with the data processing industry. About 1880 there's the time of the perforated card technique and since then history of data processing is almost identical with the history of the IBM concern. Starting with Hollerith founding the Tabulating Machine Corporation (TMC), there was founded after several fusions the Computing-Tabulating Recording Company (CTR) and finally in 1924 IBM. Driessen

[51] Hans-Jürgen Schneider, 125 Jahre Opel. Autos und Technik, Köln (Schneider & Repschläger) 1987, 472 p.

[52] Dorothea Haaland, Der Luftschiffbau Schütte-Lanz Mannheim-Rheinau (1909–1925). Die Geschichte einer innovativen Idee als zeitlich-räumlicher Prozeß (= Südwestdeutsche Schriften, 4), Mannheim (Institut für Landeskunde und Regionalforschung der Universität Mannheim) 1987, 281 p.

[53] Tilmann Driessen, Von Hollerith zu IBM. Zur Frühgeschichte der Datenverarbeitungstechnik von 1880 bis 1970 aus wirtschaftswissenschaftlicher Sicht (= Wirtschafts- und Rechtsgeschichte, 5), Cologne (Müller Botermann) 1987, 245 p.

shows that IBM's control of the market induced to keep relatively low the expenditure for research and development. Only when in the sixties competition became more keen, IBM increased its research and development expenditure.

Friedrich Jerchow, economic historian from Hamburg, has written a commemorative paper on the occasion of the 150th anniversary of the factory of nautical instruments, C. Plath.[54] Based on sources from numerous Hamburg archives and on interviews, Jerchow has presented a precise study of the family enterprise which has only 300 employees and which since 1963 is a subsidiary of the American technology combine Litton Industries. With that he shows that not only big enterprises can edit a serious and well researched business history.

2.8 Chemicals, Plastics, Glass

Wolfgang Feiter has published his graduate work in business economics on the product and advertising history of the washing powder Persil in commemoration of the product's 80th anniversary.[55] The washing powder Persil belongs to the group of traditional consumer goods. Until 1959 advertising for this product has been done by the manufacturer Henkel in Düsseldorf itself and since then by always the same advertising agency. The Henkel enterprise, which was founded in 1876, introduced the product Persil to the market in 1907. The advertising, which at that time was still called "publicity", deliberately aimed at a mixing up of information and emotion. The well written, short, but nevertheless readable publication is cleverly illustrated by photos.

Karl-Heinz Manegold, the economic and technical historian from Hanover, has written a well illustrated and clearly chronographically arranged history of the enterprise Goetze AG in Burscheid, which has been made more accessible through a register of people and subjects.[56] It was published on occasion of the 100th anniversary of Europe's largest piston ring manufacturer which at the same time is one of the largest employers in this area. The publication concentrates on the technical development, but it also portrays the entrepreneurial family Goetze as a family closely connected with the area of the Bergisches Land.

In 1987 the Flachglas AG in Gelsenkirchen could look back on a 500 year tradition in glass production. That's why the historians Adalbert Busl and Mark Spoerer and the glass specialist Heinz A. Krewinkel have published a history of the concern.[57] With the help of good photos they meticulously show the varying development from the forest hut in the upper Palatinate, which did not produce for several decades because of the Thirty Years' War, to a highly technical technology combine which today has its main selling in the construction and in the car industry.

---

[54] Friedrich Jerchow, Vom Sextanten zur Satellitennavigation 1837–1987. 150 Jahre C. Plath, Hamburg (publ. by the firm) 1987, 144 p.

[55] Wolfgang Feiter, 80 Jahre Persil: Produkt- und Werbegeschichte (= Schriften des Werksarchivs der Henkel KGaA Düsseldorf, 20), Düsseldorf (publ. by the firm) 1987, 96 p.

[56] Karl-Heinz Manegold, Goetze: 100 Jahre Unternehmensgeschichte, Düsseldorf (Econ) 1987, 192 p.

[57] Adalbert Busl/Mark Spoerer/Heinz W. Krewinkel, 500 Jahre Flachglas. 1487–1987. Von der Waldhütte zum Konzern, Schorndorf (Karl Hofmann) 1987, 248 p.

2.9 Textiles

Michael Knieriem, head of the Engels-Haus in Wuppertal and researcher on Friedrich Engels, has interpreted the archives of the firm Ermen & Engels, which for a long time has been considered lost, and thus he has made a contribution to Friedrich Engel's commercial situation.[58] Knieriem reconstructs, from an economic point of view, the history of the different enterprises of the Engels family in the Bergisches Land and in Manchester. In doing this the financial situation of the socialist Friedrich Engels becomes clearer. Unfortunately this presentation in its documentation-like style with reprints of several sources, is not available in book shops and therefore will possibly remain unknown to the research on Engels at home and abroad.

The history of the firm Ermen & Engels in Engelskirchen is also theme of the museum catalogue written by Thomas Schleper.[59] The Rheinisches Industriemuseum (Industrial Museum of the Rheinland) has opened a permanent exhibition on business history in the second of eight external showroom, in the former textile factory of Ermen & Engels, which has been founded in 1837 i.a. by the entrepreneur Friedrich Engels senior from Barmen. In addition to the concern history of Ermen & Engels, which had the function of a pioneer for the industrialization in the area of the Bergischen Land, the factory, which was closed in 1979, also contains a changing exhibition on children's and women's work which was commonly known in the textile industry. The still preserved, extensive ensemble of factory buildings, villa of the entrepreneur and attached church, which was situated thus that water as a source of energy could be made the best of, is used as a museum now.

Susanne Müller's thesis in business economics, written in Cologne under the economic and social historian Friedrich-Wilhelm Henning, studies the market situation and selling policy of the velvet and silk industry in Krefeld from the end of the 17th till the end of the 19th century.[60] The selling aspect has up to now been neglected in the history of individual industries. This is particularly true for the change from pre-industrial to industrial production where selling was of great importance for the growth of the concerns. Production got many impulses from the adaptation to changing selling conditions, which was accomplished very quickly by the enterprises in Krefeld. First the Krefeld trades could also exist under unfavourable conditions due to a directed selling policy, which intensified essential aspects of the idea of modern marketing, until their influence on the economic life in the area of the Niederrhein finally declined in the 20th century. The thesis is based on material from the Scheibler Peltzer company archives and the town archives in Krefeld.

As answer to Volkmar Leohold's work, published in 1986, on the history of the Bremen wool combing plant, which he describes from the trade unions' view,

---

[58] Michael Knieriem, "Gewinn unter Gottes Segen". Ein Beitrag zu Firmengeschichte und geschäftlicher Situation von Friedrich Engels. Aus dem Archiv der Firma Ermen & Engels in Engelskirchen, ed. by Engels Haus, Wuppertal (publ. by the ed.) 1987, 120 p.

[59] Thomas Schleper, Ermen & Engels in Engelskirchen: Industrialisierung einer ländlichen Region (= Schriftenreihe des Rheinischen Industriemuseums, 3), Cologne (Rheinland) 1987, 92 p.

[60] Susanne Müller, Marktsituation und Absatzpolitik der Krefelder Samt- und Seidenindustrie in der Zeit von Ende des 17. bis zum Ende des 19. Jahrhunderts (= Wirtschafts- und Rechtsgeschichte, 7), Cologne (Müller Botermann) 1987, 244 p.

Friedrich Jerchow has dealt with the distorted picture and the reality of industrial life at the Bremen wool combing plant.[61] In the local region the very polemic discussion on the official presentation of the concern's history written by Friedrich Jerchow in 1983 got much attention. Central point of the discussion was i.a. the large number of forced labourers having been employed at the Bremen wool combing plant. Jerchow proves that Leohold has very often been inaccurate in his use of the sources and he questions most of his statements whereby, as far as an outsider can judge, he seems to base on the more exact facts and their more correct interpretation.

2.10 Breweries and Foodstuffs

The regional researcher Bernd Winkler has written down the history of beer brewing in the Bavarian Kulmbach.[62] His work is based on documents from the municipal archives there and contains a lot of details and quotations, unfortunately without a detailed reference to sources. The registers of people and firms help to disclose many facts on the production of beer which are of interest for business history.

In commemoration of the 150th anniversary of the Süddeutschen Zucker AG the business historian Manfred Pohl has written a history of this Mannheim concern using sources from five archives.[63] The sugar industry is one of the oldest industries and since the 1830's sugar factories have been an important factor for the development of agricultural areas. With its industrial production sugar developed from a luxury good to an everyday article. A change in the feeding habits also led to a higher sugar consumption. The Süddeutsche Zucker AG and the Zuckerfabrik Franken GmbH, the history of which is inserted into the general economic and social history, have been the main supporters of the sugar industry.

2.11 Trade

The 150th company anniversary was also reason for the publication of the history of the Hamburg trading-house C. Woermann.[64] Five authors have written the book, the company history itself is presented by the historian and journalist Dirk Bavendamm. The trading-house which is now managed by the fifth generation as family enterprise, has from the start been active in the risky overseas trade. The book which has been provided with good photographs, does unfortunately not contain any footnotes and a list of literature.

---

[61] Friedrich Jerchow, Zerrbild und Wirklichkeit des Arbeitslebens auf der Bremer Woll-Kämmerei. Ein Kommentar zu V. Leoholds "Die Kämmeristen", Bremen (publ. by the firm) 1987, 114 p.

[62] Bernd Winkler, Das Bierbrauen in Kulmbach (= "Die Plassenburg" für Heimatforschung und Kulturpflege in Ostfranken, 46), Kulmbach (Freunde der Plassenburg e.V.) 1987, 264 p.

[63] Manfred Pohl, Südzucker 1837–1987. 150 Jahre Süddeutsche Zucker-Aktiengesellschaft Mannheim, Mainz (v. Hase & Koehler) 1987, 210 p.

[64] Wagnis Westafrika: 150 Jahre C. Woermann. Die Geschichte eines Hamburger Handelshauses 1837–1937 (= Veroffentlichungen der Wirtschaftsgeschichtlichen Forschungsstelle e.V., 47)., Hamburg (Hanseatischer Merkur) 1987, 210 p.

2.12 Insurance Companies

Martina Gilles' business economical thesis, written in Cologne under Friedrich-Wilhelm Henning, is concernd with the question of location of the insurance industry since 1914.[65] There are also studied historical problems of the choice of location at the rise of new classes of insurance and new insurance companies and the role of political influences on this choice. The chronologically arranged work investigates the question until the present time, basis for this is an inquiry of about 25 German insurance companies.

The German Reich was the first state in the world creating an insurance for accidents on sea and the See-Berufsgenossenschaft which had been founded for this reason in 1887, was charged with its execution. Co-workers of the sphere of the Deutsches Schiffahrtsmuseum (German Shipbuilding Museum) in Bremerhaven have presented an omnibus volume to commemorate the 100th anniversary of the Hamburg See-Berufsgenossenschaft.[66] Of interest to business history are the contributions of Lars U. Scholl on the history of the See-Berufsgenossenschaft and of Klaus-Peter Kiedel on the sailors' lodging on board during the last 100 years, a question which up to now hasn't been dealt with. Since the archives material of the insurance has been destroyed, the authors base their work on printed material.

The Miners' Relief Association is the most important trade-based national insurance in Germany, but nevertheless it has hardly been examined. In his Munich historical thesis which ensued from a suggestion of the Bundesknappschaft[67] Martin Geyer has dealt with the special insurance of mining during the first half of this century. The author concentrates in his study on the Weimar period which is characterized by the permanent discussion of reforms within the Miners' Relief Association, leading to greater unification and centralization. The presentation uses extensive contemporary magazine literature and sources from the Federal Archives in Koblenz, the Central State Archives in Potsdam and the Mining Archives in Bochum.

Dieter Brosius, archives director in Hanover, has written a short scientific paper on the struggle for admission of the Magdeburger Feuerversicherungs-Gesellschaft in the Kingdom of Hanover.[68] In 1844 the Magdeburger, like many other fire insurance companies, has been founded by traders as result of the fire catastrophe in Hamburg in 1842. Using new margin methods, the Magdeburger became the largest fire insurance company world-wide. For the first time Brosius interprets

---

[65] Martina Gilles, Die Standortfrage in der Versicherungswirtschaft. Eine empirisch-historische Analyse der Standortwahl von Versicherungsunternehmen und der Standortentwicklung in der deutschen Versicherungswirtschaft seit 1914 (= Wirtschafts- und Rechtsgeschichte, 4), Cologne (Müller Botermann) 1987, 320 p.

[66] Klaus-Peter Kiedel/Uwe Schnall/Lars U. Scholl (Eds.), Arbeitsplatz Schiff. 100 Jahre See-Berufsgenossenschaft 1887–1987 (= Schriften des Deutschen Schiffahrtsmuseums, 23), Hamburg (Ernst Kabel) 1987, 301 p.

[67] Martin H. Geyer, Die Reichsknappschaft. Versicherungsreformen und Sozialpolitik im Bergbau 1900–1945 (= Bergbau und Bergarbeit), Munich (C.H. Beck) 1987, 520 p.

[68] Dieter Brosius, Der Kampf der Magdeburger Feuerversicherungs-Gesellschaft um die Zulassung im Königreich Hannover, Hanover (publ. by the firm) 1987, 52 p.

sources on the process of the foundation and the reasons of the company's licensing 130 years ago whereby state policy and economic interests first of all faced incompatible. Solution and permission were finally granted by King George V. of Hanover.

[illegible]

A Review of the New Literature on Banking History

Monika Pohle

Stock Markets

In a short work commissioned by the Institut für Kapitalmarktforschung Ralf Joachim Götz discusses Big Bang and its effects on the German stock markets.[1] The study covers data up to 1 September 1987.

Carsten P. Claussen, Lothar Hübl and Hans-Peter Schneider have produced a Festschrift to mark the bicentenary of the Lower Saxony stock exchange in Hanover.[2] The numerous contributions by different authors deal with regional, general, micro- and legal aspects of stock exchange trading.

Private and Joint Stock Banks

The Festschrift by the mortgage bank Deutsche Hypothekenbank Frankfurt-Bremen AG to mark its 125th anniversary successfully blends illustration and scholarly text.[3] Dierk Hartwig, deputy chief editor of the Börsen-Zeitung, has given an account of the history of the establishment of the bank and its development, while historian Maria R. Alföldi has contributed an essay on mortgage loans and banking business in Antiquity.

To mark the 100th anniversary of the Deutsche Überseeische Bank in Buenos Aires Manfred Pohl has presented the history of the bank in a two-language edition. Particular attention is given to the importance of the overseas banks generally for banking and German trade. The political and economic development of Argentina provides the framework to the study.[4]

Small brochures giving a vivid account of their histories come from three other banks on their anniversaries, the Liquidations-Casse in Hamburg AG (centenary)[5],

---

[1] Ralf Joachim Götz, Big Bang und die deutschen Börsen, ed. Institut für Kapitalmarktforschung, Steinmann & Boschen, Frankfurt am Main 1987, 40 pages.

[2] Zweihundert Jahre Geld und Brief, Herausforderung an die Kapitalmärkte (Festgabe an die Niedersächsische Börse zu Hannover aus Anlaß ihres 200jährigen Bestehens), ed. Carsten P. Claussen, Lothar Hübl, Hans Peter Schneider, Fritz Knapp Verlag, Frankfurt am Main 1987, 332 pages.

[3] 125 Jahre 1862–1987 Deutsche Hypothekenbank Frankfurt-Bremen Aktiengesellschaft, ed. ibid, printed by Walter Thiele GmbH & Co., Frankfurt am Main 1987, 93 pages.

[4] Manfred Pohl, Deutsche Bank Buenos Aires 1887–1987, Mainz (v. Hase & Kochler) 1987, 2455 pages.

[5] 1887–1987 Liquidations-Casse in Hamburg Aktiengesellschaft 100 Jahre, published by the bank, Hamburg 1987, 8 pages.

the Viehmarktsbank der Unterweserstädte GmbH (75th anniversary)[6] and the Westfälische Hypothekenbank AG (25 years).[7]

Savings Banks

The development of the German savings banks is traced by Jürgen Mura in a collection of his own essays on the history of this sector, some of which are revised or summarised for this volume.[8] The author first poses the question of the purpose and use of research into savings banks history and then gives a brief survey of this in Germany. Then follow essays on historical events – the inflation from 1920 to 1923, the banking crisis in 1921, individual aspects of banking, such as consumer credit or foreign business, the legal and technical foundations of the savings banks organisation and an article on the savings banks in the GDR. The bibliography is subdivided according to the aspects covered, and a chronology of German savings banks history concludes the work.

Marlis Lippik has examined the emergence of the savings bank movement in Schleswig-Holstein between 1790 and 1864. She traces the objectives and motives of the founders of the savings banks in the rising and ambitious bourgeoisie, as well as the social composition of savers and the savings behaviour of individual groups. The history of the savings banks in Schleswig-Holstein deserves particular interest for its private banks; of the twelve which are still operating in the Federal Republic of Germany, eight are in Schleswig-Holstein. It may also be noted that the history of the German savings banks has been enriched by what is a "undeniably… first savings bank ": the Ersparungsclasse in Hamburg (p. 16f.).[9]

To mark the 40th anniversary of the Hessische Sparkassen- und Giroverband, the head association of the Hesse Savings and Giro banks, its President, Dr. Adolf Schmitt-Weigand, gave an address which has now been published in the series by the Association: Sparkassen, Wirtschaft, Gesellschaft.[10]

The Festschrift by the Wesermünde-Hadeln district savings bank to mark its 150th anniversary is similar in design to the other small brochures, but very much

---

6 1912–1987, 75 Jahre Viehmarktsbank der Unterweserstädte GmbH, published by the bank, 1987, 20 pages.

7 25 Jahre Westhyp, published by the Westfälische Hypothekenbank AG, Dortmund 1987, 54 pages.

8 Jürgen Mura, Entwicklungslinien der deutschen Sparkassengeschichte (Sparkassen in der Geschichte, Section 3, Research, Vol. 2), Deutscher Sparkassenverlag GmbH, Stuttgart 1987, 351 pages.

9 Marlis Lippik, Die Entstellung des Sparkassenwesens in Schleswig-Holstein 1790–1864 (Studien zur Wirtschafts- und Sozialgeschichte Schleswig-Holsteins, Bd. 10), Neumünster (Karl Wachholtz) 1987, 152 pages.

10 Adolf Schmitt-Weigand, 40 Jahre HSGV Hessischer Sparkassen- und Giroverband (Sparkassen Wirtschaft Gesellschaft, Vol. 1), published by the Hessische Sparkassen- und Giroverband, Frankfurt am Main 1987, 345 pages.

larger, with 360 pages. It also has relatively few pictures.[11] This is a very detailed account of the history of the bank; the text contains no footnotes but is very well documented, with extensive source lists and indices of names and places. A carefully written and expensively produced book, which will be of great interest particularly to economic and social historians.

To mark its 150th anniversary, the Ostunterfranken Savings Bank has issued a Festschrift which will be of great interest especially to banking historians, but to general, economic and social historians as well.[12] The authors, Uwe Klauer for the savings bank history section and Josef Wysocki for the economic and social history, consulted archive material not only in the bank itself but also in the main state archives in Munich and the state archive in Würzburg. The text is supplemented with numerous informative statistical data and tables on the history of the population and the structure of the economy in the East Lower Franconian area.

Smaller illustrated publications come from several other savings banks on their anniversaries: the Bersenbrück district savings bank (centenary)[13], the Edenkoben district and municipal savings bank (150 years)[14], Dinkelsbühl savings bank (150 years)[15], the Neumarkt/Parsberg savings bank (150 years)[16], the Rottal-Inn savings bank (150 years)[17] and the Bad Sachsa municipal savings bank (100 years).[18] Only the jubilee publication by the Bad Oeynhausen municipal savings bank (125th anniversary) has a longer text and deserves special mention.[19]

Cooperative Banks

The reorganisation of the cooperative banking sector which began in the second half of the sixties in the Federal Republic of Germany brought the liquidation of the Association of German Cooperative Banks in 1983. The last act of the Association was to produce a book on its founder, Hermann Schultze-Delitzsch, to honour the

---

[11] "... das herrliche Institut ..." Die Geschichte der Kreissparkasse Wesermünde-Hadeln und ihrer Vorgänger-Institute 1837–1987, with articles by Friedrich Jüchter and Heinrich E. Hausen, published by the Kreissparkasse Wesermünde-Hadeln, Ditzen Druck- und Verlags-GmbH, Bremerhaven 1987, 360 pages.

[12] Unser Land. Unsere Leute. Unser Geld, ed. Sparkasse Ostunterfranken aus Anlaß ihres 150jährigen Jubiläums, Deutscher Sparkassenverlag GmbH, Stuttgart 1987, 124 pages.

[13] Unser Bersenbrücker Land, Heimat gestern und heute (Mitteilungen des Kreisheimatbundes Bersenbrück e.V., Vol. 26), Druckerei Oelkers, Quakenbrück 1987, 159 pages.

[14] Zum Jubiläum 150 Jahre 1937–1987, published by the Kreis- und Stadtsparkasse Edenkoben, Neustadt a.d. Weinstrasse 1987, 40 pages.

[15] Tradition und Fortschritt 150 Jahre Sparkasse Dinkelsbühl, Hrsg. v. ders., Wenng – Druck, Dinkelsbühl 1987, 495 pages.

[16] Tradition und Fortschritt, 150 Jahre Sparkasse Neumarkt/Parsberg, published by the bank, Neumarkt i.d. Opf 1987, 30 pages.

[17] Sparkasse Rottal-Inn, wegweisend im Landkreis, published by the bank, Passavia Druckerei GmbH, Passau 1987, 33 pages.

[18] 1887–1987 gestern – heute – morgen, 100 Jahre Stadtsparkasse Bad Sachsa, published by the bank, Bad Sachsa 1987, 12 pages.

[19] 125 Jahre Stadtsparkasse Bad Oeynhausen, Deutscher Sparkassenverlag GmbH, Stuttgart 1987, 146 pages.

personality of the founder of the movement and his work in realising the concept of cooperative banking. The articles by Rita Aldenhoff, Eberhard Dülfer, Volker Beuthien, Walter Hamm and Peter Klös are concerned mainly with the economic, social and legal activities of Schulze-Delitzsch.[20]

Ingrid Bauert-Keetman has added another volume to the series of Raiffeisen biographies.[21] The book is highly compressed and contains many illustrations. There are no footnotes or list of titles and sources.

Smaller Festschriften have been issued by several cooperative banks to mark their jubilees: Ehninger Bank (75 years)[22], Raiffeisenbank Grossauheim (centenary)[23], Raiffeisenkasse Hallein (80 years)[24], Raiffeisen-Volksbank Schriesheim[25], Volksbank Diez-Nastätten (125 years)[26], Volksbank Dreieich (30 years in the building in Offenbacher Strasse, Sprendlingen)[27], Volksbank Sandhausen (centenary)[28] and Volksbank Schorndorf (125 years)[29].

The Festschriften by the Volksbank Greven (centenary)[30] and the Volksbank Mössingen (centenary)[31] have more text and altogether more pages.

Credit Guarantee Associations

In 1987 two works appeared on the establishment and development of the credit guarantee associations. Karlheinz Montag has analysed the development of these associations in Hesse from 1969 to 1983[32], and Roland Giebitz has given a comprehensive account of the history of the associations in Germany from their origins in the 1920s to 1985.[33] Both authors see the medium-sized sector as the main

[20] Schulze-Delitzsch – ein Lebenswerk für Generationen, ed. Deutscher Genossenschaftsverband (Schulze-Delitzsch) e.V.i.L., Deutscher Genossenschaftsverlag, Wiesbaden 1987, 246 pages.

[21] Ingrid Bauert-Keetman, Friedrich Wilhelm Raiffeisen, Ein Leben für die Zukunft, Steinbock Verlag, Hanover 1987, 143 pages.

[22] 25 Jahre die Bank der Ehninger. Von der Rechenstube zu einer modernen Bank 1912–1987, published by the bank, Ehningen 1987, 16 pages.

[23] 100 Jahre Raiffeisenbank Großauheim eG 1887–1987, ed. by the bank, Otto Herbert KG, Hanau-Großauheim 1987, 48 pages.

[24] 80 Jahre Raiffeisenkasse Hallein 1907–1987, published by the bank, Hallein 1987, 4 pages.

[25] Raiffeisen, Volksbank Schriesheim eG 100 Jahre 1887-1987, published by the bank, Schriesheim 1987, 76 pages.

[26] 125 Jahre Volksbank Diez-Nastätten eG, published by the bank, printed by Druckerei Schmidt und Kramm, Diez 1987, 96 pages.

[27] Unser neues Haus, Volksbank Dreieich eG, published by the bank, printed by Schäfer-Druck GmbH, Dreieich 1987, 43 pages.

[28] Festschrift zum 100jährigen Jubiläum 1887–1987, published by the bank, Sandhausen 1987, 36 pages.

[29] 125 Jahre Volksbank Schorndorf 1862–1987, published by the bank, Schorndorf 1987, 12 pages.

[30] 100 Jahre Volksbank Greven eG, published by the bank, Greven 1987, 60 pages.

[31] Volksbank Mössingen eG, published by the bank, printed by Fritz-Druck, Mössingen 1987, 95 pages.

[32] Karlheinz Montag, Entwicklung und Aufgabenstellung der hessischen Kreditgarantiegemeinschaften seit 1969, Fritz Knapp Verlag, Frankfurt am Main 1987, 249 pages.

[33] Roland Giebitz, Kreditgarantiegemeinschaften. Entstehung, Entwicklung und aktuelle Fragen (Schriftenreihe des Instituts für bankhistorische Forschung e.V., Vol. 8), Fritz Knapp Verlag, Frankfurt am Main 1987, 188 pages.

pillar of the social market economy and praise the role of the credit guarantee associations in securing a supply of capital to medium-sized firms in their competition with larger companies that have easier access to the capital market.

Figures, Coins and Measures

In his "Universal History of Numbers" (Universalgeschichte der Zahlen) Georges Ifrah gives a full but compressed account of the history of figures and numbers, from the non-abstract methods of counting still used today by primitive peoples to the Arabic numerals and the decimal system.[34] The book is in narrative style and has many illustrations and notes, together with a bibliography, a list of names and a subject index.

In 1972 the Deutsche Bundesbank acquired the "Walle Treasure" from East Frisia for its money museum. The collection consists of 468 silver coins and is one of the largest discoveries of coin in this area in the early modern age. This monograph gives numerous illustrations of the find and classifies the coins using scientific analysis and comparisons with other finds in the same region.[35] In addition to the metal analyses the texts include articles on the legal aspects of treasure trove.

A reference work by Helmut Kahnt and Bernd Knorr provides information on the nature and size of old measures, coin, weights and units of time, explaining their absolute or relative values in certain periods and regions.[36] The many illustrations are mainly of old coin and measuring instruments.

Economic and Monetary History

In his thesis "Volksbank oder Aktienbank? Parlamentsdebatten, Referendum und zunehmende Verbandsmacht beim Streit um die Nationalbankgründung 1891–1905" Rolf Zimmermann concentrates his analysis on the controversy over the establishment of the Swiss Nationalbank between the radical democratic majorities in the Bundesrat and parliament and the Swiss Association of Trade and Industry. The author has consulted numerous works of secondary literature and sources from the Swiss federal archives.[37]

In her thesis on Ludwig Bamberger, subtitled "Ideology instead of Realpolitik" Marie-Luise Weber considers her subject mainly as a social politician.[38] But the

---

[34] Georges Ifrah, Universalgeschichte der Zahlen, Campus Verlag, Frankfurt am Main 1987, second and revised edition, 600 pages.

[35] Münzschatzfunde. Das Beispiel Walle, Deutsche Bundesbank, Fritz Knapp Verlag, Frankfurt am Main 1987, 193 pages.

[36] Helmut Kahnt and Bernd Knorr, Alte Maße, Münzen und Gewichte. Ein Lexikon, Meyers Lexikonverlag, Mannheim 1987, 399 pages.

[37] Rolf Zimmermann, Volksbank oder Aktienbank? Parlamentsdebatten, Referendum und zunehmende Verbandsmacht beim Streit um die Nationalbankgründung, 1891–1905, Zürich (Chronos) 1987, 301 S.

[38] Marie-Luise Weber, Ludwig Bamberger, Ideologie statt Realpolitik, Frankfurter Historische Abhandlungen, Vol. 28, Fritz Steiner Verlag Wiesbaden GmbH, Stuttgart 1987, 310 pages.

chapter on monetary reform and the public interest (pp. 138–160) does full justice to Bamberger as the son of a banker and co-founder of the Deutsche Bank and the Reichsbank.

The ninth national symposium, held by the Institute for Bankhistorical Research in 1985, was devoted to the theme "From the Gold Standard to the Multi-Reserve Currency Standard."[39] Gerald D. Feldman of the University of Berkeley spoke on politics, banks and the gold standard in the interwar years, and Günther Schleiminger, former Director-General of the Bank for International Settlements, outlined the evolution of the international monetary system since 1945.

One of the concerns of Marxist-Leninist financial historians is to examine in how far financial preparations for war affect social change. In this context the East German writer Reinhold Zilch studies the complexities of the "financial readiness for war" on the eve of the First World War. He sees the activities of the Reichsbank as responsible for the collapse of the gold standard and maintains that the collapse initiated "the permanent crisis of the capitalist monetary system" (p. 9). The study is based on archive material in the Central State Archive in the GDR and the Secret State Archive of the Foundation for Prussian Cultural Heritage in Berlin (West).[40]

In his account of the international monetary and stabilisation policy in 1923 and 1924 and the influence of the national interests of France, Great Britain and the United States Hans Otto Schötz discusses international relations in an approach that will find more sympathy with historians and considers the question of how national interests may function as categories of international politics.[41] The author uses empirical analysis of a concrete historical situation, limited in time and controversial: the monetary policy conflict over the stabilisation of the Mark in 1923/24.

In his book on the problems of monetary control in socialist planned economies Karl-Hans Hartwig considers the role of money in such economies and its influence on economic processes.[42] This is a work by an economist and it is mainly concerned with the development in the GDR, Poland and the Soviet Union from 1950 to 1985.

---

[39] Vom Goldstandard zum Multireservewährungsstandard, Neuntes Nationales Symposium zur Bankengeschichte, Bankhistorisches Archiv, Series 11, Wissenschaftlicher Beirat des Instituts für Bankhistorische Forschung e.V., Fritz Knapp Verlag, Frankfurt am Main 1987, 70 pages.

[40] Reinhold Zilch, Die Reichsbank und die finanzielle Kriegsvorbereitung 1907 bis 1914 (Forschungen zur Wirtschaftsgeschichte, Vol. 20), Akademie-Verlag, Ost-Berlin 1987, 239 pages.

[41] Hans Otto Schötz, Der Kampf um die Mark 1923/24. Die deutsche Währungsstabilisierung unter dem Einfluss der nationalen Interessen Frankreichs, Grossbritanniens und der USA (Beiträge zur Inflation und Wiederaufbau in Deutschland und Europa 1914–1924, Vol. 9, Veröffentlichungen der Historischen Kommission zu Berlin, Vol. 68), de Gruyter Verlag Berlin, New York 1987, 205 pages.

[42] Karl-Heinz Hartwig, Monetäre Steuerungsprobleme in sozialistischen Planwirtschaften (Schriften zum Vergleich von Wirtschaftsordnungen, Vol. 39), Gustav Fischer Verlag, Stuttgart, New York 1987, 146 pages.

Regional History

In his economic history of Baden-Württemberg from the Romans to today Willi A. Boelcke presents the first comprehensive such account of South-West Germany.[43] Economic change in the region is shown from an examination of population movements, agricultural development, manufacturing, transport, local and longdistance trade and money and banking. The articles on the development of banking each form the conclusion to a chapter. Boelcke begins with an account of coinage in the High Middle Ages (pp. 55f.), and follows this with accounts of coinage problems and credit businss in the late Middle Ages (pp. 86–88), credit and banking, public indebtedness (pp. 156–163) in the Age of Absolutism, industry finance, savings banks, pawn shops, insurance, capital formation and problems of the money supply in the nineteenth century (pp. 202–210), the capital market, cooperative banks, the pawn shop controversy and insurance during the peak of the industrialisation phase (pp. 298–306) and money and credit, inflation, national income and the economic cycle between 1914 and 1945 (pp. 432–441). The banking history closes with articles on credit markets and integration in the world economy after the Second World War. The extensive work has many illustrations (photographs and tables).

Andreas Ranft has studied the municipal accounts and cash books of the City of Lüneburg in the late Middle Ages, and in his thesis on the structure of the city's finances in the mid-15th century he examines the municipal budget as an indicator of the city's economic and social development in this contribution to modern municipal history.[44]

Collective Volumes

Volume 6 of the "Handbuch der Europäischen Wirtschafts- und Sozialgeschichte (Handbook of European Economic and Social History) deals with the period from the First World War to the present (1980).[45] In the first part the banking historian will be mainly interested in the article on money and credit (pp. 159–167). The second part describes the development in individual countries, with money and currency policy and the development of banking each considered under the heading "The Economy".

Colleagues and pupils have honoured Professor Karl Erich Born of the University of Tübingen on his 65th birthday with a Festschrift. With 493 pages this is a large

---

[43] Willi A. Boelcke, Wirtschaftsgeschichte Baden-Württembergs von den Römern bis heute, Konrad Theiss Verlag, Stuttgart 1987, 725 pages.

[44] Andreas Ranft, Der Basishaushalt der Stadt Lüneburg in der Mitte des 15. Jahrhunderts. Zur Struktur der städtischen Finanzen im Spätmittelalter (Veröffentlichungen des Max-Planck-Instituts für Geschichte, Vol. 84), Vandenhoeck & Ruprecht, Göttingen 1987, 314 pages.

[45] Handbuch der Europäischen Wirtschafts- und Sozialgeschichte, Vol. 6, Europäische Wirtschafts- und Sozialgeschichte vom Ersten Weltkrieg bis zur Gegenwart, ed. Wolfram Fischer, Ernst Klett Verlag GmbH, Stuttgart 1987, 1136 pages.

work, and it includes altogether 17 articles on economic and social history, with subjects ranging from the 15th century to today.[46]

Hermann Kellenbenz and Hans Pohl published a Festschrift to mark the 65th birthday of Wolfgang Zorn. This is a supplement to the quarterly periodical on social and economic history and it includes articles by numerous distinguished writers in this field.[47] For those mainly interested in financial history I should like to draw attention to the essays by Karl Heinrich Kaufhold on research on German price and wage history since 1930 (pp. 81–101), Hans Mauersberg on the financial structures of the budgets of the Kingdom of Hanover, the Principality of Hesse and the Duchy of Nassau in the nineteenth century (pp. 293–307) and Hugo Ott on Constantin von Schaezler (1927–1880) and Olga von Leonrod geb. von Schaezler (1828–1901). This last article is concerned wit the conflict between the churches and is more of interest to the family historian, since it deals less with the business activities of the Schaezlers, a well-known banking family.

Uwe Bestmann, Franz Irsigler and Jürgen Schneider published a Festschrift in 1987 for Wolfgang von Stromer's 65th birthday, so honouring a renowned scholar in social, economic, technical and cultural hitory.[48] This is a three-volume work containing altogether 46 articles, most of which concentrate on high finance, economic regions and innovations. Of interest to the banking historian are mainly the articles by Victor J. Rutenburg: Sistema di tassazioni e credito pubblico a Firenze nei seculi XII–XV (pp. 17–34), Natalie Fryde on the levers of British royal finance under the first five Plantagenets (pp. 127–146), Bernd Ulrich Hucker on Nuremberg as a money market for the Staufen kings (pp. 147–188), Martin Körner on the Kawersches, Lombards and the beginnings of banking in Lucerne (pp. 245–267), Franz Irsigler on Reinhard von Schönau and financing the election of Charles IV in 1346, a study in the history of high finance between the Rhine and the Maas (pp. 357–382). Of further interest are the articles by Harald Witthöft "Sizilische Tari – Italienische Libbra – Nordwesteuropäische Mark. Pegolottis 'Pratica della Mercatura' (1310–1340) in modern research" (pp. 421–468), Alfred Wendehorst and Gerhard Rechter on a moneylender in late mediaeval Franconia, Philipp von Seckendorff-Gutend (pp. 487–529) and Karlheinz Blaschke on the importance of church institutions for the capital market in the 15th and 16th centuries (pp. 559–570).

[46] Hansjoachim Henning u.a. (Hrsg.), Wirtschafts- und sozialgeschichtliche Forschungen und Probleme. Karl Erich Born zur Vollendung des 65. Lebensjahres angeeignet von Kollegen, Freunden und Schülern, St. Katharinen (Scripta Mercaturae) 1987, 493 S.

[47] Historia Socialis et Oeconomica, Festschrift für Wolfgang Zorn zum 65. Geburtstag (Vierteljahrschrift für Sozial- und Wirtschaftsgeschichte, Supplement 84), ed. Hermann Kellenbenz and Hans Pohl, Franz Steiner Verlag Wiesbaden GmbH, Stuttgart 1987, 369 pages.

[48] Hochfinanz, Wirtschaftsräume, Innovationen. Festschrift für Wolfgang von Stromer, ed. Uwe Bestmann, Franz Irsigler, Jürgen Schneider, 3 vols., Auenthal Verlag, Trier 1987, 1281 pages.

Cooperation in the Form of Banking Consortia

Second Scientific Colloquium held by the Institute for Bankhistorical Research on 15 May 1987 in the premises of the Creditanstalt-Bankverein, Vienna.[1]

Monika Pohle

Gerhard Randa of the Board of Management of the hosting Creditanstalt-Bankverein, welcomed the participants and referred to the topicality of the subject "Cooperation in Banking Consortia". The amendment to the Austrian banking act had introduced more stringent regulations on bank's own funds and limited risks, such those on large loans. This would require more cooperation between banks.

In his introduction Professor Dr. Hans Pohl of the University of Bonn gave a survey of the large number of consortial banking transactions and defined the consortium as compared with other forms of cooperation between banks. Consortia are mainly used for bond issues for public finance and for loans and bond issues to finance companies in the private sector. This has not changed principally during the period covered by the conference, from the Middle Ages to today. But the size and scope of the consortia have changed greatly and consortial business now ranges beyond the traditional forms of financing to new banking business.

The introduction was followed by three historical papers: Dr. Wilfried Forstmann of the University of Frankfurt spoke on the period before 1870 and gave a review of the establishment of the issue consortium for the Austrian Métalliques loan of 1818.

Dr. Manfed Pohl, head of the Historical Archive of Deutsche Bank AG, spoke on the great days of the consortia between 1870 and 1914, giving details of the construction of the Santa Katharina railway in Brazil.

Dr. Dieter Stiefel of the Economics University in Vienna dealt with the banking consortium in the interwar years, in a paper entitled "Cooperation in Crisis". This was when banks joined mainly in active risk prevention. Worldwide crisis tendencies were countered by these international consortia through a kind of "financial diplomacy".

The survey was concluded by Professor Dr. Hans-Egon Büschgen from the University of Cologne, who spoke on the work of the consortia from 1945 to the present. This was a period when consortial banking business went through a large number of striking changes which can be summarised as greater fragmentation, a wider range of activities and a strong increase in internationalisation. Today a few world renowned major banks dominate the international consortium business and they have the necessary know-how, innovative ability and staff quality to meet the ever-growing requirements.

The panel discussion with representatives of banks, historians and bank economists dealt mainly with the following aspects of consortial business: risk spreading, competition from outside the consortium, the aim of consortia in strengthening financing capital, the value of information and consortia in the financial reorganisation of industrial firms.

---

[1] The papers and discussions are published as a supplement to Bankhistorisches Archiv (Beiheft 15), Fritz Knapp Verlag, Frankfurt am Main 1989.

Socialized Companies – Yesterday – Today – Tomorrow

12th Programme of Public Lectures Organized by the Company for Corporate History (GUG) on the 22nd May 1987 in Bonn

Horst A. Wessel

Readers of papers, panel chairman and participants were agreed on one point: they all praised the GUG's courage to organize a public event focussed on the scientific discussion of the social economy topic. This had little to do with the fiasco recently suffered by the German Trade Unions Association with its socialized enterprise, in particular with "Neue Heimat" (which, surprisingly enough, was not a matter of discussion), but rather with the private sector's obvious aversion to express itself on social economy and a notion of social economy which was interpreted at will and deprived a highly topical matter of its explosiveness.

Dr. Franz Schoser, executive manager of DIHT which acted as host, and Dr. Reinhart Freudenberg, Chairman of the board of management of GUG, were able to welcome more than 100 guests from trade and industry, science and the press. In his paper, Freudenberg outlined the scientific discussion on social economy since the last third of the 19th century. The first phase was dominated by the idea of an autonomous economic sector existing between state economy and private economy. During the twenties, social economy was understood to be, together with state economy, a necessary component part of economic life, the two exercising control and pace-making functions, wherever private initiative failed. After World War II – when housing and food were in short supply and the economy plagued by financing problems – social economy experienced a new upswing in the form of cooperative self-help. In our time, the trade unions have caused havoc and insecurity. For them who used to be its most fervent champions, social economy is at its end.

Dr. Achim von Loesch, former director of the trade unions' holding company and of Bank für Gemeinwirtschaft, dealt with the history of socialized enterprises from the 19th century until 1945. His notion of social economy encompassed all economic activities and all companies motivated by the public interest rather than by the interests of individuals or groups. In the opinion of the speaker, the phenomenon is more suitably defined by its aims than by its owners. This definition enabled a more pragmatic understanding of social economy and of the conception it has of itself and placed socialized enterprises on the same track with public ones. In economics, various attitudes towards social economy can be made out: classics and neo-classics were generally against it. The liberals at first considered public enterprises as a means of controlling monopolies, but later saw them to be troublemakers on the privately organized market. The social-conservative reformers of the 19th century established social economy as a necessary component part of the economy, together with private economy.

The Christian and socialist co-operatives of the 19th century confronted the ruling individualism of the classics with their idea of solidary action – although not all co-operatives belonged to social economy. Whereas Marxists were always hostile to social economy, socialists for some time understood it to provide an opportunity for a partial realization of their aims. In the twenties and especially in the years after 1945, Social Democrates and trade unions had, according to the speaker, developed a positive relationship with social economy. Social economy was de-ideologized and its relatively unprejudiced use in the public interest was possible. Von Loesch warned against regarding social economy superfluous or even dangerous because of the repeated human failure of people charged with safeguarding its interests. Now as before, social economy was a stimulating element in the economic structure.

Professor Dr. Peter Eichhorn, holder of the chair of managerial economics, public administration and publicly-owned enterprises and, in parciular, hospital management and administration at Mannheim University, began his lecture with a report on a visit to a pit coal mine. This mine ought to be closed down for managerial reasons, while, for reasons innate in social economy, it is actually being subsidized. Eichhorn defined social economy by figures; as far as ownership is concerned, the distinction he gave was between publicly-owned and socialized enterprises. The enterprises committed to the public economic interest were primarily striving to meet the needs of major groups not belonging, as a rule, to the enterprise, up to and including the public in general. While serving the public interest, they, unlike the Church and some other institutions, got their services paid for. Eichhorn's was a wide notion of social economy in which he included all publicly-owned enterprises which he assumed to pursue goals in the public interest. The definition of the many socialized enterprises of various descriptions being problematic, it was difficult to reach general agreement on the notion.

In addition to their promoting the public interest, socialized enterprises were related by a common field of activity: they provided, maintained and operated a technical, social, healthrelated, educational and financial infrastructure. This infrastructure constituted a fundamental material basis for the other economic entities. The question as to the subsidiary nature of public managerial activity, in particular, did not arise, because socialized enterprises fulfilled original economic and societal duties in the public interest.

Retrospectively, says Eichhorn, the socialized enterprises appeared as a supporting element in the post-war upswing and as a stabilizing factor during the boom and the recession of the sixties. In the years thereafter, new tasks were added and developments in the recent past could be defined as a consolidation. Our social order and economic system could not be imagined without socialized enterprises; privately orientated companies could not, in the long run, exist without them. It may be doubted though that the need of self-justification under which the socialized enterprises find themselves, is exclusively or primarily caused by their profit-making nature which follows from their actual corporate doctrine. The author feels that, to a large extent, it may be due to the fact that according to common opinion and even in the opinion of the associates of some of the institutions, the social economy notion is being filled with the most different contents, that theory and practice often fail to correspond and that the public interest they serve is frequently represented by surprisingly small groups and even individuals.

The discussion chaired by Professor Dr. Hans Besters, Bochum, first expanded on the definitions given by the speakers. It showed, in particular, that the wider notion presented by Eichhorn was problematic. So far, an operational and verifiable notion is still lacking and may not easily be found.

Other points of the panel discussion in which Manfred Arenz, member of the board of management of Stadtwerke Essen AG, Dr. Werner Lamby, member of the board of management of VIAG and Professor Dr. Erich Potthoff, Cologne, Participated concerned the tax privilege, profit distribution, return on net worth and the competitive function of socialized companies. The absence of profit and loss accounting in this sector was regretted; it is certainly difficult, but should be possible as part of an individual company's accounting.

Trends in the Savings Banks' Deposits-Taking Business

Report on the Symposium of the History of Savings Banks, Heidelberg, September 23/24/1987

Jürgen Mura

'Trends in the Savings Banks' Deposits-Taking Business' was the general theme of the Symposium on the History of Savings Banks in Heidelberg, September 23/24, 1987, chaired by Mr. Gustav Adolf Schröder, managing director of the German Savings Banks and Giro Association*, Bonn, and Professor Dr. Bernd Rudolph, University of Frankfurt/Main; the organizer and sponsor was the Gesellschaft zur Förderung der Wissenschaftlichen Forschung über das Spar- und Girowesen, e.V., Bonn.

In his opening address, Mr. Schröder once again underlined the importance of history to the savings banks when defining their own position. Here again the historical dimension allowed a sufficiently deep background field against which current processes were developing. The fact that – historically speaking – the taking of deposits was *the* original line of business of the saving banks signified the importance of this topic to the savings banks when defining their own position in this area as well.

Professor Rudolph, who chaired the academic part of the discussion, explained in his introductory that by choosing the Symposium's general theme he wanted to focus the discussion on a topic that was of fundamental importance to the credit industry and even more to the savings banks system and of current relevance at the same time.

Dr. Dr. Josef Wysocki, professor for economic history, Salzburg, who spoke on 'The Savings Deposit', covered the first part of the chronology of the German savings bank movement till 1908, when the institutes took on the banking function as well.

Under the term savings deposit defined as a genuine innovative and constitutive product of the savings banks, Professor Wysocki discussed five of the general elements he had elaborated from the Statutes of the Hamburger Sparkasse founded in 1778. The wording ".... to enable people to put aside even in times of low wages safely and against some interest a little something for a rainy day or for the bride's wedding day" described the product in a general way that retained its normative validity for at least a century. Further topics for discussion concerned organizational issues such as 'Inpayment Vouchers or Passbooks' as well as the problem field relating to 'The Savings Deposits in the Market'.

Subsequently, Professor Dr. Werner Ehrlicher, University of Freiburg, discussed 'The Deposits-Taking Business in Times of War, Inflation and Emergency' between 1908 and 1948. His paper thus covered the period from the commencement of cashless payment transactions by the savings banks system to the post-World War

* Deutscher Sparkassen- und Giroverband, Bonn.

II monetary reform in 1948 reflecting basic trend changes in the deposits-taking business which affected the savings banks' position in the credit industry on a lasting basis and their share in the volume of cashless payment transactions as well as their contribution to monetary capital formation within the economy and, thus, to the financing of real capital formation or of the increasing activities of the public sector.

Professor Dr. Bernd Rudolph's paper discussed 'Differenciation and Diversification in the Deposits-Taking Business' of the savings banks since the monetary reform in 1948. For the period under review and after 1967 in particular, when government-fixed interest rates ceased to exist, Professor Rudolph's diagnosis was that the "classical triad of the roughly homogenous blocks of sight, savings and time deposits were split into a multitude of differential monetary investment facilities" and that the deposits-taking business, especially important to the savings banks, had been subject to "substantial differenciation" having resulted in a wide variety of investment facilities. "Product differenciation on the liabilities side" has been "a major characteristic in this field since the 1948 monetary reform". Diversification, e.g. a breakdown of deposits by maturities and notice periods, by demographic, regional and social groups of investors, by volumes of deposits, types of interest and securitization, was referred to as a special trend in the deposits-taking business of the savings banks as well. Over time, decreasing diversification would make institutes more dependent on the capital market.

In conclusion, Dr. Jürgen Miethke, President of the Savings Banks and Giro Association for Schleswig-Holstein, Kiel, covered the latest trends by drawing the contours of the "Perspectives of the Savings Banks' Deposits-Taking Business'. He discussed the factors influencing this business as well as a few conclusions to be derived therefrom and the response of these institutes to changes that have occurred. Against this background, Dr. Miethke ventured the prognosis that savings deposits, investments in securities and insurance will be the three most important forms of investment in future.

A podium discussion among renowned savings bank managers of about one and a half hour moderated by Professor Rudolph was the concluding event of the Symposium and allowed a variety of new insights and new food for thinking in this important business sector of the savings banks as well.

In order to give general access to the results of the Symposium, the papers read and discussions held at the Symposium have been combined in a brochure also this time.*

---

* Gesellschaft zur Förderung der Wissenschaftlichen Forschung über das Spar- und Girowesen e.V., Bonn (Publ.), Sparkassenhistorisches Symposium 1987. Entwicklungslinien im Einlagengeschaft der Sparkassen. Deutscher Sparkassenverlag. Stuttgart 1988.

The Private Customer

Eleventh National Symposium of the Institute for Bank-Historical Research held in October 16, 1987, at the Deutsche Genossenschaftsbank, Frankfurt am Main.[1]

Monika Pohle

In the decisive battle for market shares in the retail banking sektor, banks are not merely competing against one another (take, for example, new opening hours, aggressive canvassing for home-building savings, etc.) but, as a group, they are also competing against non-banks which take away a substantial portion of the non-cash payment business from banks through credit cards, for instance. How much of a threat are these competitors to banks? Are the endeavours to issue a "joint credit card" an adequate response to this challenge? After all, it seems that private customers have something of an aversion to being part of an automated impersonal business, and would greatly appreciate decidedly more individual treatment. Are banks aware of this need, and what are they going to do about it?

This and other questions were the issues discussed by the panel chaired by Mr. Hans-Konradin Herdt, Editor-in-Chief of the Börsen-Zeitung, at the Eleventh National Symposium of the Institut für bankhistorische Forschung e.V. dedicated to "The Private Customer".

The panel discussion was preceded by fundamental papers presented by Professor Dr. Günter Ashauer, director of the Sparkassenakademie (saving banks academy), and Dr. Ulrich Weiss, member of the Board of Governors of the Deutsche Bank.

In this paper on the historical background, Professor Ashauer described the origins and development of retail banking, starting with its predecessors in the High Middle Ages – the "Monti di Pietà" in Perugia and Orvieto – right up to the introduction of noncash wage and salary remittances and the "small personal loan" in 1959. His paper focussed on the presentation of developments in the 19th and 20th centuries up to 1959. The very long period of extremely low income for the masses – much of it, it should be remembered, was paid in kind – was succeeded by a "take-off" in real income in the middle of the nineteenth century, which for the first time permitted large sectors of the population to save. The first institutions to seek the deposit of these saving were the savings banks and the credit cooperatives founded in large numbers in the forties of the nineteenth century. By the end of the nineteenth century, however, the big Berlin banks began to accept savings deposits as well as share capital to finance their lending business. Since the twenties of this century, the big banking corporations have been expanding their deposits network and have come to appreciate savings as an increasingly profitable sector of business. However, well into that time, socialist ideology was another factor hampering the savings business, since saving instead of consuming was thought to promote unemployment. At the same time, special banks were established – banks for civil servants, wage-

1 The papers and discussions are published as a supplement to Bankhistorisches Archiv (Beiheft 16), Fritz Knapp Verlag, Frankfurt am Main 1990.

earners, salary-earners and for the trade unions – whose business primarily concentrated on the financing of hire-purchase transactions. To the end of the fifties, advocates of saving continued to maintain that the granting of personal loans – mostly for hire-purchase – should not be allowed to turn the economy into a "country living on credit". The attitude to the consumer business, in other words, to the "small loan" business changed only gradually. The introduction of salary payment by remittance in 1959 provided the Deutsche Bank with sufficient security for small personal loans.

In his topical paper, Dr. Weiss described how essential it was for private banks to open their doors to the general public – a step that recognized private customers as one of the mainstays of "universal" banking institutes. Services to private customers, if properly run and providing the advice such customers need, are by no means performed at the expense of other banking sectors. Since payment transactions play a key role in retail banking, more attractive services should be offered, and any additional costs could be covered by providing payment services as part of the general cooperation between banks. The competitive challenge coming from services provided by non-banks should be met by greater mobility and flexibility on the part of banks (more automation, for instance). This must not go so far as to impair personal contacts between customer and bank staff, however. If all these caveats are born in mind, Dr. Weiss sees considerable growth and earnings potential in the retail sector.

The panel discussion that followed the papers focussed on competitors in the retail banking sector – non-banks, such as insurance companies and banks established by manufacturers. The panelists gave different answers to the question of how banks are reacting to this trend, or at least placed their emphasis on different aspects. To woo private customers, Dr. Weiss suggested that banks could use certain means which are now available to at least some competitors: flexible opening hours and even a mobile field service which is quite normal in the insurance business. Flexible opening hours should have ceased to be a taboo for the trade unions by now, since, sooner or later, competitive disadvantages will put bank jobs at risk.

Professor Dr. Joachim Süchting from the University of Bochum and Mr. Hans Peter Sorg, Director General of Schweizerische Kreditanstalt, concurred, that the classification of private customers according to income and property, and the services offered to them (as has long been the practice in Switzerland), promotes higher growth rates in retail banking. Professor Süchting cannot see how any classical all-round bank will be able to swim against the current in the matter of segmentation.

The representatives of the savings and cooperative banks see smallness as their biggest handicap in competing for private customers. Dr. Paul Wieandt, Chairman of the Management Board of the Landesbank Rheinland-Pfalz – Girozentrale – and Dr. Wulf von Schimmelmann, Member of the Management Board of the DG BANK recommend associations as the solution to prevent the loss of private customers. Nevertheless, Dr. von Schimmelmann believes that the number of branches in the cooperative sector will continue to decline. But, as Dr. Weiss said in his concluding remarks, banks must become more mobile and flexible also in defending their network of branch offices.

The Contributions to the Yearbook Were First Published in the Following Journals

Yearbook 1988

Beate Brüninghaus
A Review of the New Literature on Business History (first printing)

Lothar Burchardt
Zwischen Kriegsgewinn und Kriegskosten: Krupp im Esten Weltkrieg. In: Zeitschrift für Unternehmensgeschichte 1987, pp. 71–123

Volker Hentschel
Indikatoren der realen effektiven Wechselkurse großer Handelsnationen 1922–1937. In: Vierteljahrschrift für Sozial- und Wirtschaftsgeschichte 1986, pp. 183–209

Johannes Houwink ten Cate
Hjalmar Schacht als Reparationspolitiker (1926–1930). In: Vierteljahrschrift für Sozial- und Wirtschaftsgeschichte 1987, pp. 186–228

Jürgen Mura
Entwicklungslinien im Einlagengeschäft der Sparkassen. Bericht über das Sparkassenhistorische Symposium 1987 am 23. und 24. September in Heidelberg. In: Archiv und Wirtschaft 1988, pp. 34–35

Monika Pohle
A Review of the New Literature on Banking History. Revised Version of the "Literaturbericht 1987". In: Bankhistorisches Archiv 1988, pp. S. 62–69

Monika Pohle
Der Privatkunde. Elftes Nationales Symposium des Instituts für bankhistorische Forschung e.V. am 16. Oktober 1987 im Hause der Deutschen Genossenschaftsbank, Frankfurt am Main. AHF Information. Arbeitsgemeinschaft außeruniversitärer historischer Forschungseinrichtungen in der Bundesrepublik Deutschland e.V., Nr. 14 v. 11.3.1988

Monika Pohle
Cooperation in the Form of Banking Consortia. Second Scientific Colloquim held by the Institute for Bankhistorical Research on 15 May 1987 in the premises of the Creditanstalt-Bank, Vienna (first printing)

Harm G. Schröter
Kartelle als Form industrieller Konzentration: Das Beispiel des internationalen Farbstoffkartells von 1927 bis 1939. In: Vierteljahrschrift für Sozial- und Wirtschftsgeschichte 1987, pp. 479–513

Horst A. Wessel
Gemeinwirtschaftliche Unternehmen – gestern – heute – morgen. 12. öffentliche Vortragsveranstaltung der Gesellschaft für Unternehmensgeschichte am 22. Mai 1987 in Bonn. In: Archiv und Wirtschaft 1987, pp. 118–120

MIX
Papier aus verantwortungsvollen Quellen
Paper from responsible sources
FSC® C105338

If you have any concerns about our products,
you can contact us on
ProductSafety@springernature.com

In case Publisher is established outside the EU,
the EU authorized representative is:
Springer Nature Customer Service Center GmbH
Europaplatz 3, 69115 Heidelberg, Germany

Printed by Libri Plureos GmbH
in Hamburg, Germany